DAVID W. JOHNSON
University of Minnesota

REACHING OUT

Interpersonal Effectiveness and Self-Actualization

SECOND EDITION

PRENTICE-HALL, INC., ENGLEWOOD CLIFFS, NEW JERSEY 07632

Library of Congress Cataloging in Publication Data

JOHNSON, DAVID W. (date)
   Reaching out.

   Bibliography
   Includes index.
   1. Interpersonal relations.   2. Self-realization.
   3. Youth—United States.   I. Title.
HM132.J64   1981   302   80-20522
ISBN 0-13-753327-6
ISBN 0-13-753319-5 (pbk.)

Editorial supervision and interior design: Serena Hoffman
Cover design: Mario Piazza
Manufacturing buyer: Edmund W. Leone
Cartoons: Nancy Valin Waller

Printed in the United States of America
10   9   8   7   6   5   4

PRENTICE-HALL INTERNATIONAL, INC., *London*
PRENTICE-HALL OF AUSTRALIA PTY. LIMITED, *Sydney*
PRENTICE-HALL OF CANADA, LTD., *Toronto*
PRENTICE-HALL OF INDIA PRIVATE LIMITED, *New Delhi*
PRENTICE-HALL OF JAPAN, INC., *Tokyo*
PRENTICE-HALL OF SOUTHEAST ASIA PTE. LTD., *Singapore*
WHITEHALL BOOKS LIMITED, *Wellington, New Zealand*

*To my brothers and sisters, who have significantly contributed
to the development of my interpersonal skills
and to my self-actualization:*
Frank, Helen, Roger, Edythe, Keith, Dale

Contents

List of Exercises

Preface

Reaching Out seeks to provide the theory and experience necessary to develop effective interpersonal skills. It is more than a book that reviews current psychological knowledge on how to build and maintain friendships. It is more than a book of skill-building exercises. The theory and exercises are *integrated into an experiential approach* to learning about interpersonal skills.

Some of the material in this book was originally developed to train high school and college students to establish relationships with lonely and alienated peers. It was assumed that many adolescents and young adults would never seek professional help for their personal problems and unhappiness, but they would be receptive to the support and friendship of someone their own age. It was also assumed that supporting and caring friendships are a missing and important part in the lives of many alienated and lonely young people. The material in this book can be, and has been, used for peer-outreach and peer-counseling programs.

I wish to thank many people for their help in writing this book. My younger sister, Edythe Holubec, contributed most of the questions the reader will find in the text, and she helped revise and improve many parts of the book. I owe much to those psychologists who have influenced my theorizing and to my colleagues with whom I have conducted various types of experimental learning sessions. Whenever possible, I have tried to acknowledge the source of any exercises that are not original in this book, but a few of the exercises are so commonly used that the originators are not traceable. If I have inadvertently missed giving recognition to anyone, I apologize.

Special thanks go to the many friends who have helped me improve my interpersonal skills and to my wife, Linda Mulholland Johnson, who contributed her support to the rewriting of this book. All photographs not otherwise credited were taken by the author. Finally, I wish to thank Nancy Valin Waller, who drew the cartoon figures appearing in the book.

D.W.J.

1

The Importance
of Interpersonal Skills

THE RELATIONSHIP IMPERATIVE

The human species seems to have a *relationship imperative:* We desire and seek out relationships with others, and we have personal needs that can be satisfied only through interacting with other humans. Career success, family success, friendships, and companionships, all depend on building and maintaining relationships with other people. In fact, the most distinctive aspect of being alive is the potential for joy, fun, excitement, caring, warmth, and personal fulfillment in our relationships with other people. Making new friends, deepening existing relationships, falling in love, and negotiating alliances with other people to achieve mutual goals— all these give life meaning and richness. How fulfilling, productive, meaningful, and satisfying our lives turn out to be depends on the quality of the relationships we form with other people. There is no way to overstate the importance of interpersonal relationships in our lives.

In this chapter the importance of interpersonal relationships for personal well-being, for the well-being of society, and for self-actualization will be examined. In addition, the specific interpersonal skills needed to build and maintain relationships will be discussed, along with the procedures for learning interpersonal skills from the experiential exercises included in this book. In subsequent chapters, each major interpersonal skill will be discussed at length.

Interpersonal relationships are essential for our personal well-being in many ways, helping us to grow and develop cognitively and socially, to build a positive and coherent personal identity, to feel we are firmly in touch with reality, and to gain and maintain psychological and physical health. *Human development* follows a pattern of expansion of interdependence with other people. Growing children are impelled to become aware of and interact with a widening social circle. From having to relate to members of the family, children move on to interaction with peers and other people in the neighborhood. The social world of children is expanded dramatically when they begin formal schooling. When young adults enter a career organization and become members of a community, they must build and maintain relationships with a larger and larger number of people. And it is from their family, peers, friends, colleagues, and teachers that children and young adults learn new skills and competencies, and acquire knowledge, attitudes, and values (Johnson 1979). As we grow and develop there is an ever-expanding number of people with whom we must build and maintain relationships; we are required to cooperate with others in family, school, career, community, and societal settings; and we learn how to do so from the people with whom we interact. Both our social and our intellectual growth and development are determined by the quality and nature of our relationships with other people.

Our *identity* is built out of our relationships with other people. As we interact with others we note their responses to us, we seek feedback as to how they perceive us, and we learn how to view ourselves as they view us. From the reflections of others, we develop a clear and accurate picture of ourselves. When others view us as worthwhile, we tend to view ourselves similarly. We try to incorporate into ourselves characteristics that we admire in other people. In our relationships with other people we adopt social roles such as "student" or "engineer" that we incorporate into our view of ourselves. It is within our relationships that we discover who we are as a person.

As we strive to make sense of the world around us, to determine what is real and what is illusory, we depend on other people to validate our perceptions and impressions. Many questions concerning *reality cannot* be answered by our physical senses. While we can touch a leaf or smell a flower we cannot tell for sure what is fair or unfair, whether we are fast or slow, what is good or bad, or whether something is beautiful or ugly, without checking our opinions with the opinions of others. In order to make sense of the world, we need to share our perceptions and reactions with other people and find out whether or not other people perceive and react similarly.

Our *psychological health* depends almost entirely on the quality of our relationships with other people. The ability to build and maintain co-operative, interdependent relationships with other people is often cited as a primary manifestation of psychological health (Johnson 1980). People who, for one reason or another, are unable to establish acceptable relationships often develop considerable anxiety, depression, frustration, and alienation. They tend to be afraid and to feel inadequate, helpless, and alone. They often cling to unproductive and unskilled ways of reaching out to others, and they seem unable to change to more successful methods of building and maintaining relationships. Having poor interpersonal skills seems to be a major cause of psychological pathology.

Within any given period of several weeks, many American adults feel painfully lonely. The incidence of loneliness is considerably higher among adolescents. In order not to be lonely, each of us has a need for two different types of relationships: intimate relationships that provide a sense of attachment with a spouse, lover, or friend of the opposite sex, and more casual relationships with a network of friends who share our interests and concerns and provide a sense of community (Weiss 1973). Loneliness, based on the absence of attachment and community, is a feeling that is particularly prevalent and intense during adolescence. Loneliness varies with the time of day and time of year. Winter is widely believed to be the loneliest season. Christmas is the loneliest time of all for many people who lack strong family ties. Almost everyone needs to be involved in an intimate relationship, which provides a sense of attachment, and in a network of friendships, which provides a sense of community. There is even evidence that loneliness and social isolation bring emotional and then physical deterioration. Many serious illnesses, such as heart disease, occur more frequently among socially isolated individuals. As W. H. Auden once stated, "We must love one another or die."

Most of all, perhaps, we need to be *confirmed* as a person by other people. Confirmation consists of response from other people in ways that indicate we are normal, healthy, and worthwhile. Being *disconfirmed* consists of responses from other people suggesting that we are ignorant, inept, unhealthy, unimportant, or of no value, and, at worst, that we do not exist. In most interpersonal interactions, we implicitly request, "Please validate me as a person." In our relationships we need to give and receive such confirmations. This book explains how to do so.

A BROADER VIEW

The evolution and survival of our species are intimately intertwined with our ability to initiate, develop, and stabilize our relationships with other people. *Biologically*, interpersonal relationships are required for our conception, survival, and development. It takes two humans to conceive a child, and when the child is born it must depend on other people in order to survive. Infants depend on other people for their food and care due to the biological pattern of growth and development genetically structured into our species. Our biological nature is such that we also have to be educated by other people into the language, competencies, and appropriate behavior patterns of our society and culture.

There is growing evidence that we owe our *evolution* as a species to a uniquely intense social contract among individuals formed three million years ago in an economy based on reciprocal sharing of plant and animal foods. It was this cooperative interdependence that pushed humans to develop conceptual abilities, which, in turn, fostered the development of language and technology. The foundation of our evolution as a species was the interpersonal relationships formed to achieve the mutual goals involved in short-term and long-term survival.

The foundation of all *civilizations* and *societies* is the ability of humans to collaborate with each other and coordinate their actions to achieve common goals. The more complex and technical our society becomes, the greater the need to establish warm, personal, human relationships. In most situations there is no possibility of achieving our goals unless we combine our efforts with the efforts of others. A great deal of our time is spent in forming coalitions with one or more people to achieve goals that we cannot hope to achieve individually. Through our relationships we commit ourselves to actions that result in mutual benefit—we share a problem, trade help and resources, or work together to complete a project. Such commitments allow us to rely on others to behave in ways that are mutually beneficial and to pool such resources as materials, energy, time, and money. Much of our lives is spent working directly with other people, negotiating arrangements and divisions of labor with them, and developing new procedures and activities for mutual benefit.

All members of our society are highly interdependent and therefore must be skilled in building and maintaining relationships with each other. Other people make the cars we drive, the clothes we wear, the buildings we live and work in, and even the money we spend. Our economy is a vast division of labor; our legal system specifies the boundaries of acceptable interpersonal interaction within our society; our traffic control systems determine how people move in and out of buildings and cities; our language is a shared system of symbols; our political system is based on the cooperative and orderly use and transfer of power and authority—the list goes on and on. Every society is a vast collaborative system of human relationships that is maintained through interpersonal interaction.

Much of human society and action seems to be based on the liking people have for each other. The words that name degrees of interpersonal attraction, such as like, love, dislike, and hate, are among the most frequently used words in the English language. We are a social species; most of our happiness and fulfillment rests on our ability to relate effectively to other humans. Especially in our highly technical and bureaucratic society, the yearning for closer personal ties is a major need.

What makes us human is the way we interact with other people. To the extent that our relationships reflect kindness, mercy, consideration, tenderness, love, concern, compassion, cooperation, responsiveness, and caring, we are becoming more human. In *humanizing* relationships, individuals are sympathetic and responsive to human needs. They invest each other with the character of humanity, and they treat and regard each other as human. It is positive involvement with other people that we label humane. In a *dehumanizing* relationship, people are divested of those qualities that are uniquely human and are turned into machines, in the sense that they are treated in impersonal ways that reflect unconcern with human values. To be inhumane is to be unmoved by the suffering of others, to be unkind, even cruel and brutal. In a deep sense, the way we relate to others and the nature of the relationships we build and maintain determine what kind of people we become.

There is nothing more important in our lives than our interpersonal relationships. The quality of our relationships, as well as the number, depends on our interpersonal skills. It takes skills to build and maintain fulfilling and productive relationships. The purpose of this book is to help you understand and master these important interpersonal skills.

SELF-ACTUALIZATION

The rapid technological change we have been experiencing for the past several decades has resulted in rapid cultural change within our society. Our culture seems to be changing from its emphasis from materialism to self-actualization, from self-control to self-expression, from independence to interdependence, from endurance of stress to a capacity for joy, from full employment to full lives. The values of our society seem to be moving toward emphasis on self-actualization and development of personal resources. We are seeking a sense of fulfillment. Mobility has become a hallmark of our society; the people we know and love today may be hundreds of miles away tomorrow. Several times during our lives we may be faced with beginning new relationships with a group of people we do not know and ending relationships with old neighbors. The ability to develop relationships that actualize our personal resources and in which we find joy and a sense of fulfillment is becoming more and more important. The ability to begin and end relationships is becoming more and more of a necessity.

Many psychologists believe that there is in all of us a drive to actualize our potentialities. It is apparent that such self-actualization consists primarily of being *time competent,* that is, of having the ability to tie the past and the future to the present effectively while living fully in the present. The self-actualized person appears to be less burdened by guilts, regrets, and resentments from the past than is the nonself-actualized person, and the self-actualized person's aspirations are tied realistically to present goals.

Self-actualization is also dependent on being autonomous. In order to understand autonomy, it is necessary to contrast inner- and other-directedness. The *inner-directed person* adopts a small number of values and principles early in life that are rigidly adhered to, no matter what the situation is like. The *other-directed person* receives guidance and direction from the people he or she is relating to—whatever is necessary to gain the approval of other people is done. The *autonomous person* is liberated from rigidly adhering to parental values or social pressures and expectations. The autonomous person applies values and principles flexibly in order to act in ways that are appropriate to the current situation.

The time competence and the autonomy of the self-actualizing person are related, in the sense that a person who lives primarily in the present relies more on his or her own support and expressiveness than does a person living primarily in the past or in the future. To live fully in the present means that you must be autonomous—free not only from rigid inner values but also from excessive need to conform to social prescriptions in order to get approval from other people.

Self-actualization is achieved by relating to other people in time-competent and autonomous ways. Your interpersonal skills are the foundation for your self-actualization. Whether you are six, sixteen, or sixty years old, your ability to relate effectively to other people determines how productive and happy you are.

Interpersonal skills are essential for building and maintaining the relationships that promote your personal well-being, the well-being of society, and your self-actualization. In the following section, we discuss the specific interpersonal skills that are needed.

INTERPERSONAL SKILLS

To initiate, develop, and maintain caring and productive relationships, certain basic skills must be present. These skills generally fall into four areas:

1.   Knowing and trusting each other
2.   Communicating with each other accurately and unambiguously

3.   Accepting and supporting each other

4.   Resolving conflicts and relationship problems constructively

The first area of skill development involves self-disclosure, self-awareness, self-acceptance, and trust. There must be a high level of trust between you and the other person in order for you to get to know each other. Getting to know each other involves telling or in some other way disclosing how you are reacting to what is presently taking place and how you feel about it. Such openness depends on your self-awareness and self-acceptance; if you are unaware of your feelings and reactions, you cannot communicate them to another person, and if you cannot accept your feelings and reactions, you will try to hide them. Telling other people who you are and listening carefully when they tell you who they are is how you begin and prolong all relationships. Chapters 2 and 3 deal with these skills.

The second area of interpersonal-skills development involves communicating your ideas and feelings accurately and unambiguously. Especially important is communicating warmth and liking. Unless you believe the other person likes you and the other person believes that you like him or her, a relationship will not grow. Communication skills begin with sending messages that are phrased so that the other person can easily understand them. They also include listening in ways that ensure that you have fully understood the other person. It is through sending and receiving messages that all relationships are initiated, developed, and stabilized. Chapters 4, 5, and 6 cover these skills.

When a friend asks you for help, what is the best way to respond? When someone you know is going through a personal or family crisis and needs your personal support, what is the best way to express your concern? The third area of interpersonal-skills development concerns mutual acceptance and support. Responding in helpful ways to another person's problems and concerns, communicating acceptance and support, using reinforcement and modeling to increase the constructiveness of another person's behavior are all important relationship skills. Chapters 7 and 8 cover this material.

Finally, learning how to resolve interpersonal conflicts and problems in ways that bring you and the other person closer together and help the relationship grow and develop is vitally important to maintaining a relationship. Conflicts will arise no matter how much two people care about each other and no matter how often they provide opportunities to increase their closeness and commitment. Important aspects of conflict management include being aware of your usual strategies for managing conflicts, defining conflicts in ways that faciliate or help bring about a constructive resolution, being able to negotiate resolutions that are beneficial both to you and to the other person, and being able to manage your feelings (such as anger) constructively. Conflicts are inevitable, even among the best of friends, and ensuring that conflicts deepen rather than weaken a relationship involves a vital set of interpersonal skills. This material is covered in chapters 9, 10, 11, and 12.

THE APPLICATION OF SOCIAL SCIENCE RESEARCH TO INTERPERSONAL SKILLS

Relating to other individuals in effective and productive ways is a vital need in modern society. We have at our disposal a vast amount of social science research on interpersonal dynamics. Yet this knowledge has not been translated into a form useful to individuals who wish to apply it to increase their interpersonal skills. This book aims to fill the gap between the findings of the research on interpersonal interaction and the application of this knowledge to the development of interpersonal skills.

To make this book as readable as possible, a minimum of footnotes and references to research and theory are included. This does not mean that there is no empirical support for the behaviors recommended. The basic skills that determine a person's interpersonal effectiveness have been identified from the results of the author's research (Johnson 1971, 1980), from the results of the research on effective therapeutic relationships (for example, Gurman and Razin 1977), and from the results of the social-psychological research on interpersonal relationships (Watson and Johnson, 1972; Johnson and Johnson 1975; Johnson 1979). In addition, much of the material in this book has been used in a variety of training programs aimed at increasing interpersonal skills. The evaluation of these programs indicates that the material in this book is effective in increasing the interpersonal skills of readers.

Any person concerned with increasing his or her interpersonal skills and any practitioners who work with people will find this book helpful. It is not a review of theory and research for scholars; it translates theory and research findings into a program for developing the skills necessary to form productive and fulfilling relationships with other people. Anyone, young or old, will be able to understand and use the material in this book.

CO-ORIENTATION

In building a relationship, two individuals must be *co-oriented;* that is, they must operate under the same norms and adhere to the same values. The co-orientation does not have to be perfect; rewarding relationships are quite common between individuals from different backgrounds and even different cultures. But in order to develop a relationship, you must agree on the norms and values that will determine your behavior in that relationship.

Norms refer to common expectations about the behavior that is appropriate for you and the other person in the relationship: Do you ask each other to do favors? How personal are your discussions? What types of things can you depend upon each other for? Norms depend to a large extent upon the values two individuals agree to adhere to in a relationship. The skills emphasized in this book will establish norms about expected behavior in a relationship (that is, you should self-disclose, build trust, be supportive and accepting, try to help each other, and so on). They are based upon a set of humanistic values (that is, you should assume responsibility for your ideas and feelings, strive toward self-actualization, engage in cooperative interaction, and build the capacity for intimate and personal relationships). If you use the skills presented in this book, your interactions with other people will promote norms that will help you develop effective and fulfilling relationships.

Often, establishing mutual norms and values concerning how you and the other person are going to relate is more important than the actual level of interpersonal skills the two of you have. For example, if you are mutually committed to facing conflicts and resolving them constructively, this may be more important in facilitating the growth of the relationship than the actual level of your conflict resolution skills. Or the mutual commitment to be self-disclosing and genuine with each other may be more important in creating intimacy and comradeship than the actual skill with which you disclose your feelings and reactions. This book emphasizes developing your interpersonal skills. It should be remembered, however, that whenever you apply the skills discussed in this book, you are also promoting a set of norms and values for your relationships.

There is a set of interpersonal skills identified by social science research as essential for building and maintaining constructive and fulfilling interpersonal relationships. These skills not only facilitate the development of relationships, but also help establish a constructive set of norms and values for the relationship. The next two sections of this chapter describe the procedures by which you can master these important interpersonal skills.

LEARNING FROM EXPERIENCE

We all learn from our experiences. From touching a hot stove we learn to avoid heated objects. From dating we learn about male-female relationships. Every day we have experiences we learn from. Many things about relating to other people can be learned only by experience. Seeing a movie about love is not the same as experiencing love. Hearing a lecture on friendship is not the same as having a friend. It takes more than explanations to teach interpersonal skills.

To learn interpersonal skills, you first need to understand what the skills are and when they should be used, and second, you need the opportunity to actually practice the skills. The best way to learn about the skills and to master them is through structured exercises. The plan in this book is for you to learn interpersonal skills through experiences as well as through reading. Each chapter has a series of exercises that provide opportunities to experience and master the interpersonal skills as well as to read about them. To learn skills you must understand them conceptually as well as behaviorally. Experiential learning is the best way to do this.

There is a four-stage cycle in experiential learning, as shown in Figure 1.1. The learner reflects on his or her concrete personal experiences and examines their meaning in order to formulate a set of concepts or principles to help understand such experiences. The sequence is: (1) concrete personal experiences are followed by (2) observation of, reflection on, and examination of one's experiences; this leads to (3) the formulation of abstract concepts and generalizations, which leads to (4) hypotheses to be tested in future action. Experiential learning results in personal theories about effective behavior and continuously reoccurs as a person tests out and confirms or modifies his or her personal theories.

Experiential learning is based on three assumptions: (1) people learn best when they are personally involved in the learning experience; (2) knowledge has to be discovered if it is to mean anything or make a difference in behavior; and (3) commitment to learning is highest when people are free to set their own learning goals and actively pursue them

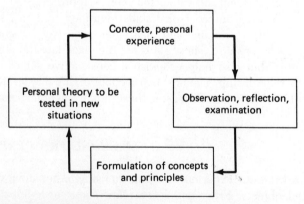

FIGURE 1.1: Experiential Learning Cycle

within a given framework. Learning by experience is a process of making generalizations and conclusions about your own direct experiences. It emphasizes experiencing directly what you are studying, building a personal commitment to learn, and being responsible for organizing the conclusions you draw from your experiences.

Learning from your experiences is especially useful when you want to learn skills. No one wants to ride in an airplane with a pilot who has read a book on how to fly but has never actually flown a plane. Reading about how to communicate is not enough to make you skillful in communicating with others; you need practice and experience in good communication skills. The next section examines skill learning in greater depth.

LEARNING INTERPERSONAL SKILLS

You are not born with interpersonal skills nor do they appear magically when you need them. You have to learn them. Interpersonal skills are learned just as any other skills are learned. Learning how to phrase messages so they will be easily understood is no different from learning how to play the piano or throw a football. All skills are learned in the same way, through the following steps:

1. *Understand why the skill is important and how it will be of value to you.* To want to learn a skill, you must see a need for it.

2. *Understand what the skill is and the component behaviors you have to engage in to perform the skill.* To learn a skill, you must have a clear idea of what the skill is, and you must know how to perform it. Often it is helpful to have someone who has already mastered the skill go through it several times while describing it step by step.

3. *Find situations in which you can practice the skill.* To master a skill, you have to practice it again and again. Try practicing the skill for a short time each day for several days until you are sure you have mastered it completely.

4. *Get someone to watch you and tell you how well you are performing the skill.* Feedback is necessary for correcting mistakes in learning a skill and for identifying problems you are having in mastering the skill. Through feedback, you find out how much progress you are making in mastering the skill. Feedback lets you compare how well you are doing with how well you want to do.

5. *Keep practicing!* With most skills, there is a period of slow learning, then a period of fast improvement, then a period in which performance remains about the same (a plateau), then another period of fast

improvement, then another plateau, and so forth. Plateaus are quite common in skill learning. You just have to stick with it until the next period of rapid improvement begins.

6. *Load your practice toward success*. Set up practice units that you can easily master. It always helps to feel like a success as you practice a skill.

7. *Get friends to encourage you to use the skill*. Your friends can help you learn by giving you encouragement to do so. The more encouragement you receive, the easier it will be for you to practice the skill.

8. *Practice until it feels real.* The more you use a skill, the more natural it feels. While learning a skill, you may feel self-conscious and awkward. Practicing a skill is like role playing—it does not feel like *real* behavior. But you should not let this awkwardness stop you from mastering the skill. Ever try learning to type by typing only when it feels natural? It is through role playing and drill that all skills are learned. If you keep practicing, the awkwardness will pass, and soon you will become comfortable and *natural* in using the skill.

This book is designed to provide you with information concerning the nature of, and the need for, the interpersonal skills discussed. The behaviors involved in engaging in the skills are specified. Questions to test your comprehension and understanding of the material presented are included in each chapter. You are given instructions for participating in exercises that provide you with an opportunity to practice the skills, and you receive feedback on how well you are mastering them. Often the exercises let you diagnose the present level of your skills. After you engage in the exercises, it is up to you to practice the skills until you feel comfortable doing them. At the end of each chapter you will be asked to evaluate the extent to which you have mastered the skills presented.

A mechanical process is involved in practicing the behaviors that constitute a skill. While you do the exercises, you may, at times, feel that the process is somewhat mechanical and unreal. But that is true of every kind of skill development. Learning how to play a piano, for example, also involves the mechanical practice of specific behaviors that seem unreal compared to the performance of a beautiful piano concerto. It is only when you apply your new skills to real situations that they will gain the fire and life that may sometimes be lacking while practicing.

This book provides you with guidance for increasing your interpersonal skills. It is up to you to take advantage of the material and exercises presented and use it in ways that will increase your interpersonal skills. The extent of your learning and skill development rests entirely on your commitment to using this book effectively.

In learning any new skills, the approval of a group is a powerful source of motivation and support. Readers of this book may find it most rewarding to go through the exercises as part of a group. The group should make a point of giving approval to those members who are seriously trying to increase their interpersonal skills. The more a member practices and develops interpersonal skills, the more group approval he or she should receive. Everyone's progress will be enhanced if the group supports members' attempts to experiment with new behavior and to take risks in trying out their new skills. There are few influences upon our behavior more powerful than the support and approval of a group of friends. Using the group's influence to facilitate our learning is one of the most constructive ways of ensuring that we will increase our interpersonal skills.

SUMMARY

Interpersonal skills are essential for many aspects of our personal well-being. They help us to grow and develop socially and cognitively, to build a positive and coherent personal identity, to feel we are firmly in touch with reality, and to gain and maintain psychological and physical health. Interpersonal skills are also essential for the well-being of the society in which we live. Human evolution and survival are intimately intertwined with our ability to initiate, develop, and stabilize our relationships with each other. Furthermore, our interdependence requires us to be skillful in building and maintaining productive interpersonal relationships. Our self-actualization is based on our ability to relate to other people. As a species we seem to have a relationship imperative that is based on needs that can be satisfied only through interacting with other humans and that requires us to seek out relationships with others.

The essential interpersonal skills generally fall into four areas: (1) knowing and trusting each other, (2) communicating with each other accurately and unambiguously, (3) accepting and supporting each other, and (4) resolving conflicts and relationship problems constructively. Each of these areas is covered in this book. This book is constructed to faciliate your mastery of the essential interpersonal skills by providing discussions of the skills and exercises that enable you to practice and experience the skills.

2

Self-Disclosure

INTRODUCTION

By letting you know me, I allow you to like me. By disclosing myself to
you, I create the potential for trust, caring, commitment, growth, and self-
understanding. How can you care for me if you do not know me? How can
you trust me if I do not demonstrate my trust in you by disclosing myself
to you? How can you be committed to me if you know little or nothing
about me? How can I know and understand myself if I do not disclose
myself to friends? To like me, to trust me, to be committed to our relationship, to facilitate my personal growth and self-understanding, and to
be my friend you must know me. In order for me to feel free to disclose
myself to you, I must accept and appreciate myself. This chapter will focus
on self-awareness and the disclosure of oneself to other people. A later
chapter will focus on self-acceptance.

SELF-DISCLOSURE

Relationships begin with two people getting to know one another. To establish a fulfilling relationship, two people must disclose themselves to
each other. Without self-disclosure you cannot form a personal relationship
with another person. A relationship grows and develops as two people be-

come more open about themselves and with each other. If you cannot reveal yourself, you cannot become close to others, and you cannot be valued by others for who you are. Two people who let each other know how they are reacting to situations and to each other are pulled together; two people who stay silent about their reactions and feelings stay strangers.

Self-disclosure may be defined as revealing how you are reacting to the present situation and giving any information about the past that is relevant to an understanding of your reactions to the present. Reactions to people and events are not facts as much as they are feelings. To be self-disclosing means to share with another person how you feel about something he or she has said or done, or how you feel about events that have just occurred. Self-disclosure does not mean revealing intimate details of your past life. Making highly personal confessions about your past may lead to a temporary feeling of intimacy, but a relationship is built by disclosing your reactions to events you both experience or to what the other person says or does. A person comes to know and understand you not through knowing your past history but through knowing how you react. Past history is helpful only if it clarifies why are you reacting in a certain way.

BEING AWARE OF MYSELF, OF WHO I AM, AND OF WHAT I AM LIKE	BEING AWARE OF YOU, WHO YOU ARE, AND OF WHAT YOU ARE LIKE
+	+
BEING ACCEPTING OF MYSELF, AWARE OF MY STRENGTHS AND ABILITIES	BEING ACCEPTING OF YOU, AWARE OF YOUR STRENGTHS AND ABILITIES
+	+
TRUSTING YOU TO ACCEPT AND SUPPORT ME, TO COOPERATE WITH ME, AND TO BE OPEN WITH ME	BEING TRUSTWORTHY BY ACCEPTING AND SUPPORTING YOU, COOPERATING WITH YOU, AND BEING OPEN WITH YOU
results in	results in
BEING OPEN <u>WITH</u> YOU, SHARING MY IDEAS AND FEELINGS, AND LETTING YOU KNOW WHO I AM AS A PERSON	BEING OPEN <u>TO</u> YOU, BEING INTERESTED IN YOUR IDEAS AND FEELINGS AND IN WHO YOU ARE AS A PERSON

BEING OPEN <u>WITH</u> YOU + BEING OPEN <u>TO</u> YOU
= AN OPEN RELATIONSHIP

There has been a considerable amount of research on the effects of self-disclosure on interpersonal relationships (Johnson 1973). There is, for example, considerable evidence that indicates that healthy relationships are built on self-disclosure. If you hide how you are reacting to the other person, your concealment can sicken the relationship. The energy you pour into hiding adds to the stress of the relationship and dulls your awareness of your own inner experience, thus decreasing your ability to disclose your reactions even when it is perfectly safe and appropriate to do so. Hiding your reactions from others through fear of rejection and conflict or through feelings of shame and guilt leads to loneliness. Being silent is not being strong; strength is the willingness to take risks in a relationship, to disclose yourself with the intention of building a better relationship.

Several aspects of a relationship influence self-disclosure. The more self-disclosing you are to another person, the more likely it will be that that person will like you. You are more likely to self-disclose to a person you know and like than to a person you do not know or do not like. The amount of self-disclosure you engage in will influence the amount of self-disclosure the other person engages in; the more you self-disclose, the more the other person will tend to self-disclose.

Willingness to engage in self-disclosure is related to several characteristics. The research done in this field indicates that persons willing to be self-disclosing will likely be competent, open, and socially extroverted individuals who feel a strong need to interact with others. They are likely to be flexible, adaptive, and perhaps more intelligent than less self-revealing peers. They are objectively aware of the realities of the interpersonal situations in which they are involved, and they perceive a fairly close congruence between the way they are and the way they would like to be. Finally, they view others as generally good rather than evil.

Communicating intimately with another person, especially in times of stress, seems to be a basic human need. Disclosing yourself to another person builds a relationship that allows for such intimate communication, both by yourself and by the other. If neither you nor the other person feels free to engage in self-disclosure, you can be of little or no help to each other during periods of stress.

Being self-disclosing means being "for real." It is important that your self-disclosures are as honest, genuine, and authentic as possible. This chapter will focus on some of the skills involved in effective self-disclosure, but the communication of the sincerity, genuineness, and authenticity of your self-disclosures is one of the most important aspects of building a relationship.

In addition to being *open with* other people, you must be *open to* others to build good relationships. Being open to another person means showing that you are interested in how he feels about what you are saying and doing. It is being receptive to his self-disclosure. This does not mean prying into the intimate areas of another's life. It means being willing to listen to his reactions to the present situation and to what you are doing and saying.

In responding to another's self-disclosure, it is important to show acceptance and support, if possible. Being accepting and supportive will increase the other person's tendency to be open with you. It will strengthen the relationship and help it grow. Even when a person's behavior seriously offends you, it is possible for you to express acceptance of the person and disagreement with the way she behaves. To be open with another person is to risk rejection; to self-disclose is to ask for support and acceptance in trying to build a better relationship. You should be careful, therefore, to give the support and acceptance necessary for the relationship to grow.

COMPREHENSION TEST A

Test your understanding of self-disclosure by answering true or false to the following statements. Answers are found at the end of the chapter

True	False	1.	Self-disclosure is revealing how you are reacting to the present and giving relevant information about the past.
True	False	2.	Self-disclosure helps a relationship grow.
True	False	3.	Self-disclosure means revealing the intimate details of your past life.
True	False	4.	Hiding your reactions to another person's behavior helps your relationship with that person grow.
True	False	5.	When a person's behavior seriously offends you, you should reject him as a person.
True	False	6.	Jim meets Mary at a party. Mary immediately begins to tell Jim about her relationship with her father. This is a good example of self-disclosure.
True	False	7.	Communicating intimately with another person is a human need.
True	False	8.	Sandy and Bill are watching a sunset. Bill begins to explain to Sandy the way he is reacting to the sunset and goes into a childhood incident that has affected the way he reacts to sunsets. This is a good example of self-disclosure.

True   False   9. You should be self-disclosing at all times in all relationships.

True   False   10. Being open to others involves being interested in their self-disclosures.

APPROPRIATENESS OF SELF-DISCLOSURE

Self-disclosure must be relevant to your relationship with the other person and appropriate to the situation you are in. You can be too self-disclosing. A person who reveals too many of her reactions too fast may scare others away; a relationship is built gradually except in rare and special cases. Being too self-disclosing will create as many relationship problems as disclosing too little. Although you should sometimes take risks with your self-disclosure to others, you should not be blind to the appropriateness of your behavior to the situation. Self-disclosure is appropriate when:

1. It is not a random or isolated act but rather part of an ongoing relationship.
2. It is reciprocated.
3. It concerns what is going on within and between persons in the present.
4. It creates a reasonable chance of improving the relationship.
5. It takes account of the effect it will have upon the other person.
6. It speeds up when a crisis develops in the relationship.
7. It moves gradually to a deeper level.

While relationships are built through self-disclosure, there are times when you will want to hide your reactions to a particular situation from another person. If a person has clearly shown himself to be untrustworthy, it is foolish to be self-disclosing with him. If you know from past experience that the other person will misinterpret or overreact to your self-disclosure, you may wish to keep silent.

SELF-DISCLOSURE AND SELF-AWARENESS

You can't disclose your feelings and reactions if you do not know what they are. Unless you are aware of your reactions and feelings, you cannot consciously communicate them to others. Being aware of how you react to various situations and what you like and dislike as a person is the first step in being self-disclosing with other people and building strong relationships with them. Self-awareness is also the first step toward understanding yourself and making a choice as to whether or not you wish to change current patterns of behavior to more effective ones.

There are two major ways of becoming more self-aware. The first involves "listening" to yourself in order to understand how you are feeling and reacting and what is causing your feelings and reactions. You have a reaction to everything you do and notice. Most of these reactions are ignored. Yet they can become conscious if you work on it. The procedures for becoming more aware of your internal reactions are discussed in chapter 5. In addition, when you express your feelings, perceptions, reactions, and experiences in words, they become clear in your mind and take on a new meaning for you. Disclosing your feelings and reactions to friends whom you trust can lead to a new awareness of yourself and your experiences. Disclosure can lead to increased self-awareness and self-understanding, providing in turn the opportunity for further disclosures that will promote even greater self-understanding and awareness.

The second way of becoming more self-aware is to request feedback from other people as to how they see you and how they are reacting to your behavior. Before considering feedback, however, it may be helpful to examine Figures 2.1, 2.2, and 2.3 (Luft 1969). Figure 2.1 is known as the Johari Window after its two originators, Joe Luft and Harry Ingham. It illustrates their point that there are certain things you know about yourself and certain things you do not know about yourself as well as certain things other people know about you and certain things they do not know. It is

	Known to Self	Unknown to Self
Known to Others	1. Free to Self and Others	2. Blind to Self, Seen by Others
Unknown to Others	3. Hidden Area: Self Hidden from Others	4. Unknown Self

FIGURE 2.1:   Identification of Areas of the Self

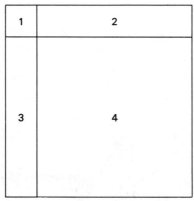

FIGURE 2.2: At the Beginning of a Relationship

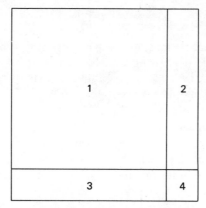

FIGURE 2.3: After the Development of a Close Relationship

assumed that it takes energy to hide information from yourself and others and that the more information that is known, the clearer communication will be. Building a relationship therefore often involves working to enlarge your free area while decreasing your blind and hidden areas. As you become more self-disclosing, you reduce the hidden area. As you encourage others to be self-disclosing with you, your blind area is reduced. Through reducing your hidden area you give other people information to react to, thus enabling them to help you reduce your blind area. Through reducing your blind area, you increase your self-awareness; this helps you to be even more self-disclosing with others.

COMPREHENSION TEST B

Test your understanding of the Johari Window by answering the following questions. Answers are at the end of the chapter.

1. Write "free," "hidden," "blind," or "unknown" in the appropriate space.

_____ a. A man is reluctant to express his resentment for another member of his group.

_____ b. A woman is not aware that she, herself, and others think she is a critical person.

_____ c. A man expresses his religious doubts to his friends.

_____ d. Unexpectedly, a woman expresses anger at a group she is a member of and cannot explain why she is angry.

2. The Johari Window illustrates (indicate the correct answer):

   a. Building a relationship involves enlarging your blind and hidden areas while decreasing your free areas.

   b. Building a relationship involves enlarging your free areas while decreasing your blind and hidden areas.

   c. Building a relationship involves opening your windows so other people can see you.

Look around at the members of your group. How large is your free area with each of the other members? How large is each of their free areas with you?

SELF-AWARENESS THROUGH FEEDBACK FROM OTHERS

Personal growth involves self-disclosure in words and actions, feedback from a trusted person, a comparison between what you are now and your vision of what you might become, attempts to change, followed by further feedback and self-evaluation, and so on. Feedback from people you trust can confirm your view of yourself or reveal to you aspects of yourself and consequences of your behavior you never knew. And it is through feedback from other people that you increase your self-awareness.

When other people disclose how they are reacting to your behavior, they are giving you *feedback*. The purpose of feedback is to provide constructive information to help you become aware of how your behavior af-

fects others and is perceived by others. The key benefit of feedback is that it tells you when you are off course with respect to your desired objectives. Often the most helpful feedback is that which tells you that your behavior is not being as effective as you want it to be and, therefore, helps you modify your actions so that they become more productive.

When you disclose how you are reacting to the actions of another person, you are providing the other person with feedback. Helpful feedback tells the other person what effect her actions are having on you. It is important to give feedback in a way that will not be threatening to the receiver and make the receiver defensive. The more defensive a person is, the less likely it is that she will hear and understand your feedback correctly. The person receiving feedback, furthermore, is always responsible for deciding whether or not her present behavior is to be continued or changed. By increasing another person's self-awareness through feedback, you provide her with a more informed choice for future behavior. Some characteristics of helpful, nonthreatening feedback are:

1. *Focus your feedback on the person's behavior, not on his personality.* Refer to what the person does, not to what you imagine his traits to be. Thus, you might say the person "talked frequently in the meeting" rather than saying the person "is a loudmouth." The former is an observation of what you see and hear and the latter is an inference about, or interpretation of, the person's character.

2. *Focus your feedback on descriptions rather than on judgments.* Refer

to what occurred, not to your judgments of right or wrong, good or bad, or nice or naughty. You might say, "You do not pronounce words clearly, and you speak too softly to be heard," rather than, "You are a terrible, rotten, lousy public speaker." Judgments arise out of a personal frame of reference or value system and should be avoided, whereas description represents, as much as possible, neutral reporting.

3. *Focus your feedback on a specific situation rather than on abstract behavior.* What a person does is always related to a specific time and place. Feedback that ties behavior to a specific situation and is given immediately after the behavior has occurred increases self-awareness. Instead of saying, "Sometimes your face lights up and happiness shines out of your eyes," say, "When you and John were talking just now your face lit up and you smiled in a way that made me feel warm."

4. *Focus your feedback on the "here and now" not on the "there and then."* The more immediate the feedback, the more helpful it is. Instead of saying, "Three years ago when I saw you in the hall you didn't speak to me," say, "Hey, I just said hello and you didn't reply. Is something wrong?"

5. *Focus your feedback on sharing your perceptions and feelings rather than on giving advice.* By sharing perceptions and feelings you leave other people free to decide for themselves, in the light of their own goals in a particular situation at a particular time, how to use the perceptions, reactions, and feelings. When you give advice, you tell other people what to do with the information and thereby take away their freedom to determine for themselves what is for them the most appropriate course of action. Let the other people decide for themselves what behavior they want to change. You can give feedback such as, "You look away and blush whenever John says hello to you," without giving advice such as, "You are too shy. Go ask John for a date."

6. *Do not force feedback on other people.* Feedback is given to help people become more self-aware and to improve their effectiveness in relating to other people. It is not given to make you feel better. Feedback should serve the needs of the receiver, not the needs of the giver. Giving feedback does release tension and increase the giver's energy, but help and feedback need to be given and heard as an offer, not as something being forced on the receiver. If other people do not want to hear your feedback, do not force it on them. If

you do not want to hear other people's feedback to you, do not let them force it on you. Even if you are upset and want more than anything else in the world (at that moment) to give a friend some feedback, do not give it if your friend is too defensive or uninterested to understand it.

7. *Do not give people more feedback than they can understand at the time.* If you overload other people with feedback, it reduces the chances that they will use it. When you give people more feedback than they can understand, you are satisfying some need for yourself rather than helping the other people become more self-aware.

8. *Focus your feedback on actions that the person can change.* It does no good to tell people that they have a lopsided head, that you don't like the color of their eyes, or that they are missing an ear. These are things the other people cannot change.

The giving and receiving of feedback requires courage, skill, understanding, and respect for yourself and others as well as involvement. Do not give feedback lightly. Make sure you are willing to be responsible for what you say and to clarify as much as the receiver wants. Be sure the timing of your feedback is appropriate. Excellent feedback presented at an inappropriate time may do more harm than good. Finally, remember that the purpose of feedback is to increase other people's self-awareness and feelings that "I am liked, I am respected, I am appreciated, I am capable, I am valued." To invest in a relationship by providing accurate and realistic feedback is a sign of caring and commitment.

COMPREHENSION TEST C

Test your understanding of feedback by answering true or false to the following statements. Answers are at the end of the chapter.

True   False   1. You should focus feedback on the person rather than on his or her behavior.

True   False   2. You should focus on judgment rather than on description.

True   False   3. You should focus on a specific time and place, not on an abstract behavior.

True   False   4. You should focus on the "here and now" rather than on the "there and then."

True   False   5. You should focus on giving advice rather than on sharing information.

True   False   6. You should focus on giving feedback that will make you feel better.

True   False   7. You should give as much feedback as you can think of without worrying about how much the person can use.

True   False   8. You are giving feedback when you tell another person what is wrong with him.

True   False   9. You are giving feedback when you explain how you are reacting to the way another person is behaving.

True   False   10. You are giving feedback when you tear this book into small pieces and stomp on them.

INTERPERSONAL EFFECTIVENESS

The effectiveness of your behavior depends in large measure on your self-awareness; your self-awareness depends in large part upon receiving feedback from other individuals; the quality of the feedback you receive from other persons depends largely upon how much you self-disclose. In order to improve your interpersonal effectiveness, you need to be aware of the consequences of your behavior and decide whether those consequences match your intentions. *Interpersonal effectiveness* can be defined as the degree to which the consequences of your behavior match your intentions.

When you interact with another person, you have no choice but to make some impact, stimulate some ideas, arouse some impressions and observations, or trigger some feelings and reactions. Sometimes you make the impression you want to, but at other times you may find that some people react to your behavior much differently than you would like them to. An expression of warmth, for instance, may be seen as your being condescending; an expression of anger may be seen as a joke. Your interpersonal effectiveness depends upon your ability to communicate clearly what you want to communicate, to create the impression you wish, to influence the other person in the way you intend. You may improve your interpersonal effectiveness by disclosing your intentions, receiving feedback on your behavior, and modifying your behavior until other individuals perceive it as you mean it, that is, until it has the consequences you intend it to have.

EXERCISE 2.1: INITIATING RELATIONSHIPS

The following is a simple experience in initiating relationships. The objectives of the exercise are:

1. To initiate relationships with other individuals whom you do not know.
2. To share initial feelings and thoughts with other individuals.
3. To take risks in revealing yourself to other individuals.
4. To experience a variety of ways to disclose yourself to others.
5. To encourage openness, trust, risk taking, and feedback with other individuals.

The activities are:

1. Everyone stand up and mill around the room, making sure that you pass by everyone present. Greet each person nonverbally. This greeting may be a handshake, a smile, a wink, a sock on the arm, or any other nonverbal way you may think of to say hello. After five minutes of milling, find a person you don't know. If you know everyone present, find the person you know least well.
2. Sit down with the person; each of you then take 2½ minutes to introduce yourself to the other. Do this by discussing the question of who you are as a person.
3. Turn around and find someone else near you whom you don't know or know least well of the other people present. Sit down with your new partner; each of you then take 2½ minutes to discuss the most significant experience you have had recently.
4. Find someone else you don't know. Sit down with your new partner and take 5 minutes (2½ minutes each) to exchange views on what you hope to accomplish by participating in this program.
5. Find another person whom you don't know. Sit down with your new partner and take 5 minutes (2½ minutes each) to share a fantasy or daydream that you often have. It may be connected with success, such as becoming president of the United States, or it may be connected with love, such as meeting a terrific person who immediately falls in love with you, or it may be about what you would like to do with your next vacation.
6. Now form a group no larger than ten or twelve people. Try to be in a group with as many of the individuals as you have talked with in the previous activities. In the group discuss:
   a. How you feel about the different members on the basis of the previous activities, first impression, or past experience if you knew them previously.
   b. Which activity you felt was most helpful in getting to know the person you were interacting with.
   c. What you have learned from this exercise.
   d. What individuals in the group need to share if you are to get to know them during this session.
   e. Anyhing else that seems relevant to initiating relationships. This discussion may continue for as long as you like.

7. Alternative topics for discussion in pairs are
   a. What animal I would like to be and why.
   b. What song means the most to me and why.
   c. What it is that I like most about myself.
   d. How I would change myself if I had complete power to do so.
   e. What my most significant childhood experience was.
   f. What my immediate impressions of you are.
   g. The ways in which we are similar or different.

EXERCISE 2.2: NAME TAGGING

The purpose of this exercise is to get to know other members of your group or class while at the same time letting them know more about you. The procedure is:

1. Working alone, write your first name in the center of a three-by-five-inch index card. Write it large enough so other people can read it at some distance. In the upper left-hand corner, write the names of two places: where you were born and your favorite place. In the upper right-hand corner, write two of your favorite activities. These may be sports, hobbies, pastimes, jobs, or other ways you spend your time. In the lower left-hand corner, write three adjectives that describe you. In the lower right-hand corner, describe something you are looking forward to, something you are excited about doing in the future—for example, a vacation or a new job.

2. Pin the card on the front of your shirt or blouse.

3. Mill around, find people you don't know, and discuss each other's cards. You should try to meet as many people as possible in the time allowed (about twenty minutes).

4. Keep your name tag and wear it at subsequent sessions until you know everyone present and they all know you.

Indiana British Columbia		Mountain climbing Working
	DAVE	
Intense Hard-working Fun-loving		Backpacking in the Canadian Rockies

EXERCISE 2.3: SHARING YOUR PAST

The purpose of this exercise is to let other people get to know you by sharing your family history with them and to get to know them by learning more about their past. The procedure is:

1.   Fill in the following chart with the names (first and last) of your grandparents and parents. If you are not sure of all the names, ask your parents what they are. If you did not grow up with your parents, use whatever parent figures you have.

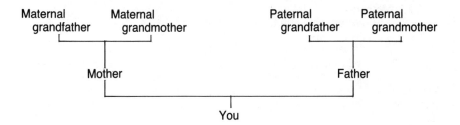

2.   In small groups (from two to seven members), tell your answers to the following questions and listen carefully to the answers of the other group members.
   a.   Maternal grandfather:
      1.   Where was he born and raised?
      2.   What was his early life like?
      3.   What are (were) his outstanding characteristics?
      4.   What is (was) his career?
      5.   Can you trace any of your characteristics or attitudes back to him?
      6.   Do any family traditions (activities, foods, places, etc.) come from him?
   b.   Maternal grandmother:
      1.   Where was she born and raised?
      2.   What was her early life like?
      3.   What are (were) her outstanding characteristics?
      4.   What is (was) her career?
      5.   Can you trace any of your characteristics or attitudes back to her?
      6.   Do any family traditions (activities, foods, places, etc.) come from her?
   c.   Paternal grandfather:
      1.   Where was he born and raised?
      2.   What was his early life like?
      3.   What are (were) his outstanding characteristics?
      4.   What is (was) his career?
      5.   Can you trace any of your characteristics or attitudes back to him?
      6.   Do any family traditions (activities, foods, places, etc.) come from him?
   d.   Paternal grandmother:
      1.   Where was she born and raised?
      2.   What was her early life like?

  3. What are (were) her outstanding characteristics?
  4. What is (was) her career?
  5. Can you trace any of your characteristics or attitudes back to her?
  6. Do any family traditions (activities, foods, places, etc.) come from her?
  e. Mother:
  1. Where was she born and raised?
  2. What was her early life like?
  3. What are (were) her outstanding characteristics?
  4. What is (was) her career?
  5. Can you trace any of your characteristics or attitudes back to her?
  6. Do any family traditions (activities, foods, places, etc.) come from her?
  f. Father:
  1. Where was he born and raised?
  2. What was his early life like?
  3. What are (were) his outstanding characteristics?
  4. What is (was) his career?
  5. Can you trace any of your characteristics or attitudes back to him?
  6. Do any family traditions (activities, foods, places, etc.) come from him?
3. In the same small groups, discuss the following questions:
  a. How did you feel about doing this exercise?
  b. Did you learn anything new about yourself?
  c. Is it important for you to know about your family?
  d. How do you think an adopted person deals with this issue? (If you are adopted, how do you deal with it?)
  e. How did you react to what other members of your group said about their family roots?

EXERCISE 2.4: SELF-DISCLOSURE AND SELF-AWARENESS

The purpose of this exercise is to allow participants to focus on three of the areas described in the Johari Window: the free area, the blind area, and the hidden area. It is to be used with people who know each other, at least a little. Each participant needs a number of three-by-five-inch index cards. The procedure is:

1. Working by yourself, review the material on the Johari Window. Then on a sheet of paper, write down several of your characteristics that you think other people in the room know (free area) and several of your characteristics that you think no one in the room knows (hidden area). Leave room on your paper to add characteristics in your blind area.
2. Form into groups of five. Each person then takes five three-by-five-inch index cards. Working by yourself, write a different group member's name on the front of each card (make one for yourself also). Turn the cards over and write two positive characteristics of the person whose name appears

on the front. On your own card write two positive characteristics you think the other group members do not know about you (from your hidden area) that you are willing to have them know.

3. Collect all the cards, shuffle them, and place them face down in a pile in the center of the group. Then, one by one, take each card, read the description aloud, and decide by group consensus whom the card belongs to (do not look at the name on the front of the card). Place the card, with the name still facing down, in front of the person the group decides it belongs to. Repeat this procedure until all the cards have been distributed.

4. One by one, members of the group turn the cards they have been given face up. Each member gives his or her reactions to the cards received. If someone receives a card that does not belong to him, the card is given to the person it really belongs to. The group then discusses:
    a. Why were the cards given to the right or wrong person?
    b. Are the descriptions on the cards accurate for the people for whom they are intended?
    c. What has been learned from the exercise?

5. Working by yourself, take the cards you received and classify them into the free, hidden, and blind areas of the Johari Window. If your cards mention any characteristics you did not write down at the beginning of the exercise, add them to your sheet. Pay special attention to characteristics that are in your blind area.

Self-Awareness Sheet

Name _____ Date _____

Free Area

1.   6.
2.   7.
3.   8.
4.   9.
5.   10.

Hidden Area

1.   6.
2.   7.
3.   8.
4.   9.
5.   10.

Blind Area

1.   6.
2.   7.
3.   8.
4.   9.
5.   10.

EXERCISE 2.5: YOUR UNKNOWN AREA

The purpose of this exercise is to increase your awareness of aspects of yourself that may be in your unknown area. The procedure is:

1. As the instructor reads a list of topics, write down in a "free association" way the first responses that come into your mind.
2. Study your written responses. What conclusions about yourself as a person can you make from your responses? What characteristics, needs, goals, fears, or worries do your responses reflect?
3. Form into groups of five members. If you feel comfortable doing so, share your responses with the group and ask for their help in describing what you have learned about yourself. If a member of your group does not wish to report her responses, protect her right to remain silent. Be supportive of those group members who do reveal their responses to the group.
4. Working by yourself, summarize on a sheet of paper what you have learned about yourself from the exercise.

Topics

tool	musical instrument	fruit
geographic location	vacation	article of clothing
color	human	god or goddess
hero or heroine	legendary figure	piece of furniture
season of the year	food	retreat
weapon	animal	protect

EXERCISE 2.6: LABELING

The purpose of this exercise is to provide feedback concerning first impressions. Each participant needs ten blank name tags or labels. The procedure is:

1. The instructor gives each participant ten blank name tags or labels and a copy of the Category List.
2. Participants copy each category on a separate blank name tag or label.
3. Participants then mill around the room and choose a person who best fits each category. They then attach a category label on the clothing of the person and engage in a one-minute conversation with the person.
4. Participants form groups of five and discuss reactions to being labeled (or not labeled) by people's first impressions. Did you learn anything about yourself?

Category List

happy	warm	fun
smart	friendly	spontaneous
sincere	aloof	aggressive
mysterious		

The purpose of this exercise is to get acquainted with other members of a group. Each participant needs a copy of the Interview Sheet. The procedure is:

1. Choose a partner. Make sure it is a person you would like to know better. Choose five questions from the Interview Sheet and interview your partner. He or she will then interview you by asking you five of the questions. Each of you will later introduce the other to a group, so you may want to take notes.
2. Form groups of six. Each person introduces his or her partner to the group.
3. Pick a new partner and repeat the interview and introduction procedure. The whole process may be repeated as often as there is time for.
4. Discuss in your group:
    a. How does it feel to be interviewed and introduced?
    b. Did you learn anything about yourself from the experience?

Interview Sheet

What is difficult for you to do?

What is a favorite joke of yours?

How do you define friendship?

What value is most important to you?

When do you feel most comfortable?

If you weren't what you are, what would you be?

How do you deal with your own anger?

Where do you go to be alone?

What is your favorite object?

What do you most often dream about?

Whom do you trust the most?

When do you feel most uncomfortable?

Under what circumstances would you tell a lie?

What is difficult for you to do?

Where would you most like to live?

What is your major life goal?

What is the thing your worst enemy would say about you?

What is the thing your best friend would say about you?

EXERCISE 2.8: FRIENDSHIP RELATIONS

The following exercise is based on the Johari Window. The objectives of the exercise are to examine your and the group's receptivity to feedback, willingness to self-disclose, and willingness to take risks in relations with friends. The procedure for the exercise is:

1. Working by yourself, complete the Friendship Relations Survey.
2. Score the results according to the instructions on pages 36 and 37.
3. Follow the directions on the Friendship Relations Survey Summary Sheet that follows to get the final results of the survey for yourself and your group.
4. Form into groups of six. Complete a new Friendship Relations Survey Summary Sheet for the group as a whole, using the average of the members' scores. The group average is found by adding the scores of every member and dividing by the number of persons in the group.
5. Discuss the results in the group, using the following questions:
   a. What are your thoughts and feelings about when it is appropriate to receive feedback from your friends and to self-disclose to them?
   b. What are your thoughts and feelings about when you want other members of the group to give feedback to you and when you want to self-discose to them?
   c. Do you have a conservative or a risky group?
   d. How does trust affect your receptivity to feedback and willingness to give feedback?
   e. Would you like to change the way you are now behaving?
   f. What changes in your behavior would be productive and useful in developing better relationships with your friends?

Friendship Relations Survey

This questionnaire was written to help you assess your understanding of your behavior in interpersonal relationships. There are no "right" or "wrong" answers. The best answer is the one that comes closest to representing your quest for good interpersonal relationships. In each statement, the first sentence gives a situation and the second sentence gives a reaction. For each statement indicate the number that is closest to the way you would handle the situation.

     5 = You *always* would act this way

     4 = You *frequently* would act this way

     3 = You *sometimes* would act this way

     2 = You *seldom* would act this way

     1 = You *never* would act this way

Try to relate each question to your own personal experience. Take as much time as you need to give a true and accurate answer for yourself. *There is no right or wrong answer.* Trying to give the "correct" answer will make your answer meaningless to you. *Be honest with yourself!*

1. You work with a friend, but some of her mannerisms and habits are getting on your nerves and irritating you. More and more you avoid interacting with or even seeing your friend.
   Never 1—2—3—4—5 Always
2. In a moment of weakness, you give away a friend's secret. Your friend

finds out and calls you to ask about it. You admit to it and talk with your friend about how to handle secrets better in the future.
Never 1—2—3—4—5 Always

3. You have a friend who never seems to have time for you. You ask him about it, telling him how you feel.
Never 1—2—3—4—5 Always

4. Your friend is upset at you because you have inconvenienced him. He tells you how he feels. You tell him he is too sensitive and is overreacting.
Never 1—2—3—4—5 Always

5. You had a disagreement with a friend and now she ignores you whenever she's around you. You decide to ignore her back.
Never 1—2—3—4—5 Always

6. A friend has pointed out that you never seem to have time for him. You explain why you have been busy and try for a mutual understanding.
Never 1—2—3—4—5 Always

7. At great inconvenience, you arrange to take your friend to the doctor's office. When you arrive to pick her up, you find she has decided not to go. You explain to her how you feel and try to reach an understanding about future favors.
Never 1—2—3—4—5 Always

8. You have argued with a friend and are angry with her, ignoring her when you meet. She tells you how she feels and asks about restoring the friendship. You ignore her and walk away.
Never 1—2—3—4—5 Always

9. You have a secret that you have told only to your best friend. The next day, an acquaintance asks you about the secret. You deny the secret and decide to break off the relationship with your best friend.
Never 1—2—3—4—5 Always

10. A friend who works with you tells you about some of your mannerisms and habits that get on his nerves. You discuss these with your friend and look for some possible ways of dealing with the problem.
Never 1—2—3—4—5 Always

11. Your best friend gets involved in something illegal that you believe will lead to serious trouble. You decide to tell your friend how you disapprove of his involvement in the situation.
Never 1—2—3—4—5 Always

12. In a moment of weakness, you give away a friend's secret. Your friend finds out and calls you to ask about it. You deny it firmly.
Never 1—2—3—4—5 Always

13. You have a friend who never seems to have time for you. You decide to forget her and to start looking for new friends.
Never 1—2—3—4—5 Always

14. You are involved in something illegal, and your friend tells you of her disapproval and fear that you will get in serious trouble. You discuss it with your friend.
Never 1—2—3—4—5 Always

15. You work with a friend, but some of her mannerisms and habits are getting on your nerves and irritating you. You explain your feelings to your friend, looking for a mutual solution to the problem.
    Never 1—2—3—4—5 Always

16. A friend has pointed out that you never seem to have time for him. You walk away.
    Never 1—2—3—4—5 Always

17. Your best friend gets involved in something illegal that you believe will lead to serious trouble. You decide to mind your own business.
    Never 1—2—3—4—5 Always

18. Your friend is upset because you have inconvenienced him. He tells you how he feels. You try to understand and agree on a way to keep it from happening again.
    Never 1—2—3—4—5 Always

19. You had a disagreement with a friend, and now she ignores you whenever she's around you. You tell her how her actions make you feel and ask about restoring your friendship.
    Never 1—2—3—4—5 Always

20. A friend who works with you tells you about some of your mannerisms and habits that get on his nerves. You listen and walk away.
    Never 1—2—3—4—5 Always

21. At great inconvenience, you arrange to take your friend to the doctor's office. When you arrive to pick her up, you find she had decided not to go. You say nothing but resolve never to do any favors for that person again.
    Never 1—2—3—4—5 Always

22. You have argued with a friend and are angry with her, ignoring her when you meet. She tells you how she feels and asks about restoring the friendship. You discuss ways of maintaining your friendship, even when you disagree.
    Never 1—2—3—4—5 Always

23. You have a secret that you have told only to your best friend. The next day, an acquaintance asks you about the secret. You call your friend and ask her about it, trying to come to an understanding how to handle secrets better in the future.
    Never 1—2—3—4—5 Always

24. You are involved in something illegal, and your friend tells you of her disapproval and fear that you will get in serious trouble. You tell your friend to mind her own business.
    Never 1—2—3—4—5 Always

Friendship Relations Survey Answer Key

In the Friendship Relations Survey there are twelve questions that deal with your willingness to self-disclose and twelve questions that are concerned with your receptivity to feedback. Transfer your scores to this answer key. Reverse the scoring for all questions that are starred; that is, if you answered 5, record the score of 1; if you answered 4, record the score of 2; if you answered 3, record the score of 3; if you answered 2, record the score of 4; and if you answered 1, record the score of 5. Then add the scores in each column.

Willingness to Self-Disclose	Receptivity to Feedback
*1. _____	2. _____
3. _____	4. _____
*5. _____	6. _____
7. _____	*8. _____
*9. _____	10. _____
11. _____	*12. _____
*13. _____	14. _____
15. _____	*16. _____
*17. _____	18. _____
19. _____	*20. _____
*21. _____	22. _____
23. _____	*24. _____
Total _____	**Total** _____

On the Friendship Relations Survey Summary Sheet below, add the totals for receptivity to feedback and willingness to self-disclose to arrive at an index of interpersonal risk taking which you will use in chapter 3.

Friendship Relations Survey Summary Sheet

Draw horizontal and vertical lines through your scores (Part a) and the group's receptivity to feedback and willingness to self-disclose (Part b). The results should look like the Johari Window.

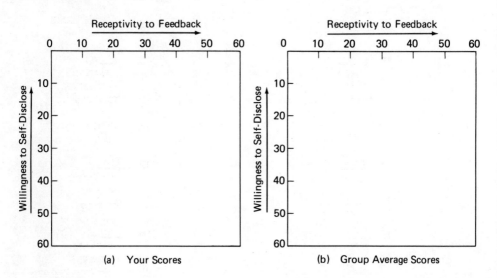

	Your Score	Group Average Scores
Receptivity to Feedback:		
Willingness to Self-Disclose:	(+)	(+)
Interpersonal Risk-Taking:		

(a) Your Scores

(b) Group Average Scores

EXERCISE 2.9: ADJECTIVE CHECKLIST

The following exercise is aimed at providing an opportunity for participants to disclose their view of themselves to the other members of their group and to receive feedback on how the other group members perceive them. The activities are:

1. Members should each go through the list of adjectives and circle the six adjectives they think are most descriptive of themselves.

2. Each member of the group then tells the group which adjectives he circled. Members of the group then tell the person what adjectives they would have checked if they were to describe him. Do not spend more than five to ten minutes on each person in the group.

able	authoritative	careless	confident
accepting	belligerent	caring	conforming
adaptable	bitter	certain	controlled
aggressive	bold	cheerful	courageous
ambitious	brave	clever	cranky
annoying	calm	cold	critical
anxious	carefree	complex	cynical

demanding	irritable	pragmatic	serious
dependable	jealous	precise	shy
dependent	jovial	pretending	silly
derogatory	juvenile	pretentious	simple
determined	kind	principled	sinful
dignified	knowledgeable	progressive	skillful
disciplined	lazy	protective	sly
docile	learned	proud	sociable
dogged	lewd	quarrelsome	spontaneous
domineering	liberal	questioning	stable
dreamy	lively	quiet	strained
dutiful	logical	radical	strong
effervescent	loving	rational	stubborn
efficient	malicious	rationalizing	sympathetic
elusive	manipulative	reactionary	taciturn
energetic	materialistic	realistic	tactful
extroverted	maternal	reasonable	temperamental
fair	mature	reassuring	tenacious
fearful	merry	rebellious	tender
foolish	modest	reflective	tense
frank	mystical	regretful	thoughtful
free	naive	rejecting	tough
friendly	narcissistic	relaxed	trusting
genial	negative	reliable	trustworthy
gentle	nervous	religious	unassuming
giving	neurotic	remote	unaware
greedy	noisy	resentful	uncertain
gruff	normal	reserved	unconcerned
guilty	oblivious	resolute	uncontrolled
gullible	objective	respectful	understanding
happy	observant	responsible	unpredictable
hard	obsessive	responsive	unreasonable
helpful	organized	retentive	unstructured
helpless	original	rigid	useful
honorable	overburdened	sarcastic	vain
hostile	overconfident	satisfied	vapid
idealistic	overconforming	scientific	visionary
imaginative	overemotional	searching	vulnerable
immature	overprotecting	self-accepting	warm
impressionable	passive	self-actualizing	willful
inconsiderate	paternal	self-assertive	wise
independent	patient	self-aware	wishful
ingenious	perceptive	self-conscious	withdrawn
innovative	perfectionist	self-effacing	witty
insensitive	persuasive	self-indulgent	worried
insincere	petty	selfish	youthful
intelligent	playful	self-righteous	zestful
introverted	pleasant	sensible	
intuitive	pompous	sensitive	
irresponsible	powerful	sentimental	

Self-disclosure is most clearly accomplished when you tell others directly how you are reacting to the present situation. Yet many times we reveal ourselves in indirect ways, for example, by the jokes we tell, the things we find funny, the books we are interested in, or the movies we see. All these actions and attitudes tell other people something about ourselves. Often we may learn something about ourselves we were not fully aware of by analyzing our dreams, our day-dreams, our interests, our values, or our humor. The following exercise lets you use your imagination in ways that may lead to a greater awareness of yourself and also may help you get to know others in a different and interesting way.

The following are a series of fantasy situations. They deal with initiating relationships with lonely people or giving help to individuals who seem to need it. The procedure for the exercise is:

1. Divide into groups of three.

2. The leader presents an unfinished fantasy situation.

3. Each member of the triad thinks about his or her ending to the fantasy situation. If you want to, write out your ending.

4. In the triad each person tells her ending to the fantasy situation.

5. Each person tells the other members of the triad what she has learned from the endings given to the fantasy situation about herself and about the other two members.

6. Switch partners and repeat steps 2, 3, 4, and 5. Do this for a series of situations, switching partners after each situation.

7. In the group as a whole, discuss what you have learned about yourself and the other members.

The fantasy situations are:

1. You are walking down a dark street, Up ahead you see a streetlight. You walk nearer and nearer to the streetlight. Underneath the streetlight is a girl crying. What do you do? What happens?

2. You are eating lunch in a school cafeteria. You get your lunch and walk into the lunchroom. The lunchroom is crowded and noisy with lots of people laughing and shouting and having a good time. Off in a corner is a boy sitting all alone at a table. What do you do? What happens?

3. You are going to a party. You enter the party, take off your coat, find something to drink, and talk to a couple of friends. Standing all by himself in the middle of the room is a person you don't know. After ten minutes the person is still standing by himself. What do you do? What happens?

4. You are at a basketball game. It is half-time. You are talking with several of your friends. A person whom you casually met the week before is nearby. He is making obnoxious and embarrassing remarks to the people he is with. They all leave. You walk over to him and he insults you. What do you do? What happens?

5. You are sitting in class. Several persons in the class are making belittling comments about another student. The student is obviously having his feelings hurt. He catches your eye and looks at you. What do you do? What happens?

6. You are watching a group of friends talking in front of a restaurant. A person whom they consider odd and strange walks up to them and tries to join in the conversation. They ignore him. Finally one of your friends says, "Why don't you get lost?" The person turns away. What do you do? What happens?

7. You are sitting in a classroom. A student you don't know has constantly bugged the teacher and caused trouble ever since the class began several months ago. Although he is often funny, everyone is fed up with his behavior. He comes into the room and takes a seat next to you. What do you do? What happens?

8. There is a new student in the school. You have often heard her say that your school is not nearly as good as the school she previously attended and that the students at your school are "really just unreal" and "really think they're cool" while she praises the students at her previous school. You meet her walking out of the school door. What do you do? What happens?

EXERCISE 2.11: BAG EXERCISE

This exercise is to be used in connection with the presentation of the Johari Window. The exercise focuses on the thinking through of the things about yourself that you commonly share with other individuals (your free areas) and the things that you do not commonly share with other individuals (your hidden areas). In addition, it opens up the opportunity for each group member to receive feedback on how the others see him. The materials needed for the exercise are:

1. A ten-pound paper bag for each person.

2. One or two popular magazines, such as *Life*, for each person.

3. Construction paper of several different colors.

4. Yarn, string, and some small toys or any other objects that will help in constructing the bags.

5. Crayons, paints, or pencils for drawing.

6. Tape, paste, or glue.

The procedure for the exercise is:

1. Each person in the group gets a paper bag. Various materials described above are scattered around the room.

2. Each person spends half an hour building his or her bag. On the outside of the bag you should attach things that represent aspects of yourself that you commonly share with other people. On the inside of the bag you should place things that represent aspects of yourself that you do not com-

monly share with others. You may cut pictures, words, phrases, or slogans out of the magazines, draw designs or pictures, make objects out of the construction paper, or use anything else that seems relevant in portraying the free and hidden aspects of yourself.

3.   After everyone has finished, a group meeting is begun in which anyone may volunteer to talk about his bag. You may want to talk just about the outside of the bag, or you may feel like talking about part or all of what you have inside your bag. Everyone should feel free to share as much or as little as he would like to. You may want to keep working on your bag for a few days, adding things to the outside and inside, and then share it with the group at a later date.

4.   After a person has shared part or all of his bag, the other members of the group may wish to comment on how their perceptions of the person match what they have heard. You may feel that the person left out qualities that you appreciate in him or perceive him as having. You may be surprised by finding that something the person felt was in his free area you have never seen in his behavior. Whatever your impressions of the person and your reactions to his bag, you should feel free to share them with him, using the characteristics of good feedback.

5.   So that everyone who wants to may share her bag, you may want to put a time limit on how long the group may focus upon one person. Try to ensure that everyone who wants to share part or all of her bag has the opportunity to do so within the time limit set for the session.

EXERCISE 2.12: FEEDBACK

Many of the exercises described in this chapter involve giving and receiving feedback. Feedback from others is the primary means by which you can increase your self-awareness. Since your ability to self-disclose depends upon your awareness of what you are like, it is important for you to receive as much feedback as possible from others on their impressions of you and how they are reacting to your behavior in the group. If not much feedback has been given and received during the other exercises, the group may wish to spend some time sharing their impressions of, and reactions to, each other. This can be done simply by stating, "My impression of you is . . . ," or "My reactions to your behavior are . . . ," or "The way I feel about you is . . . ." Be sure to observe the rules for constructive feedback.

Sometimes you may be unsure of what your impressions are of another person or of how you are reacting to her behavior. One way to clarify your impressions of, and reactions to, a person is to associate some animal, bird, song, color, weather, movie, book, food, or fantasy with the person. You may want to ask yourself, "What animal do I associate with this person: a puppy, a fox, a rabbit?" Or you may wish to ask yourself, "What books do I associate with this person; what songs do I associate with this person?" Finally, you may wish to ask yourself, "What fantasies do I associate with this person? Is he a knight in shining armor, an innkeeper in medieval England, a French chef, a conforming business executive, a professional singer?" Through telling that person what animal, song, color, weather, movie, food, book, or fantasy you associate with her you may clarify your impressions and reactions and provide her with some interesting, entertaining, and helpful feedback.

EXERCISE 2.13: INTERPERSONAL PATTERNS

The following exercise focuses upon your interaction with other individuals. It may help you think about how you behave when you initiate a relationship with another person or how you act in a group. The procedure for the exercise is:

1. Divide into groups of three. Each person fills out the adjective check list.
2. Analyze the meaning of the adjectives you checked by following the instructions that follow the check list.
3. Share with the other two members of your triad the results of the exercise and ask for their comments on whether they perceive you in the same way as or differently than the results of this exercise indicate.

The twenty verbs listed below describe some of the ways people feel and act from time to time. Think of your behavior in interaction with other people. How do you feel and act with other people? Check the five verbs that best describe your behavior in interaction with others as you see it.

_____ acquiesces	_____ disapproves
_____ advises	_____ evades
_____ agrees	_____ initiates
_____ analyzes	_____ judges
_____ assists	_____ leads
_____ concedes	_____ obliges
_____ complies	_____ relinquishes
_____ coordinates	_____ resists
_____ criticizes	_____ retreats
_____ directs	_____ withdraws

There are two underlying factors or traits involved in the list of adjectives: _dominance_ (authority or control) and _sociability_ (intimacy or friendliness). Most people tend to like to control things (high dominance) or to let others control things (low dominance). Similarly most people tend to be very warm and personal (high sociability) or to be somewhat cold and impersonal (low sociability). In the following boxes circle the five adjectives you used to describe yourself in group activity. The set in which three or more adjectives are circled out of the five represents your interpersonal-pattern tendency in that group.

	HIGH DOMINANCE	LOW DOMINANCE
HIGH SOCIABILITY	advises coordinates directs initiates leads	acquiesces agrees assists complies obliges
LOW SOCIABILITY	analyzes criticizes disapproves judges resists	concedes evades relinquishes retreats withdraws

EXERCISE 2.14: OPEN AND CLOSED RELATIONSHIPS

Are most of your relationships open or closed? Read through Figure 2.4 carefully and classify yourself on each dimension. Do you have relationships you wish to make more open? Do you have relationships you wish to make more closed? What actions are needed to make a relationship more open? What acts are needed to make a relationship more closed? Discuss your conclusions with another member of your group.

Each of the aspects of open and closed relationships summarized in Figure 2.4 will be discussed in this book.

EXERCISE 2.15: SELF-DESCRIPTION

Who am I? What am I like? How do others perceive me? What are my strengths as a person? In what areas do I want to develop greater skills? At this point you have participated in a series of exercises aimed at increasing your self-awareness and your skills in self-disclosing. You should now sit down and try to summarize what you have learned about yourself. Take a sheet of paper and write a description of what you are like. Use the five questions stated at the beginning of this paragraph as a guide.

FIGURE 2.4: OPEN AND CLOSED RELATIONSHIPS

Closed ◄----------------► Open

Content being discussed	The content is of concern to no one (weather talk).	The content consists of technical aspects of work.	The content consists of the ideas and feelings of one person.	The content consists of the relationship between the two persons.
Time reference	No time reference (jokes and generalizations).	Distant past or future being discussed.	Recent past or future being discussed.	The immediate "here and now" being discussed.
Awareness of your sensing, interpreting, feeling, intending	You never listen to yourself and try to ignore, repress, and deny feelings and reactions.		You are constantly aware of what you are sensing, the interpretations you are making, your feelings, and your intentions about acting on your feelings.	
Openness with own ideas, feelings, reactions	Your statements are generalizations, abstract ideas, intellectualizations; feelings are excluded as irrelevant and inappropriate and nonexistent.		Your personal reactions such as attitudes, values, preferences, feelings, experiences, and observations of the present are stated and focused upon; feelings are included as helpful information about the present.	
Feedback from other people	Feedback from others is avoided, ignored, not listened to, and perceived as being hostile attacks on your personality.		Feedback from others is asked for, sought out, listened to, and used to increase your self-awareness; it is perceived as being a helpful attempt to add to your growth and effectiveness.	
Acceptance of yourself	You believe that once you are known you will be disliked and rejected and, therefore, you hide your "real" self and try to make the impression you think will be most appreciated by other people.		You express confidence in your abilities and skills; can discuss your positive qualities without bragging and without false modesty; you understand how you have used your strengths in the past to achieve your goals and are confident you will do so again in the future.	
Openness to others' ideas, feelings, reactions	You avoid and disregard others' reactions, ideas and feelings; you are embarrassed and put off by others' expressions of feelings; you reject other people and try to one-up and better them; you refuse to hear their feedback on their reactions to your behavior.		You listen to and solicit others' reactions, ideas, and feelings; you are interested and receptive to what others are saying and feeling; you express a desire to cooperate fully with them; you make it clear that you see their value and strengths even when you disagree with them; you ask others for feedback on their perceptions of your behavior.	
Acceptance of other people	You evaluate the other person's actions, communicate that the other is unacceptable, show disregard for the other as a person.		You react without evaluation to the other's actions, communicate that the other is acceptable, value the other as a person.	

Test your understanding of this chapter by answering true or false to the following statements. Answers are at the end of the chapter.

True   False   1. Self-disclosure should be aimed at making the other person improve his or her behavior.

True   False   2. Self-disclosure should be a two-way street, a shared understanding of how each person is reacting to the present situation.

True   False   3. Self-disclosure involves risk taking.

True   False   4. Statements are more helpful if they are tentative, specific, and informing.

True   False   5. Wait to discuss disturbing situations until after your feelings have built up for a while.

True   False   6. It is often helpful to describe your reactions to the other person's behavior.

True   False   7. It is often helpful to disclose full details of your past life.

True   False   8. An example of constructive self-disclosure is when Edye says to Dave, "Stop bothering me!"

True   False   9. An example of constructive self-disclosure is when Dave says to Edye, "You look angry. Are you?"

True   False   10. An example of constructive self-disclosure is when Edye says to Dave, "I feel hurt and rejected by your failure to answer my questions."

In this chapter we have focused on being self-disclosing, increasing self-awareness, and giving and receiving feedback. Which of these skills have you mastered and which ones do you need further work on?

1. I have mastered the following:

    __ Self-disclosing appropriately

    __ Giving feedback constructively

    __ Receiving feedback constructively

    __ Using my experiences, self-disclosures, and feedback to increase my self-awareness.

2.   I need more work on:
— Self-disclosing appropriately
— Giving feedback constructively
— Receiving feedback constructively
— Using my experiences, self-disclosures, and feedback to increase my self-awareness.

At this point, you should have an understanding of self-disclosure and know how to self-disclose appropriately. You should also understand how to give and receive constructive feedback, and you should have increased your self-awareness. The next chapter will build on these skills by showing you how to build and maintain trust in a relationship.

ANSWERS

Comprehension Test A: 1. true; 2. true; 3. false; 4. false; 5. false; 6. false; 7. true; 8. true; 9. false; 10. true.

Comprehension Test B: 1. a. hidden, b. blind, c. free, d. unknown; 2. b.

Comprehension Test C: 1. false; 2. false; 3. true; 4. true; 5. false; 6. false; 7. false; 8. false; 9. true; 10. false.

Chapter Review: 1. false; 2. true; 3. true; 4. true; 5. false; 6. false; 7. false; 8. false; 9. true; 10. true.

3

Developing and Maintaining
Trust

INTRODUCTION

Chapter 2 emphasized that to develop a relationship with another person you must disclose yourself in order to let the other person get to know you. Engaging in self-disclosure involves being self-aware and self-accepting. In addition, self-disclosure frequently involves taking the risk of rejection and ridicule. To self-disclose in a meaningful way, you must trust the other person not to respond in a way that will hurt your feelings or make you feel rejected. Thus, a third element in the use of self-disclosure is your willingness to risk being rejected in order to build a closer relationship. When deciding to take such a risk, your trust in the other person is of central importance.

In studying this chapter you should seek to (1) arrive at an understanding of what trust is and what it is not, (2) understand how trust is developed and maintained in a relationship, (3) know the difference between appropriate and inappropriate trust, and (4) experience a situation in which trust is either developed or destroyed.

I am afraid to tell you who I am, because, if I tell you who I am, you may not like who I am, and it's all that I have.

John Powell

Trust is absolutely essential for a relationship to grow and develop. The first crisis most relationships face involves the ability of two individuals to trust themselves and each other. In order to build a relationship, you must learn to create a climate of trust that reduces your own and the other person's fears of betrayal and rejection and promotes the hope of acceptance, support, and confirmation. It is important to understand that trust in a relationship is not something stable and unchanging that exists within a person. Trust exists in a relationship and constantly changes and varies. The actions of both people are important in establishing and maintaining trust in their relationship.

What is trust and how do you create it? Trust is a word everyone uses, yet it is a very complex concept and difficult to define. Based on the writings of Deutsch (1962) and others, trust may be defined as including the following elements:

1. You are in a situation where a choice to trust another person can lead to either beneficial or harmful consequences for your needs and goals. Thus, you realize, there is a risk involved in trusting.

2. You realize that whether the beneficial consequences or the harmful consequences result depends on the behavior of another person.

3. You expect to suffer more if the harmful consequences result than you will gain if the beneficial consequences result.

4. You feel relatively confident that the other person will behave in such a way that the beneficial consequences will result.

Thus a woman who is depressed over problems she is having with her parents is making a trusting choice when she shares her problems with a friend. First, she is aware that the choice to discuss her family problems can lead to beneficial consequences (figuring out an effective course of action to improve her family relationships and feeling less burdened by her problems) or harmful consequences (being laughed at, ridiculed, rejected, or gossiped about). Second, she realizes that the consequences of her choice depend on the behavior of her friend. Third, she would suffer more from being rejected and ridiculed than she would gain from planning a course of action to try improving relationships with her parents. Finally, she is relatively confident that her friend will help her plan a course of action to solve her family problems.

Another example may help. Trust is when you lend your older brother your bicycle. You can gain his appreciation or lose your bike; which one happens depends on him. You will suffer more if your bike is wrecked than you will gain by his appreciation, yet you really expect him to take care of your bike. (Sad experience has led the author to recommend that you never lend your bike to your older brother!)

BUILDING INTERPERSONAL TRUST

In order to build a relationship, two people must establish mutual trust. This is done during a commitment period in which they risk themselves either by disclosing more and more of their thoughts, feelings, and reactions to immediate situations and to each other, or by expressing acceptance, support, and cooperativeness toward each other. If when disclosing, they do not get the acceptance they need, they may back off from the relationship. If they are accepted, they will continue to risk self-disclosure and continue to develop the relationship. As both people continue to trust and to be self-disclosing, the relationship continues to grow.

The basic elements influencing the level of trust between two people are summarized in Figure 3.1. If Person A takes the risk of being self-disclosing, he may be either confirmed or disconfirmed, depending on whether Person B responds with acceptance or rejection. If Person B takes the risk of being accepting, supportive, and cooperative, she may be confirmed or disconfirmed, depending on whether Person A is disclosing or nondisclosing.

Interpersonal trust is *built* through risk and confirmation and is *de-*

PERSON A \ PERSON B	HIGH ACCEPTANCE, SUPPORT, AND COOPERATIVENESS	LOW ACCEPTANCE, SUPPORT, AND COOPERATIVENESS
HIGH OPENNESS AND SHARING	PERSON A: Trusting, Confirmed PERSON B: Trustworthy, Confirmed	PERSON A: Trusting, Disconfirmed PERSON B: Untrustworthy, No risk
LOW OPENNESS AND SHARING	PERSON A: Distrusting, No risk PERSON B: Trustworthy, Disconfirmed	PERSON A: Distrusting, No risk PERSON B: Untrustworthy, No risk

FIGURE 3.1: The Dynamics of Interpersonal Trust

stroyed through risk and disconfirmation. Without risk there is no trust, and the relationship cannot move forward. The steps in building trust are:

1. Person A takes a risk by disclosing his thoughts, feelings, and reactions to the immediate situation and to Person B.

2. Person B responds with acceptance, support, and cooperativeness and reciprocates Person A's openness by disclosing her own thoughts, feelings, and reactions to the immediate situation and to Person A.

An alternative way in which trust is built is:

1. Person B communicates acceptance, support, and cooperativeness toward Person A.

2. Person A responds by disclosing his thoughts, feelings, and reactions to the immediate situation and to Person B.

There are three types of behavior that will decrease trust in a relationship. The first is the use of rejection, ridicule, or disrespect as a response to the other's self-disclosure. Making a joke at the expense of the other person, laughing at his disclosures, moralizing about her behavior, being evaluative in your response, or being silent and poker-faced all communicate rejection and will effectively silence the other person and destroy some of the trust in the relationship. The second is the nonreciprocation of self-disclosures. To the extent that you are closed and the other person is open, he will not trust you. If someone is self-disclosing and you do not reciprocate, she will often feel overexposed and vulnerable. The third type of behavior that will decrease trust in a relationship is the refusal to disclose your thoughts, feelings, and reactions after the other person has indicated considerable acceptance, support, and cooperativeness. If someone indicates acceptance and you are closed and guarded in response, he will feel discounted and rejected.

COMPREHENSION TEST A

Test your understanding of building trust by answering true or false to the following statements. Answers are at the end of the chapter.

| True | False | 1. Trust involves a risk that can lead to either harmful or beneficial consequences. |
| True | False | 2. Your own behavior determines whether there are beneficial or harmful consequences from your trusting actions. |

True   False   3. When you trust another person, you will gain more from the beneficial consequences than you will suffer from the harmful ones.

True   False   4. When you engaged in trusting behavior, you are relatively confident that the other person will be accepting.

True   False   5. In responding to another person's self-disclosures, you should be noncommital and non-judgmental.

True   False   6. It does not matter if the other person reciprocates your self-disclosures or not.

True   False   7. When someone self-discloses, he or she will feel disconfirmed if the other person is not accepting.

True   False   8. When people communicate acceptance, then you can risk trusting them.

True   False   9. An example of trusting behavior would be Jane telling Frank about a personal problem.

True   False   10. An example of trustworthy behavior would be Frank listening noncommitally to Jane.

BEING TRUSTING AND TRUSTWORTHY

The level of trust within a relationship changes and varies according to the individuals' abilities and willingness to be trusting and trustworthy. *Trusting behavior* may be defined as the willingness to risk beneficial or harmful consequences by making oneself vulnerable to another person and is described in some detail by Deutsch (see previous section). More specifically, trusting behavior involves your being self-disclosing and willing to be openly accepting and supportive to others. *Trustworthy behavior* may be defined as the willingness to respond to another person's risk-taking in a way that ensures that the other person will experience beneficial consequences. This involves your acceptance of another person's trust in you. Expressing acceptance, support, and cooperativeness as well as reciprocating disclosures appropriately are key aspects of being trustworthy in an interpersonal relationship.

Acceptance is probably the first and deepest concern to arise in a relationship. Two points concerning acceptance need to be made. The first point is that acceptance of others usually results from, and begins with, acceptance of oneself. This was discussed in chapter 2. The second point is that acceptance is the key to reducing anxiety and fears about being vulnerable. Defensive feelings of fear and distrust are common blocks to the functioning of a person and to the development of constructive relationships. Certainly if a person does not feel accepted, the frequency and depth of disclosures will decrease. To build trust and to deepen a relationship, a person needs to be able to communicate acceptance, support, and cooperativeness.

The major skills necessary for communicating acceptance, support, and cooperativeness involve the expression of warmth, accurate understanding, and cooperative intentions. There is considerable evidence that the expression of warmth, accurate understanding, and cooperative intentions increases trust in a relationship, even when there are unresolved conflicts between the two people involved (Johnson 1971; Johnson and Matross 1977; Johnson and Noonan, 1972). Warmth is a feeling, and therefore all the procedures for communicating a feeling are appropriate for the expression of warmth. These procedures are discussed in detail in chapters 5 and 6. Accurate understanding involves restating the content, feelings, and meaning of the other person's disclosures. This communication procedure is discussed in chapter 4. Cooperation involves coordinating efforts to achieve a common goal. In the case of building friendships, the cooperative goal is to deepen the relationship. Thus any messages you send indicating that you want to develop a relationship will imply that you wish to cooperate with the other person. Finally, when you reciprocate self-disclosures, you increase trust and influence the other person to be even more self-disclosing. Reciprocating self-disclosures makes both people in a relationship vulnerable to rejection, and this mutual vulnerability helps increase their trust that each person will be accepting and supportive of the other.

TRUSTING APPROPRIATELY

Trust is not always appropriate. There are times when you will think it inadvisable to disclose your thoughts, feelings, or reactions to another person. There are people you undoubtedly know who would behave in very untrustworthy ways if you made yourself vulnerable to them. To master the skills in building and maintaining trust, therefore, you need to be able to tell when it is appropriate to be trusting and when it is not. A person must develop the capacity to size up situations and make an enlightened decision about when, whom, and how much to trust others. Remember not to reveal yourself so fast to another person that he is overpowered and bewildered. And remember there are situations in which trust is inappropriate and destructive to your interests.

Trust is appropriate only when you are relatively confident that the other person will behave in such a way that you will benefit rather than be

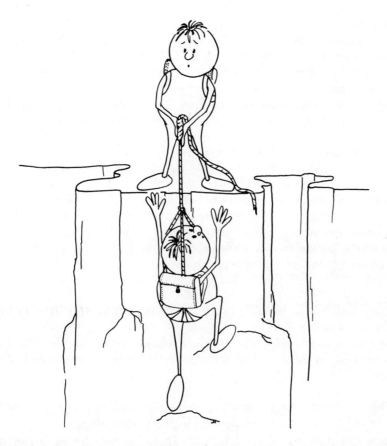

harmed by your risk, or when you are relatively sure the other person will not exploit your vulnerability. In some situations, such as competitive ones, trust is not appropriate. When you have a mean, vicious, hostile boss who has taken advantage of your openness in the past, it is inappropriate to engage in trusting behavior in the present.

TRUSTING AS A SELF-FULFILLING PROPHECY

Tom joins a new group expecting the members to dislike and reject him. He behaves, therefore, in a very guarded and suspicious way toward the other group members. His actions cause them to withdraw and look elsewhere for a friendly companion. "See," he then says, "I was right. I knew they would reject me." Sue, who joins the same group at the same time Tom does, expects the members to be congenial, friendly, and trustworthy. She initiates warmth and friendliness, openly discloses her thoughts and feelings, and generally is accepting and supportive of the other members. Consequently, she finds her fellow members to be all that she expected. Both Tom and Sue have made a self-fulfilling prophecy.

A self-fulfilling prophecy is, in the beginning, a false definition of a situation that evokes a new behavior, one that makes it possible for the originally false impression to come true. The assumptions you make about other people and the way in which you then behave often influence how other people respond to you, thus creating self-fulfilling prophecies in your interpersonal relationships. People usually conform to the expectations others have for them. If other people feel that you do not trust them and expect them to violate your trust, they will often do so. If they feel that you trust them and expect them to be trustworthy, they will often be that way. In building trust in a relationship, the expectations you have about the other person may influence how you act toward that person, thus setting up the possibility of a self-fulfilling prophecy. There is a lot to be said for assuming that other people are trustworthy.

COMPREHENSION TEST B

Test your understanding of being trusting and trustworthy by answering true or false to the following statements. Answers are at the end of the chapter.

True	False	1. Trusting behavior is being self-disclosing and accepting and supportive to others.
True	False	2. Trustworthy behavior is your accepting response to another person's self-disclosures.
True	False	3. As long as other people accept you, it doesn't matter if you accept yourself or not.
True	False	4. Your acceptance of others will reduce their anxiety about being vulnerable to you.
True	False	5. If you are self-disclosing in a relationship, trust will be increased.
True	False	6. You should trust in every situation, in hopes that you will be trusted by others.
True	False	7. A self-fulfilling prophecy is made when a true definition of a situation brings out old behavior and negates the true definition.
True	False	8. A self-fulfilling prophecy is made when a false definition of a situation brings out new behavior and confirms the false definition.

True   False   9. A self-fulfilling prophecy is made by an old Tibetan monk after he has discovered himself.

True   False   10. An example of trustworthy behavior is Keith laughing at Dale's self-disclosures.

EXERCISE 3.1: HOW TRUSTING AND TRUSTWORTHY AM I?

There is always a risk that someone will be rejecting and competitive when you attempt to build a relationship. In order for two people to trust each other, each has to expect the other to be trustworthy, and each has to engage in trusting behavior. This exercise allows you to compare the way you see your trust-building behavior in the group with the way other people see your trust-building behavior. The procedure for this exercise is:

1. Complete the questionnaire "My Group Behavior." Score your responses.

2. Take out a slip of paper for each member of your group. Write the name of one of the members on each slip of paper. Write (1) "openness and sharing" and (2) "acceptance, support, and cooperativeness" on each slip of paper. Then rate the members of your group from 1 to 7 (Low 1–2–3–4–5–6–7 High) on how open and accepting you perceive each to be. An example of a completed slip is shown below.

Member receiving feedback:	Edythe
1. Openness and sharing:	3
2. Acceptance, support, and cooperativeness:	6

Rate group members individually on the basis of how you think they have behaved during the entire time your group has met together.

3. Hand each member his or her slip. If there are six members in your group, you should have five ratings of yourself, and each of the other members should end up with five slips. Compute an average of how the other members see your behavior by adding all your ratings for openness and dividing by the number of slips and adding all your ratings for acceptance and dividing by the number of slips.

4. Record in Figure 3.2 your average openness and acceptance by: (1) drawing a dotted line for the results of the feedback slips you received and (2) drawing a solid line for the results of your questionnaire. Both the questionnaire and the feedback results should be recorded in Figure 3.2.

5. Discuss in the group how similar your self-perception and the perceptions of other group members are of your openness and acceptance. If there is a difference between the two, ask the group to give more specific feedback about your behavior and how it relates to trust in the group. Then discuss how to build trust with people in situations outside of the group.

Following is a series of questions about your behavior in your group. Answer each question as honestly as you can. There are no right or wrong answers. It is important for you to describe your behavior as accurately as possible.

1. I offer facts, give my opinions and ideas, provide suggestions and relevant information to help the group discussion.
    Never 1—2—3—4—5—6—7 Always

2. I express my willingness to cooperate with other group members and my expectations that they will also be cooperative.
    Never 1—2—3—4—5—6—7 Always

3. I am open and candid in my dealings with the entire group.
    Never 1—2—3—4—5—6—7 Always

4. I give support to group members who are on the spot and struggling to express themselves intellectually or emotionally.
    Never 1—2—3—4—5—6—7 Always

5. I keep my thoughts, ideas, feelings, and reactions to myself during group discussions.
    Never 1—2—3—4—5—6—7 Always

6. I evaluate the contributions of other group members in terms of whether their contributions are useful to me and whether they are right or wrong.
    Never 1—2—3—4—5—6—7 Always

7. I take risks in expressing new ideas and current feelings during a group discussion.
    Never 1—2—3—4—5—6—7 Always

8. I communicate to other group members that I am aware of, and appreciate, their abilities, talents, capabilities, skills, and resources.
    Never 1—2—3—4—5—6—7 Always

9. I offer help and assistance to anyone in the group in order to bring up the performance of everyone.
    Never 1—2—3—4—5—6—7 Always

10. I accept and support the openness of other group members, supporting them for taking risks and encouraging individuality in group members.
    Never 1—2—3—4—5—6—7 Always

11. I share any materials, books, sources of information, or other resources I have with the other group members in order to promote the success of individual members and the group as a whole.
    Never 1—2—3—4—5—6—7 Always

12. I often paraphrase or summarize what other members have said before I respond or comment.
    Never 1—2—3—4—5—6—7 Always

13. I level with other group members.
    Never 1—2—3—4—5—6—7 Always

14. I warmly encourage all members to participate, giving them recognition for their contributions, demonstrating acceptance and openness to their ideas, and generally being friendly and responsive to them.
    Never 1—2—3—4—5—6—7 Always

On questions 5 and 6, reverse the scoring. Then add the scores in the following way.

Openness and sharing	*Acceptance and support*
1. _____	2. _____
3. _____	4. _____
*5. _____	*6. _____
7. _____	8. _____
9. _____	10. _____

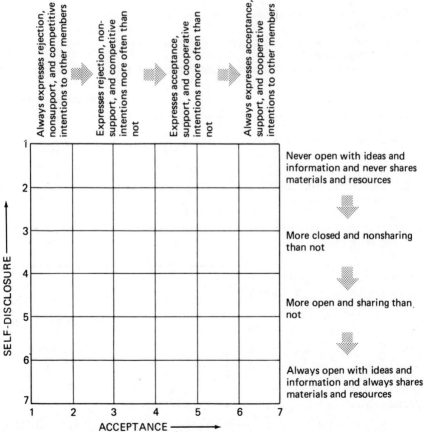

FIGURE 3.2: Johnson Trust Diagram

11. _____   12. _____

13. _____   14. _____

Total _____   **Total** _____

If you have a score of 21 or over, you are trusting or trustworthy, whichever the case might be. If you have a score under 21, you are distrustful or untrustworthy, whichever the case may be.

EXERCISE 3.2: PRACTICING TRUST-BUILDING SKILLS

This exercise is aimed at providing you with an opportunity to practice the trust-building skills needed for relationships to grow and develop. The procedure for the exercise is:

1. Form groups of six members and choose one member to observe.
2. Complete the Genetic Traits task.
3. Discuss the following questions in your group:
   a. Who engaged in what types of trust-building behaviors?
   b. What feelings do members of the group have about their participation in the group?
   c. Was trust increased or decreased by participating in this exercise?

Observation Sheet

1. Contributes ideas				
2. Describes feelings				
3. Paraphrases				
4. Expresses acceptance and support				
5. Expresses warmth and liking				

Trusting behaviors = 1 and 2
Trustworthy behaviors = 3, 4, and 5

Genetic Traits Task

Working as a group, estimate the number of people in your city (or school) who possess each of the following genetic traits. Establish the frequency of occurrence of each genetic trait, first in your group, then in the entire room. On the percentage of occurrence in your group and the room, estimate the number of people in your city (or school) who possess each trait.

1. Dimples in the cheeks versus no dimples
2. Brown (or hazel) eyes versus blue, gray, or green eyes

3. Attached versus free earlobes (an earlobe is free if it dips below the point where it is attached)

4. Little-finger bend versus no bend (place your little fingers together with your palms toward you—if your little fingers bend away from each other at the tips, you have the famous "little-finger bend")

5. Tongue roll versus no tongue roll (if you can curl up both sides of your tongue to make a trough, you have it, and it's not contagious)

6. Hairy versus nonhairy middle fingers (examine the backs of the middle two fingers on your hands and look for hair between the first and second knuckle)

7. Widow's peak versus straight or curved hairline (examine the hairline across your forehead and look for a definite dip or point of hair extending down toward your nose)

EXERCISE 3.3: PRISONER'S DILEMMA GAME

The game you are about to play is called the Prisoner's dilemma game. It is a game in which a player has to choose between increasing his own immediate gain or increasing the total gain of both players. It derives its name from the following situation:

> *Two suspects are taken into custody and separated. The District Attorney is certain that they are guilty of a specific crime, but he does not have adequate evidence to convict them at a trial. He points out each prisoner's alternatives to him: to confess to the crime that the police are sure they have committed, or not to confess. If they both do not confess, then the District Attorney states he will book them on some very minor but trumped-up charge such as petty larceny and illegal possession of a weapon for which they would both receive minor punishments; if they both confess they will be prosecuted, but he will recommend less than the most severe sentence; but if one confesses and the other does not, then the confessor will receive lenient treatment for turning state's evidence, whereas the latter will get "the book" slapped at him.*

> [*Luce and Raiffa 1957, p. 95*]

Neither prisoner is aware of the other prisoner's decision. The decision of each will be very much affected by his prediction of what the other prisoner will do. Both decisions will be very much affected by the extent to which each trusts the other not to confess. The important properties of this dilemma appear in the Prisoner's Dilemma Matrix.

Prisoner's Dilemma Matrix

In the matrix it is clear that the number of points a person receives from a choice depends not only upon his own choice, but upon what the choice of the other person is. If Person I chooses *A,* how many points he receives depends upon whether Person II chooses *C* or *D.* If Person I chooses *A,* and Person II chooses

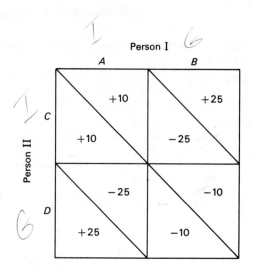

Person I

A   B

Person II

C   +10 / +10   +25 / −25

D   −25 / +25   −10 / −10

C, each will receive 10 points. If Person I chooses A, and Person II chooses D, Person I will lose 25 points and Person II will gain 25 points. If Person I chooses B, and Person II chooses C, Person I will gain 25 points and Person II will lose 25 points. And if Person I chooses B and Person II chooses D, both will lose 10 points. Study this matrix until you are sure you understand it. Then answer the following questions. Answers are at the end of the chapter.

1. If Person II chooses C and Person I chooses A, Person I receives ____ points and Person II receives ____ points.
2. If Person II chooses C and Person I chooses B, Person I receives ____ points and Person II receives ____ points.
3. If Person II chooses D and Person I chooses A, Person I receives ____ points and Person II receives ____ points.
4. If Person II chooses D and Person I chooses B, Person I receives ____ points and Person II receives ____ points.

When you understand the matrix, you are ready to play the Prisoner's Dilemma game. The objective of the game is to provide an experience in which trust is either built and maintained or violated and diminished. To play the game each person needs a small pad of paper and a pencil. The procedure for the game is:

1. Pair up with another person in the group. Sit back-to-back so that you cannot see the other player. Each person should have a pencil and a small pad of paper. One person is designated as Person I and the other as Person II.
2. When the leader gives the signal, each person should make her choice (Person I chooses between A and B, Person II chooses between C and D). Next, when the leader gives the signal, each person passes a slip of paper with her choice written on it over her shoulder to the other player.

You may not speak; no communication to the other player other than the choice you make is allowed.

3. This is repeated ten times. Each player should keep track of the number of points she has on the record sheet.

4. At the end of the tenth choice, the two players can discuss anything they want to with each other for ten minutes.

5. Ten more choices are made, following the procedure outlined in step 2.

6. At the end of the twentieth choice, total your gains and losses. Then fill out the questionnaire "Impressions of Other's Behavior."

7. In the group as a whole, discuss the following questions:

    a. What were your feelings and reactions about yourself and the other player during the game?

    b. How many points did you make during the game? How many did the other player make?

    c. How did you describe the other player's behavior during the game? How did he or she describe your behavior during the game?

    d. Did the two of you trust each other? Were the two of you trustworthy?

    e. How did it feel to have your trust violated (if that happened to you)? How did it feel to violate the other player's trust?

    f. How was trust built during the game (if it was)?

    g. What effect did the period of communication have upon the way you played the game? Did it affect the way you felt about the other player's behavior?

The essential psychological feature of the Prisoner's dilemma game is that there is no possibility for "rational" individual behavior in it unless the conditions for mutual trust exist. If each player chooses B and D to obtain either maximum gain or minimum loss for himself, each will lose. But it makes no sense to choose the other alternative, A and C, which could result in maximum loss, unless you can trust the other player. If you have to play the game, you either develop mutual trust or resign yourself to a loss by choosing competitively (that is, choosing B and D) in order to minimize your loss.

There has been a great deal of research on trust using the Prisoner's Dilemma game. Some of the conclusions from that research are:

1. Trust is often difficult to build but very easy to destroy. It may take two players a long time to arrive at a point where both consistently choose A and C, and any deviation to B or D may destroy all possibility of a cooperative solution to the dilemma.

2. Inappropriate trust may be just as dysfunctional as no trust at all; when a person consistently makes a trusting choice (A or C) and the other player consistently chooses B or D, the player exploiting the first person's trust will often feel little or no guilt, rationalizing that anyone who keeps making herself vulnerable deserves to be taken advantage of.

3. How the situation is defined will affect how easily trust may be built. If the game is defined as a problem-solving situation that the two individuals must solve, trust is relatively easy to build. If the game is defined as a competitive situation in which you must win more points than the other player, trust is very difficult to build.

	Your choice	Other's choice	Your gain or loss	Your total	Other's gain or loss	Other's total
1.	A	C	10	10		
2.	B	C	25			
3.	A	C	10	10		
4.	A	D	−25			
5.	A	D	10			
6.	A	D	10			
7.	A	D	−25			
8.	A	C	0			
9.	A	C	0			
10.	A	C	0	+45		
11.	A	C	10			
12.	A	C	10			
13.	A	C	10			
14.	A	C	0			
15.	A	C	0			
16.	A	C	0			
17.	A	C	0			
18.	A	C	0			
19.	A	C	0			
20.	A	C	0	+100		

Thus in a situation in which you are attempting to increase trust, you may want to avoid violating the other person's trust, avoid trusting the other person if he or she consistently behaves in untrustworthy ways, and ensure that the situation is defined as a problem-solving situation, not a competitive one.

Indicate, by checking the appropriate adjectives below, your impression of the other player's behavior during the game. You may know the other player; if so, ignore everything you have felt about the person in the past and rate *only* your impressions of his or her behavior during the game.

_____ warm	_____ cold
___✓___ trustworthy	_____ untrustworthy
_____ fair	_____ unfair
_____ generous	_____ selfish
_____ congenial	_____ uncongenial
___✓___ cooperative	_____ competitive
_____ kind	_____ unkind
___✓___ trustful	_____ untrustful

EXERCISE 3.4: TRUST LEVEL DISCLOSURES

The purpose of this exercise is for members of the group to disclose to one another their perceptions of the depth of the trust level in their relationship. Once this information is out in the open, the members of the group can discuss how trust could be increased in their relationship. Openly discussing issues concerning one's relationships is perhaps the most effective way to increase the closeness of the relationship. The procedure for the exercise is:

1. Pick the individual whom you trust least in the group and pair off with him.
2. For fifteen minutes, share your perceptions of why the trust level is low in your relationship. Try to avoid being defensive or hostile. Try to understand as fully as possible why the other person feels the way he does.
3. For the next ten minutes, share your impressions of how the trust level in the relationship can be increased. This may involve stating how you are going to behave differently or how you would like the other to behave differently. Be as specific as possible.
4. Answer the following questions with your partner:
   a. To what extent is the lack of self-disclosure by one or both persons contributing to the relatively low level of trust in the relationship?
   b. To what extent is the lack of communicated support and acceptance by one or both persons contributing to the relatively low level of trust in the relationship.
5. Now find the person in the group whom you trust the most. Pair up with her.
6. For fifteen minutes, share your understanding of why the trust level is high in your relationship. Try to understand as fully as possible why each of you feel the way you do.

7. For ten minutes, share your impressions of how the trust level in the relationship can be increased even more. This may involve stating how you are going to behave differently or how you would like the other to behave differently. Be as specific as possible.

8. Answer the following questions with your partner:

    a. To what extent is the level of self-disclosure by one or both persons contributing to the relatively high level of trust in the relationship?

    b. To what extent is the communication of acceptance and support by one or both persons contributing to the relatively high level of trust in the relationship?

In this exercise it is possible to focus on two important aspects of building and maintaining trust in a relationship. The first is the risk you and your partners took in self-disclosure. The second is the response you and your partners made to the other person's risk taking. Both the risks and the responses are crucial elements in building trust in a relationship.

How do you self-disclose about your perceptions of, and your feelings about, your relationship with another person in ways that will result in a closer relationship? This question will be answered in depth in the next chapter, which focuses on communication. But if your self-disclosures include the following four elements, you have a good chance of successfully moving the relationship closer:

1. *Statement of your intentions:* For example, "I'm worried about our relationship. I want to do something that will help us become better friends."

2. *Statement of your expectations about how the other person may respond:* For example, "I think you may be uncomfortable about my bringing this up but I hope that you will listen and try to understand what I am saying."

3. *Statement of what you will do if the other person violates your expectations:* For example, "If you shut me off, I will be hurt and will become defensive."

4. *Statement of how trust will be reestablished if he violates your expectations and you make your response:* For example, "If you cut me off and I become defensive, then we'll have to spend an evening talking about old times to get ourselves back together again."

To the extent that these four points become clear in the conversation in which you take a risk, you may feel more confident that the relationship will not be damaged even if the risk turns out badly.

The response you make to another person's risk taking is crucial for building trust in the relationship. The other person will feel it is safe to take risks in self-disclosure to the extent that she feels she will receive support when necessary and acceptance rather than rejection. To ensure that the relationship grows you should:

1. Make sure the other person feels supported for taking the risk.

2. If you disagree with what he is saying, make sure that it is clear that it is his ideas you are rejecting, not him as a person.

3. Make sure you disclose your perceptions and feelings about the relation-

ship. Always reward openness with openness when you are dealing with friends or individuals with whom you wish to develop a closer relationship.

EXERCISE 3.5: NONVERBAL TRUST

Taking a risk that makes you vulnerable to another person and receiving support can take place in a variety of nonverbal as well as verbal ways. One of the interesting aspects of the development of trust in a relationship is that sometimes the sense of physical support can be as powerful a developer of trust as can a sense of emotional support. Your group may like to try some of the following nonverbal exercises. Each of them is related to the development of trust. Before you attempt the exercises, however, you should carefully consider the following points:

1. No one with a bad back or another physical condition that might be adversely affected should participate in an exercise in which participants might be handled roughly.

2. Although these nonverbal exercises can be used as a form of play, they should be used only for educational purposes. That is, they should be done for a specific learning purpose, such as learning more about the development of trust, and they should be discussed thoroughly after they have been done.

3. Do not enter into an exercise unless you plan to behave in a trustworthy manner. If you cannot be trusted to support another person, do not enter into an exercise where you are responsible for physically supporting someone. No one should be allowed to fall or to suffer any injury.

4. No group pressure should be exerted upon individuals to participate. Participation should be strictly voluntary. If you do not feel like volunteering, however, you may find it interesting to analyze why. You may learn something about yourself and your relationships with the other members of the group from such an analysis. A lack of trust in the group or in other individuals might lead you to refuse to participate; on the other hand, a sense of adventure and fun might lead you to volunteer even though you do not trust the group of other individuals.

Trust Circle

The group stands facing into a close circle. A volunteer, perhaps a person who wishes to develop more trust in the group, is handed around the inside of the circle by the shoulders and upper torso. He should stand with his feet in the center of the circle, close his eyes, and let the group pass him around or across their circle. His feet should not move from the center of the circle. After as many people who want to try it have been passed around the circle, discuss the following questions:

1. How did it feel to be on the inside of the circle? What were you thinking about; what was the experience like?

2. How did it feel to be a part of the circle, passing others around? What were

you thinking about; what were you experiencing? Did you feel differently with different people in the center? Did the group behave differently when different people were in the center?

3.   Some of the groups take a great deal of care in passing a person around and are very gentle; other groups engage in aggressive play and toss the person from side to side. What did your group do? What does it signify about the group and the members?

Trust Walk

Each member of the group pairs up with another person. One person is designated as the guide, the other as a blind person. The blind person should close her eyes and the guide will lead her around the room. The guide should grasp the wrists of the blind person and, either from the side or from behind, guide the blind person around the room, planning as "rich" an experience as possible for the blind person using all the senses other than sight. Various touching experiences such as feeling the wall, the covering of a chair, the hair or face of another person are all interesting. If you can go outdoors, standing in the sun or the wind is enjoyable. In a large room, trust in the guide can be tested by running across the room, the blind person keeping her eyes shut. After fifteen minutes, reverse roles and repeat. After everyone has been both a guide and a blind person, discuss the following questions in the group as a whole:

1.   How did it feel to be the blind person?
2.   What were some of the best experiences your guide gave you?
3.   What did you learn about the guide?
4.   What did you learn about the blind person?
5.   How did it feel to be the guide?
6.   At this point, how do the two of you feel about each other?

Trust Cradle

The group forms two lines by the side of a volunteer. The volunteer leans back and the group picks him up, someone supporting his head. The volunteer should close his eyes and relax as much as possible. The group rocks him forward and backward. Slowly the group raises the person up, rocking him all the time, until he is as high as they can lift him. The group then slowly lowers the person to the floor, rocking him back and forth all the time. This can be repeated with several or all of the members of the group, depending upon the amount of time available. Afterwards, the group as a whole should discuss the following questions:

1.   How did it feel to be cradled? What were you thinking of while the group was cradling you? What were you experiencing?
2.   How did it feel to cradle the different members of the group? Did you have different feelings with different people?
3.   How has trust in the group been affected by the experience?

Partners stand, one with his back turned to the other's front. With his arms extended sideways, he falls backwards and is caught by his partner. Reverse roles and repeat. You may like to try the exercise with several different group partners. Then discuss in the group as a whole the following questions:

1. How did it feel to fall? Did you doubt that the other would really catch you?
2. How did it feel to catch your partner? Did you doubt that you would be able to catch him?
3. How has trust in the individuals who caught you been affected?

Elevated Trust Passing

The group lines up in a straight line, each person facing the back of the person in front of him. The person at the beginning of the line is lifted high and is passed over the top of the others to the end of the line, where she is slowly brought down. The person now at the head of the line is lifted high and is passed over the top of the others to the end of the line. If a group member does not wish to be passed, she moves to the end of the line when she finds herself at the head of the line. The exercise continues until all members who want to have been lifted and passed.

1. How did it feel to be passed?
2. What were you thinking; what were you experiencing?
3. How did it feel to pass the other members of the group?
4. How has trust in the group been affected by the exercise?

EXERCISE 3.6: DEVELOPING TRUST

The objectives for this exercise are for the members of the group to arrive at a summary statement concerning the ways in which trust can be built in a relationship. The procedure for the exercise is:

1. Divide into groups of four.
2. Arrive at the ten most important things a person can do to develop trust in a relationship. Take twenty minutes for this.
3. Share the results across the group.
4. As a whole, rank the ten most important aspects of developing trust from the most important to the least important.

Did your list include any of the following: progressively disclosing oneself to the other person; making sure your behavior regarding the other person is consistent; following through on your commitments to the other person; expressing warmth and acceptance to the other person; avoiding being judgmental of the other person; being trustworthy; being honest?

Test your understanding of this chapter by taking the following quiz. Answers are at the end of the chapter.

True False   1. In a trust situation, you can be either accepted or rejected.

True False   2. In a trust situation, you should prepare for rejection in order to keep from getting hurt.

True False   3. Once you develop trust in a situation, you will not have to work on the relationship anymore.

True False   4. What you expect from a situation can determine what you will get.

True False   5. Risk trusting in every situation.

True False   6. Your response to another person's self-disclosure determines your trustworthiness.

True False   7. An example of good risk taking is when Helen tells Roger how she expects him to respond to her self-disclosure.

True False   8. A good response to risk taking is when Roger interrupts Helen to make his own self-disclosures.

9. What four elements should you have in a conversation when you are taking a risk in self-disclosure in a relationship?
   a. An initial statement of neutral interest
   b. A statement of your intentions
   c. A statement of your expectations and how the other person may respond
   d. A comment about how good the other person looks
   e. A statement of what you will do if the other person violates your expectation
   f. A statement of how the other person bothers you
   g. A statement of how trust will be reestablished
10. When the other person takes a risk in self-disclosure, what three things should you work into the conversation?
   a. Support of the other person for taking the risk
   b. Complete acceptance of the other person's ideas
   c. Your nervousness in self-disclosing
   d. If you disagree, your rejection of the person's ideas but not of the person

    e. Your own openness in response to the other person's openness
    f. How much you've learned from reading this book

In this chapter we have focused on the skills involved in engaging in trusting and trustworthy behavior. Which of these skills have you mastered, and which ones do you need further work on?

1.   I have mastered the following:
    ____ Expression of warmth and cooperative intentions
    ____ Taking appropriate risks with self-disclosure
    ____ Responding to another person's self-disclosures with acceptance and support
    ____ Reciprocating another person's self-disclosures

2.   I need more work on:
    ____ Expression of warmth and cooperative intentions
    ____ Taking appropriate risks with self-disclosure
    ____ Responding to another person's self-disclosures with acceptance and support
    ____ Reciprocating another person's self-disclosures

At this point, you should understand what trust is and when it is appropriate to engage in trusting and trustworthy actions. You should also have an understanding of how to develop and maintain trust in a relationship. However, in order for you to self-disclose appropriately and effectively, you need to communicate effectively. The next chapter deals with increasing your communication skills.

ANSWERS

Comprehension Test A: 1. true; 2. false; 3. false; 4. true; 5. false; 6. false; 7. true; 8. true; 9. true; 10. false.

Comprehension Test B: 1. true; 2. true; 3. false; 4. true; 5. true; 6. false; 7. false; 8. true; 9. false; 10. false.

Prisoner's Dilemma: 1. +10, + 10; 2. +25, −25; 3. −25, +25; 4. −10, −10.

Chapter Review: 1. true; 2. false; 3. false; 4. true; 5. false; 6. true; 7. true; 8. false; 9. b, c, e, g; 2. a, d, e.

4

Increasing
Your Communication Skills

INTRODUCTION

To live is to communicate! All life communicates in some way. Living cells communicate by means of hormones and nerve fibers. Animals and insects communicate by means of chemicals, movements, and sounds. Humans use all of these to communicate, but they add words: a unique system based on symbols that stand for the objects and/or ideas to which humans refer. The importance of communication cannot be overemphasized. Communication is the foundation for all interpersonal relationships, and our daily lives are filled with one communication experience after another. Through communication we reach some understanding of each other, learn to like, influence, and trust each other, begin and end relationships, and learn more about ourselves and how others perceive us. Through communication we learn to understand others as individuals and we help others to understand us. Any discussion of interpersonal skills must emphasize the skills of communicating effectively.

WHAT IS COMMUNICATION?

Our basic social nature demands that we seek out communication with other people. We *have* to communicate with others. All of us have personal needs that can be satisfied only by relating to others. Interpersonal communication reflects our mutual need to establish contact and join our efforts to achieve mutual goals. The very process of communication— exchanging messages to achieve understanding of each other's perceptions, ideas, and experiences—makes people interdependent. It takes two to communicate, and through the very act of communicating with another person we begin or maintain a relationship. What prompts communication is our desire for someone else to know what we know, to value what we value, to feel what we feel, and to decide what we decide.

Two people sensing each other through sight, sound, touch, or smell will have a continuous effect on each other's perceptions and expectations of what the other is going to do. Interpersonal communication can be broadly defined as any verbal or nonverbal behavior that is perceived by another person. In other words, communication is much more than the exchange of words; all behavior conveys some message and is, therefore, a form of communication. *Interpersonal communication* is more commonly defined as a message sent by a person to a receiver (or receivers) with a conscious intent of affecting the receiver's behavior. Communication is initiated in order to change the other person in some way. A person sends the message "How are you?" to evoke the response "Fine." A teacher shakes his head to get two students to stop throwing erasers at him. Under this more limited definition, any signal aimed at influencing the receiver's behavior in any way is a communication.

This definition of communication does not mean than an orderly sequence of events in time always exists in which a person thinks up a message and sends it, and someone else receives it. Communication among people is a process in which everyone receives, sends, interprets, and infers all at the same time, and there is no beginning and no end. All communication involves people sending one another symbols to which certain meanings are attached. These symbols can be either verbal (all words are symbols) or nonverbal (all expressions and gestures are symbols). The exchange of ideas and experiences between two people is possible only when both have adopted the same ways of relating a particular nonverbal, spoken, written, or pictorial symbol to a particular experience. And all communication affects the relationship between two people, one way or the other.

Figure 4.1 represents a model of the process of communication between two individuals. In this model the communicator is referred to as the *sender* and the person at whom the message is aimed as the *receiver*. The *message* is any verbal or nonverbal symbol that one person transmits to another. The *channel* is the means of conveying the message to the receiver; the sound waves of the voice or the light waves involved in seeing words on a printed page are examples of channels. Because communication is a process, sending and receiving messages often take place

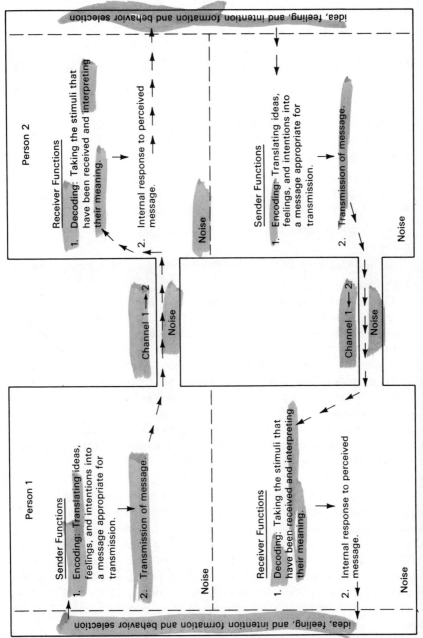

FIGURE 4.1 The Interpersonal Communication Process

simultaneously; a person can be speaking and at the same time paying close attention to the receiver's nonverbal responses.

Communication between two people may be viewed as consisting of seven basic elements (see Figure 4.1):

1. The intentions, ideas, and feelings of the sender and the way she decides to behave, all of which lead to her sending a message that carries some content.

2. The encoding of the message by the sender—she translates her ideas, feelings, and intentions into a message appropriate for sending.

3. Sending the message to the receiver.

4. The channel through which the message is translated.

5. The decoding of the message by the receiver—he interprets its meaning. The receiver's interpretation depends on how well the receiver understands the content of the message and the intentions of the sender.

6. An internal response by the receiver to this interpretation of the message.

7. The amount of *noise* in the above steps. Noise is any element that interferes with the communication process. In the sender, noise refers to such things as the attitudes, prejudices, frame of reference of the sender, and the appropriateness of her language or other expression of the message. In the receiver, noise refers to such things as his attitudes, background, and experiences that affect the decoding process. In the channel, noise refers to (1) environmental sounds, such as static or traffic, (2) speech problems, such as stammering, and (3) annoying or distracting mannerisms, such as a tendency to mumble. To a large extent, the success of communication is determined by the degree to which noise is overcome or controlled.

How do you tell whether communication is effective? *Effective communication* exists between two people when the receiver interprets the sender's message the way the sender intended it. If John tries to communicate to Jane that it is a wonderful day and he is feeling great by saying "Hi" with a warm smile, and if Jane interprets John's "Hi" as meaning John thinks it is a beautiful day and is feeling well, then effective communication has taken place. If Jane interprets John's "Hi" as meaning he wants to stop and talk with her, then ineffective communication has taken place.

Why is it so common for two individuals not to understand each other? Perhaps the most recurring and basic source of misunderstandings between two people is a communication failure resulting from the receiver's understanding the meaning of a message differently than it was intended. We do not always communicate what we mean to. Since intentions are private and known directly only to the person who experiences them, a sender's intentions are not always clear to the receiver. I know my intentions, but I must make inferences about yours. You know your intentions, but you must infer mine. Because of the private nature of intentions, difficulties in communication often result from the failure of the receiver to understand correctly the intentions of the sender.

The communication failures arising from the gap between what the sender meant and what the receiver thought the sender meant do not usually arise from word usage, grammatical form, or lack of verbal ability. Rather they are created by emotional and social sources of noise. People, for example, are often so preoccupied that they just do not listen to what others are saying. Or they can be so interested in what they have to say that they listen to others only to find an opening to get the floor to say what they want to say. Sometimes individuals are so sure that they know what the other person is going to say that they distort his statements to match their expectations—for example, when a man who has a very low opinion of himself asks a woman for a date and takes her statement "Let me think for a minute," as a refusal.

Sometimes individuals listen in order to evaluate and make judgments about the speaker, which in turn makes the speaker guarded and defensive in what he is trying to say. An example of this is when a person is presenting an argument and the receiver is constantly saying, "That's stupid; that's wrong." The speaker then becomes very careful about what he is saying.

At times individuals do fully understand the words a communicator is using without understanding the real underlying meaning of what he is trying to say. For example, a person may say, "It's a nice day," in an attempt to change the subject, and the receiver may think the speaker is really interested in the weather. All of these problems in communication will be discussed more fully later in the chapter.

Finally, a lack of trust seems to act as a principal cause of communication distortion. Distrust can cause a reduction of the information shared and a suspiciousness of what little information is communicated. To a certain extent, increasing the communication between two individuals results in greater accuracy of understanding only when trust is high.

When you stop to think of how many ways individuals can misunderstand each other, it seems at times a wonder that any effective communication can take place at all. But in the exercises in this chapter we will examine and practice communication skills that promote effective, accurate understanding of each other's communications.

Test your understanding of what communication is by taking the following quiz. Answers are at the end of the chapter.

True   False   1. If you are alive, you have to communicate something.

True   False   2. It takes two to communicate.

True   False   3. In interpersonal communication, the sender wants to affect the receiver's behavior in some way.

True   False   4. Communication is an orderly sequence of events in which a person thinks up a message and sends it, and the message is received.

True   False   5. A person's attitude can be noise that interferes with communication.

True   False   6. Effective communication exists when the receiver gets the message that was sent.

True   False   7. Effective communication is a little old lady hitting a burglar over the head with her umbrella.

True   False   8. Effective communication is your reading this book and trying to answer this question.

9. What are the seven basic elements of communication?
  a. The subject of the conversation, around which all communication occurs
  b. The intentions of the communicator
  c. The receiver's reactions to the sender
  d. Encoding
  e. Transmission of the message
  f. The receiver's understanding of the content of the message and the intention of the sender
  g. The preferred style of thinking of the sender
  h. The channel through which the message is sent
  i. The internal response of the receiver
  j. Noise
  k. The categories of response the receiver has in mind
  l. Expressing acceptance and support
10. What are three common communication faults of the receiver?
  a. Not giving the sender undivided attention
  b. Turning off the sender's hearing aid

c. Relating the conversation to something the speaker does not know about

d. Thinking about her replies instead of paying attention to the sender

e. Listening for details rather than the essential message

f. Listening to the essential message but missing details

SENDING MESSAGES EFFECTIVELY

How can you send messages effectively? What can you do to ensure effective communication of your ideas and feelings? In this and the following three chapters we discuss the answer to these questions. There are several ways senders of a message can increase the likelihood that they will be understood. The three basic requirements are: understandable messages, credibility of the sender, and optimal feedback on how the message is affecting the receiver.

Research supports the conclusion that the skills of sending messages include the following:

1. *Clearly "own" your messages by using first person singular pronouns: "I," "my."* Personal ownership includes clearly taking responsibility for the ideas and feelings that are expressed. People disown their messages when they use terms like "most people," "some of our friends," and "our group." Such terms make it difficult to tell whether the people really think and feel what they are saying or whether they are repeating the thoughts and feelings of others.

2. *Make your messages complete and specific.* Include clear statements of all necessary information the receiver needs in order to compre-

hend the message. Being complete and specific seems so obvious, but often people do not communicate the frame of reference they are using, the assumptions they are making, the intentions they have in communicating, or the leaps in thinking they are making.

3. *Make your verbal and nonverbal messages congruent.* Every face-to-face communication involves both verbal and nonverbal messages. Usually these messages are congruent, so if a person is saying that he has appreciated your help, he is smiling and expressing warmth nonverbally. Communication problems arise when a person's verbal and nonverbal messages are contradictory. If a person says, "Here is some information that may be of help to you" with a sneer on his face and a mocking tone of voice, the meaning you receive is confused by the two different messages being sent.

4. *Be redundant.* Repeating your messages more than once and using more than one channel of communication (such as pictures and written messages as well as verbal and nonverbal cues) will help the receiver understand your messages.

5. *Ask for feedback concerning the way your messages are being received.* In order to communicate effectively you must be aware of how the receiver is interpreting and processing your messages. The only way to be sure is to continually seek feedback as to what meanings the receiver is attaching to your messages.

6. *Make the message appropriate to the receiver's frame of reference.* The same information will be explained differently to an expert in the field than to a novice, to a child than to an adult, or to your boss than to a coworker.

7. *Describe your feelings by name, action, or figure of speech.* When communicating your feelings, it is especially important to be descriptive. You may describe your feelings by name ("I feel sad"), by actions ("I feel like crying"), or by figures of speech ("I feel down in the dumps"). The description will help communicate your feelings clearly and unambiguously.

8. *Describe other people's behavior without evaluating or interpreting.* When reacting to the behavior of other people, be sure to describe their behavior ("You keep interrupting me") rather than evaluating it ("You're a rotten, self-centered egotist who won't listen to anyone else's ideas").

One of the most important elements in interpersonal communication is the credibility of the sender. *Sender credibility* refers to the attitude the receiver has toward the trustworthiness of the sender's statements. Several dimensions affect the credibility of the sender:

1. The reliability of the sender as an information source—the sender's dependability, predictability, and consistency.

2. The intentions of the sender or the sender's motives. The sender should be open as to the effect she wants her message to have upon the receiver.

3. The expression of warmth and friendliness.

4. The majority opinion of other people concerning the trustworthiness of the sender. If all our friends tell us the sender is trustworthy, we tend to believe it.

5. The sender's relevant expertise on the topic under discussion.

6. The dynamism of the sender. A dynamic sender is seen as aggressive, emphatic, and forceful and tends to be viewed as more credible than a more passive sender.

There is little evidence available from the studies on sender credibility to suggest which of the above dimensions is the most important. It seems that a highly credible sender is one who is perceived in a favorable light on *all* of these dimensions. A source low in credibility, on the other hand, is one who is perceived in a negative light on *any one* of the dimensions. Unless we appear credible to the receiver, he will discount our message and we will not be able to communicate effectively with him. Sender credibility is often discussed as the perceived trustworthiness of the sender, and therefore credibility relates to the discussion of trust in chapter 3.

> *Each individual in a relationship is constantly commenting on his definition of the relationship implicitly or explicitly. Every message exchange (including silence) defines the relationship implicitly since it expresses the idea "this is the sort of relationship where this sort of message may be given."*
>
> *Donald Jackson*

COMPREHENSION TEST B

Test your understanding of sending understandable messages and having good credibility by marking the following questions true or false. The answers are given at the end of the chapter.

True   False   1. It is important to express what you think, not what other people think.

True   False   2. It is important that your verbal and nonverbal messages go together.

True   False   3. If you express yourself clearly, you will not need to repeat your message.

True   False   4. Evaluating and interpreting other people's behavior is a necessary part of effective communication.

True   False   5. As long as you express yourself clearly, you need not check on how your message is being received.

True   False   6. You must be seen as high on all the credibility dimensions in order to have high credibility.

True   False   7. The opinions of other people can influence how trustworthy the receiver sees the sender.

True   False   8. A passive sender is more credible than an aggressive one.

True   False   9. An example of good communication is Frank calling Edye a pig after she eats all the Christmas cookies.

True   False   10. An example of good credibility is a happily married psychiatrist giving his sister careful, loving advice on how to improve her marriage.

EXERCISE 4.1: ONE- and TWO-WAY COMMUNICATION*

One of the best ways a sender can make sure messages are received correctly is to obtain optimal feedback on the effects his message is having on the receiver. Feedback is the process through which the sender finds out how his message is being decoded and received. The response the receiver makes to the sender's message can subsequently cause the sender to modify his messages to communicate more accurately with the receiver. If the sender is not able to obtain information on how his message is being decoded, inaccuracies in communication may occur and never be uncovered. Open two-way communication facilitates understanding in communication, which in turn helps such things as developing a fulfilling relationship and being able to work together effectively.

One-way communication occurs when the sender is not able to determine how the receiver is decoding the sender's message. *Two-way* communication occurs when the sender is able to obtain feedback concerning how the receiver is decoding the sender's message. In this exercise we will compare one- and two-way communication. The objective is to demonstrate the differences be-

*This exercise is adapted from an exercise in Harold J. Leavitt, *Managerial Psychology*, (University of Chicago Press, 1958), pp. 118–28.

tween a situation in which two-way communication exists and ones in which communication goes only one way. For this exercise each participant needs two pieces of paper and a pencil. The leader needs copies of Square Arrangement I and Square Arrangement II, which are given in the Appendix. The leader and should copy Tables 4.1A–C onto a blackboard or a large sheet of paper.

TABLE 4.1A: MEDIANS FOR TRIALS I AND II

Medians	I	II
Time elapsed:	_____	_____
Guess accuracy:	_____	_____
Actual accuracy:	_____	_____

TABLE 4.1B: FIRST TRIAL

Number correct	Guess	Actual
5	_____	_____
4	_____	_____
3	_____	_____
2	_____	_____
1	_____	_____
0	_____	_____

TABLE 4.1C: SECOND TRIAL

Number correct	Guess	Actual
5	_____	_____
4	_____	_____
3	_____	_____
2	_____	_____
1	_____	_____
0	_____	_____

The procedure for this exercise is:

1. The leader selects a sender and two observers (if the group has less than seven members, select only one observer). The sender should be a person who communicates well and who speaks clearly and loudly enough to be heard.
2. The sender is seated either with her back to the group or behind a screen.

She is given Square Arrangement I. The leader should be careful that the group members do not see the diagram of squares that the sender will describe. The sender is told to study the first arrangement carefully for two minutes in order to be prepared to instruct the group members on how to draw a similar set of squares on their paper.

3. The first observer is asked to note the behavior and reactions of the sender during the exercise and to make notes for later comment. The second observer is asked to make notes on the behavior and reactions of the group members. Facial reactions, gestures, posture, and other nonverbal behaviors may be observed.

4. The group is given these instructions: "The sender is going to describe a drawing to you. You are to listen carefully to her instructions and draw what she describes as accurately as you can. You will be timed, but there is no time limit. *You may ask no questions of the sender and give no audible response.* You are asked to work independently."

5. Tables 4.1A–C are shown in the front of the room. The sender is then told to proceed to give the instructions for drawing the first figure of squares as quickly and accurately as she can. The leader should ensure that there are no questions or audible reactions from the group members.

6. When the sender has completed giving the instructions for Square Arrangement I, the leader records the time it took to do so in the proper space in the first table. Each member of the group is asked to write down on his paper the number of squares he thinks he has drawn correctly in relation to the preceding one.

7. The leader instructs the sender to face the group members. She gives the sender Square Arrangement II and tells her to study the relationship of the squares in this new diagram for two minutes in preparation for instructing the group members on how to draw it.

8. The group is given these instructions: "The sender is going to describe another drawing to you. This time she will be in full view of you and you may ask as many questions as you wish. She is free to reply to your questions or amplify her statements as she sees fit. She is not, however, allowed to make any hand signals while describing the drawing. You will be timed, but there is no time limit. Work as accurately and rapidly as you can."

9. The sender is told to proceed.

10. When the sender has completed giving instructions for the second figure, the time is again recorded in the appropriate space of Table 4.1A. The group members are asked to guess the number of squares they have drawn correctly and to record the number on their papers.

11. A median for guessed accuracy on the first drawing is obtained by recording the number of group members who guessed zero, the number who guessed one, and so on in Table 4.1B. The median guessed number is found by counting from zero the number of group members guessing each number until you reach half the members of the group. The median is then recorded in Table 4.1A.

12. The method is repeated to get the median of accurate guesses for the second drawing.

13. Members are shown the master drawing for the first set of squares, and the relationship of each square to the preceding one is pointed out. Each square must be in the exact relationship to the preceding one as it appears on the master drawing to be counted as correct. When this step has been

completed, the members are asked to count and record the actual number right. A similar count is taken for the second chart.

14. The median for accuracy for the first and second drawings is obtained and placed in Table 4.1A.
15. The following questions are discussed.
    a. What may be concluded from the results in terms of time, accuracy, and level of confidence?
    b. What did the observers record during the exercise? How did the behavior of the sender and the group members vary from one situation to the other? The group members and the sender should comment on what they were feeling during the two situations.
    c. How does this exercise compare with situations you find yourself in at work, school, or at home? How might you change your behavior in relating to your friends and acquaintances as a result of what you have experienced during this exercise?

The typical result of this exercise is that one-way communication is quicker and less accurate, and the level of confidence of the receiver is lower. Two-way communication takes more time, but it is also likely to be more accurate, and the level of confidence of the receiver is higher. Two-way communication promotes more accurate understanding between the sender and the receiver and builds a more cooperative relationship between the two. The sender, however, usually is more disturbed and frustrated during the two-way communication process.

Just as the sender can increase the accuracy of communication by transmitting his message through a variety of channels, it is also an aid to accuracy if feedback is available in a variety of channels. Feedback does not have to be only verbal; the nonverbal cues such as facial expression, posture, gestures, sighs, tone of voice when asking questions are often indications of how your message is being interpreted by the receiver.

COMPREHENSION TEST C

Test your understanding of one- and two-way communication by answering true or false to the following statements. Answers are at the end of the chapter.

True False	1.	Feedback is the process by which the receiver tells the sender how the message is being received.
True False	2.	Feedback is the primary process for clearing up misunderstandings in communication.
True False	3.	Feedback is not given in one-way communication.
True False	4.	One-way communication is quicker than two-way communication.
True False	5.	One-way communication is more frustrating to the sender than two-way communication.

True	False	6. Two-way communication is usually more accurate than one-way communication.
True	False	7. The confidence level of the receiver is higher in two-way communication.
True	False	8. Helen is getting feedback when Edye tells her how delicious her Christmas cookies are.
True	False	9. Edye is getting feedback when Buddy makes a face after taking a bite of her cookies.
True	False	10. David is getting feedback when no one buys his cookies.

PRACTICE IN COMMUNICATION SKILLS

You are about to receive instructions for a series of experiences dealing with effective and ineffective communication. These experiences will provide you with the opportunity (1) to become more aware of effective and ineffective communication procedures, (2) to become more aware of your own behavior in communicating with others, and (3) to practice effective communication procedures in order to develop increased skills. Such practice will increase your ability to develop and maintain effective interpersonal skills.

The suggested procedures at first may seem deceptively simple. Once you attempt them, however, you may find them more difficult than you expected. You will also find that they are very powerful when skillfully used. If you become involved in the exercise and consciously attempt both to learn as much as possible and to enjoy yourself, you will develop considerably better communication skills. If you try the activities willingly and with enthusiasm, you can have a lot of fun while learning.

The steps of the following exercise are designed to lead you from a situation in which you conduct an irrelevant, somewhat destructive conversation to a situation in which you use the tools of communicating effectively in building more personal relationships. The exercise serves the following purposes:

1. It allows you to experience two types of conversation that interfere with developing personal relationships and two kinds of conversation that facilitate development of personal relationships.

2. It provides skill practice in how to listen effectively and how to respond to messages sent by another person.

3. It provides skill practice in how to send effective messages that facilitate the development of close personal relationships.

4.   It introduces several key concepts on communication, such as (a) listening with understanding, (b) selective perception, (c) personal statements, and (d) relationship statements.

The session consists of three steps. The first two steps will contrast effective and ineffective ways of listening and responding. The final step will permit effective listening and responding in a situation emphasizing effective ways of sending messages. In each step a combination of experience, theory, and discussion will be used. At the end, a summary will be given and further skill development will be discussed.

All communication affects the relationship between the sender and the receiver. It moves the relationship forward or backward, or keeps it the same. Communication can deepen a relationship, or it can make the relationship more distant and impersonal. Many problems found in close relationships stem from failures to communicate effectively. The following activities will illustrate the skills involved in deepening relationships through communication.

You will need a partner and two more people to make groups of two and four. Communication is not a solitary activity, so find three other individuals and proceed.

EXERCISE 4.2A: INCREASING COMMUNICATION SKILLS

Step One: No Listening Versus Closely Listening; Irrelevant Response Versus Relevant Response

Part 1: Discussion on Listening. What types of problems make it difficult for two persons to understand each other? What failures in sending, listening, and responding cause communication gaps? List below at least four reasons why two persons may fail to communicate with each other.

1. _____

2. _____

3. _____

4. _____

Do your suggestions include the following?

1.   Inaccurate expression of one's thoughts
2.   Failing to listen to all that is being said
3.   Trying to say too much in one statement
4.   Two individuals not talking about the same thing while they are in a conversation with each other

Part 2: No Listening and Irrelevant Response. Divide into groups of four.

1. Conduct a discussion on establishing close friendships or on relating to others. Allow five minutes of discussion. During the discussion, you must talk about the assigned topic, and what you say must be *unrelated* to what others in the group say. It is as though you did not hear them.
2. After the discussion, jot down answers to the following questions to use later:
   a. How did it feel to make a statement and have no one respond to it?

   _____

   _____

   _____

   b. How did it feel to ignore a statement made by others in the group?

   _____

   _____

   _____

Part 3: Close Listening and Relevant Response. Within the group of four divide into pairs. Designate one member of each pair *A*, the other *B*.

1. *A* makes a statement to *B* either about himself, about *B*, or about the relationship between them. Try not to make bland statements, but say something that you have some feelings about and that can have real meaning for both of you.
2. *B* paraphrases *A*'s statement, stating in his own words what *A*'s remark meant to him. There is to be no discussion of the statements. *A* simply makes the statement; *B* paraphrases it back. Some general rules for paraphrasing reponse are
   a. Restate the other person's expressed feelings and ideas in your own words; don't mimic or parrot the exact words of the other person.
   b. Preface reflected remarks with "You feel . . . ," "You think . . . ," "It seems to you that . . . ," "It sometimes appears to you that . . . ," and so on.
   c. In paraphrasing another person's statements, avoid any indication of approval or disapproval. Refrain from blaming, interpreting, giving advice, or persuading.
3. *A* makes a second statement to *B*. *B* paraphrases it.
4. *A* makes a third statement to *B*. *B* paraphrases it.
5. Reverse the process. *B* makes three statements to *A;* after each one *A* paraphrases it back.
6. Jot down answers to the following questions to use later:
   a. How did it feel to make a statement and have your partner paraphrase it?

   _____

   _____

   _____

   b. How did it feel to paraphrase a statement made by your partner?

   _____

   _____

   _____

7. Discuss your experiences in the group of four. Some questions you may use in the discussion are

a. Did you find that you had difficulty in listening to others during the exercise? Why?

b. Did you find that you were not getting across what you wanted to say?

c. What was your reaction to the paraphrasing of your partner? Was he receiving what you intended to send?

d. Was the manner of presentation by your partner affecting your listening ability? In what way?

e. What were the differences in your feelings during the two types of experiences?

THEORY ON LISTENING AND RESPONDING

Give every man thine ear, but few thy voice.

Polonius (Hamlet)

To speak precisely and to listen carefully presents a challenge. You have just been through an exercise in which you both sent and received messages. There are several common faults that people often make when they communicate. Were you guilty of any of these mistakes in communicating?

____ Not organizing your thoughts before speaking

____ Including too many (and sometimes unrelated) ideas in your messages

____ Making short statements that did not include enough information and repetition to be understood

____ Ignoring the amount of information the receiver already had about the subject

____ Not making your message appropriate to the receiver's point of view

____ Not giving your undivided attention to the sender

____ Thinking about your reply before listening to everything the sender had to say

____ Listening for details rather than for the entire message

____ Evaluating whether the sender was right or wrong before you fully understood the message

These are not the only mistakes you can make in communicating, but they all need to be avoided if you are to be effective in communicating with other people.

The way you listen and respond to another person is crucial for building a fulfilling relationship. You can either listen and respond in ways that make the relationship more distant and impersonal, or you can listen and respond in ways that bring you and the sender into a closer, more personal relationship. It is crucial in a close relationship for you to communicate that you have clearly heard and understood the sender. It is characteristic of impersonal relationships that the receiver communicates that he has not heard and has not understood the sender. When you listen accurately and respond relevantly, you communicate to the sender, "I care about what you are saying, and I want to understand it." When you fail to listen and respond irrelevantly, you communicate to the sender, "I don't care about what you are saying, and I don't want to understand it." The previous experiences have highlighted the two different ways of listening and responding.

There are other ways of listening and responding that alienate the sender (Rogers and Roethlisberger 1952; Rogers 1965). Perhaps the major barrier to building close relationships is the very natural tendency we have to judge, evaluate, approve, or disapprove of the statements made by the sender. For instance, the sender makes a statement and you respond silently or openly with, "I think you're wrong," "I don't like what you said," "I think your views are right," or "I agree entirely."

Although the tendency to give evaluative responses is common in almost all conversations, it is heightened in situations where feelings and emotions are deeply involved. The stronger the feelings, the more likely it will be that two persons will evaluate the other's statements, each from only his own point of view.

More effective communication occurs, and this evaluative tendency is avoided, when the receiver gives understanding responses (para-phrases). An understanding response not only communicates desire to understand the sender without evaluating his statements; it also helps the receiver to see the expressed ideas and feelings from the sender's point of view. When paraphrasing is skillfully done, the receiver is able to achieve the sender's frame of reference in regard to the message. Although para-phrasing sounds simple, it is often very difficult to do. Yet it has powerful effects. Many counselors and psychotherapists have found that listening intently to what a person says, understanding how it seems to him, seeing the personal flavor it has for him, is very helpful to the sender. If you paraphrase a message, the act tends to reduce the sender's fears about revealing himself to you and decreases the sender's defensiveness about what he is communicating. It facilitates psychological health and growth. There is every indication that such empathetic understanding is such an effective approach to building close interpersonal relationships that it can bring about major positive changes in personality.

How do you improve your skills in listening empathetically to others? One way is simply to follow this rule the next time you get deeply involved in a conversation or argument: *Each person can speak up for himself only after he has first restated the ideas and feelings of the previous sender accurately and to the sender's satisfaction.* This means that before presenting your own point of view, it would be necessary for you to achieve the other's frame of reference, to understand his thoughts and feelings so well that you could paraphrase them for him. Sound simple? Try it. You will find that it is one of the most difficult things you ever attempted. You will also find that your arguments will become much more constructive and productive if you are able to follow the above rule successfully.

COMPREHENSION TEST D

You may wish to assess your comprehension of the above material on listening and responding by answering the following questions. Answers are at the end of the chapter.

1. What is the effect of judgmental or evaluative responses on communication?
    a. They increase the accuracy of communication.
    b. They encourage the sender to elaborate on her statements.
    c. They increase the sender's fears about disclosing her ideas and feelings to the receiver.
    d. They spice up the conversation.
    e. They increase the sender's defensiveness about what she is saying.
    f. They alienate the sender.
2. Three rules for effective paraphrasing are:
    a. Repeat the sender's words exactly and with the same inflections.
    b. Restate the sender's message in your own words.
    c. Preface your paraphrasing with such remarks as, "You feel . . . ."
    d. Indicate whether you approve or disapprove of his message.
    e. Do not indicate any approval or disapproval of the sender's statements.
3. How does giving an understanding response, a paraphrase, facilitate communication?
    a. It helps the receiver to see the expressed ideas and feelings from the sender's frame of reference.
    b. It communicates to the sender that the receiver cares about the message and wants to understand it.
    c. It increases the amount of time two individuals talk with each other.

EXERCISE 4.2B: INCREASING COMMUNICATION SKILLS

Step Two: Partial Listening versus Listening for Meaning; Asyndetic Response versus Attending and Negotiating for Meaning Response

Part 1: Partial Listening and Asyndetic Responding. Divide into groups of four.

1. Conduct a discussion about establishing a close friendship, relating to others, or some other related topic. Discuss the topic for five minutes.
2. This time you are to listen to what the others say but only for the purpose of using some small part of what they say in order to change the discussion to something more interesting to you. In other words, you acknowledge their statement but use it only as a polite way of introducing your own ideas into the conversation. This is called an *asyndetic response.*
3. Jot down answers to the following questions for use in a later discussion:
   a. How did it feel having others change the subject right after your statement?
   b. How did it feel changing the subject right after others had made a statement?

Part 2: Listening for Meaning and Attending and Negotiating for Meaning Response. Divide into pairs. Designate one person *A,* the other *B.*

1. *A* makes a statement about herself, about *B,* or about their relationship.
2. *B* responds by saying, "What I think you mean is . . ." (He then says what he thinks *A* meant.) He does not try to speculate about why he thinks that or about why *A* might be saying that. He simply tells *A* exactly what he thinks *A* meant by the statement. *A* and *B* then negotiate until they are in complete agreement about what *A* really meant, and *A* is able to respond to *B* with, "Yes, that is exactly what I meant." Do not add to or go beyond the original meaning, and don't try to analyze each other. Simply attempt to get at the exact meaning of what was said.
3. *A* makes a second statement. *B* responds with, "What I think you mean is . . ." The two then negotiate the exact meaning of the statement.
4. *A* makes a third statement. *B* responds as before.
5. Reverse the process. *B* makes three statements and *A* responds.
6. Answer these questions:
   a. How did it feel to make a statement and have my partner reply with what he thought it meant, then for us to negotiate the exact meaning of the statement?
   b. How did it feel to listen to my partner's statements and respond with what I thought it meant, then for us to negotiate the exact meaning of the statements?
7. Discuss the experiences in your group of four. Some questions you may use in the discussion are:

a. Did you always communicate what you wanted to communicate?
b. Did you find the listener responding to only part of what you said?
c. Was it ever unclear what the speaker had in mind? What made it unclear?

THEORY ON SELECTIVE PERCEPTION IN LISTENING AND RESPONDING

Did you notice that in responding to your partner's statement you selected part of her message to respond to and did not respond to other parts? This is very common in communication. It is based on the fact that our perceptions have to be selective. A message has too many aspects, both verbal and nonverbal, for a receiver to respond to all of them. Even when a persons says, "How are you?" a receiver may ignore the tone of voice, facial expression, gestures of the sender, and the appropriateness of the message to the situation; he may respond only to the usual meaning of the words. Most communication is so complex that we have to be selective about what we perceive and what we respond to. Selective perception, however, is one of the sources of "noise" in the communication process. Some of the factors that influence what we respond to in a message are our expectations, our needs, wants, and desires, and our opinions, attitudes, and beliefs.

If you expect a person to act unfriendly, you will be sensitive to anything that can be perceived as rejection and unfriendliness. If your past experience has led you to expect certain people to be hostile, you will be sensitive to any expression that can be seen as hostile. Such sensitization may make you completely blind to friendly expressions.

If you need and want someone to give you support, on the other hand, you may be highly sensitive to any expressions that can be perceived as supportive. If you are hungry you may be sensitive to any messages about food; or if you want to go home after a long evening you may be sensitive to how tired others are. Your wants and your needs constantly affect what you perceive in interpersonal-communication situations.

Finally, there is evidence that you will be more sensitive to perceiving messages that are consistent with your opinions and attitudes. You will tend to misperceive or fail to perceive messages that are opposite to your opinions, beliefs, and attitudes. You learn and remember material that is consistent with your attitudes, believes, and opinions. In many ways your attitudes, beliefs, and opinions affect what you perceive in interpersonal communication.

In listening and responding appropriately to others, it is important to be aware of the likelihood of selectivity in what you perceive and to be ready to change your perceptions when it becomes evident that you have misperceived a message. Your interpretations of what messages mean will always be tentative until confirmed by the sender; that is one reason it is so important to negotiate the meaning of a message before you respond to it.

COMPREHENSION TEST E

You may wish to answer the following questions to see how well you have understood the material on selective perception. Answers are at the end of the chapter.

1. What is selective perception?
   a. Responding to all the aspects, both verbal and nonverbal, of a message
   b. Responding only to a few of the verbal and nonverbal aspects of a message
   c. The name of a famous race horse
2. Which of the following are factors that influence selective perception?
   a. Self-disclosure
   b. Expectations
   c. The weather
   d. Needs, wants, desires
   e. Opinions, attitudes, beliefs
   f. Trust
3. How can you avoid misunderstandings due to selective perception?
   a. Do not try to communicate.
   b. Keep all interpretations of messages tentative until confirmed by the sender.
   c. Do not have expectations, needs, or opinions.

EXERCISE 4.2C: INCREASING COMMUNICATION SKILLS

**Step Three: The Use of Effective Communication Skills—
Clarifying Personal Strengths and Clarifying Relationships**

Part 1: Clarifying Strengths. Divide into pairs.

1. A takes two minutes to share with B what she considers to be his personal strengths, including things he thinks he does well, things he likes about himself, and things he thinks others like about him.

2.   *B* bombards *A* with any observations he has about *A*'s strengths and personal assets. In each case, when *A* receives an item of feedback she responds (a) by paraphrasing the feedback and (b) by stating what she thinks *B* means and by negotiating the meaning. Do not take more than five minutes to do this.

3.   Reverse roles and repeat the same process.

PERSONAL STATEMENTS

One of the most basic sending skills is speaking for oneself. When you speak for yourself, you take responsibility for and acknowledge ownership of your thoughts, opinions, observations, and feelings. You are an expert on *your* ideas, feelings, and needs, while other people are experts on *their* ideas, feelings, and needs. You speak for yourself when you use the personal pronouns, "I," "me," "my," and "mine." *Personal statements* are messages referring to yourself—about what you are feeling, what you are doing, what you are thinking, how you see yourself and your behavior, and so on. Whenever you refer to yourself the discussion target is "personal." You take *ownership* of your ideas, feelings, and needs when you say, "I think . . . ," "I feel . . . ," and "I want . . . ." The more you speak for yourself, the clearer your messages will be. The less you speak for yourself, the more confused your messages will be.

There are two ways you can confuse the ownership of your messages. The first is to *speak for no one*. To speak for no one you substitute words like "it," "some people," "everyone," or "one" for a personal pronoun. Or you can use no pronoun at all. As a result, it is not clear who is the owner of the ideas or feelings. Examples are, "Most people believe that students from Southeast Central are chickens!" or "It is commonly believed that students from Southeast Central have a big yellow streak down their back!"

The second way to confuse ownership of a message is to *speak for others*. When you speak for others you substitute pronouns such as "you" or "we" (or the person's name) for a first-person-singular pronoun. Examples are, "Bill doesn't like you—he thinks you're a lousy boss," and "We are bored, bored, bored!" Speaking for other people may make them angry or, at the very least, boxed in by your statements. And other people will be confused as to what your thoughts, feelings, and needs are.

Personal statements reveal who you are to the receiver and they increase the personal quality of the relationship. They also communicate personal involvement and trust in the relationship. Not "owning" your messages is a symbol of mistrust and decreases the possibilities of a closer relationship developing between you and the person you are talking with.

Part 2: Practicing Personal Statements. With your partner, decide which of the following are personal statements *(P)*, which speak for no one *(N)*, and which speak for someone else *(O)*. Answers are at the end of the chapter.

___ 1. Everyone here hates Bill.

___ 2. I love you.

___ 3. I hate you.

___ 4. Rumor has it that you are a beautiful person.

___ 5. We think flying is for the birds.

___ 6. Anyone can tell from looking at your face that you feel terrible.

___ 7. I want to find a better job.

Then discuss with your partner the following questions.

1.   In making statements about your strengths, to what extent were the statements clearly personal ones?

2.   What is your reaction to making personal statements and to receiving personal statements?

3.   How do you think personal statements help develop a relationship and improve communication between the sender and the receiver?

Part 3: Clarifying Relationships. Divide into pairs.

1.   Person *A* says, "One thing you could do to improve our relationship is . . ."

2.   Person *B* (a) paraphrases the statement and (b) states what he thinks *A* meant by the statement; they then negotiate its meaning. Once the meaning is clearly agreed upon, *B* states, "My reaction to that is . . ."

3.   Repeat the process.

4.   Reverse roles and repeat steps 1–3.

RELATIONSHIP STATEMENTS

Happiness is having good relationships. With some people, you will automatically become friends or enemies. But most relationships do not "just happen." They have to be built and maintained. At times your relationships will be smooth and enjoyable. At other times, conflicts and problems will arise and will have to be solved. At such times, you will have to sit down with the other person and discuss the current problems in the relationship and negotiate a solution. During such a conversation, you will need to make relationship statements.

A *relationship statement* is a message describing how you view the relationship or how you view some aspect of the relationship. It focuses on the relationship, not on you or the other person, and it speaks only for yourself. An example of a relationship statement is, "I appreciate your listening to me carefully." A good relationship statement indicates clear ownership and describes the relationship. A poor relationship statement speaks for the other person and makes judgments about the relationship. Relationship statements change the relationship; they consider clearly where the relationship is and what needs to happen in order for it to develop. Making relationship statements clarifies where two individuals stand and facilitates the expression of feelings and perceptions that can lead to a deeper, more satisfying relationship. Relationship statements also decrease the possibility of faulty communication.

Part 4: Understanding Relationship Statements. With your partner, decide which of the following are good relationship statements *(R)* and which are poor ones *(No)*. Then review your answers for all poor relationship statements. Decide which ones are about a person and not a relationship *(P)*, which ones make a judgment about the relationship *(J)* rather than describing how you perceive the relationship, and which ones speak for the other person *(O)* rather than for the speaker. The answers are given below.

__ **1.** We really enjoyed ourselves last night.

__ **2.** Our relationship is really lousy!

__ **3.** For the past two days, you have not spoken to me once. Is something wrong with our relationship?

__ **4.** You look sick today.

__ **5.** You really make me feel appreciated and liked.

__ **6.** You're angry again. You're always getting angry.

__ **7.** My older brother is going to beat you up if you don't stop doing that.

__ **8.** This job stinks.

__ **9.** I'm concerned that when we go to lunch together we are often late for work in the afternoon.

Answers

1. "We really enjoyed ourselves last night." This is a poor relationship statement because it speaks for the other person as well as for oneself. It should be marked *O*.

2. "Our relationship is really lousy!" This is a poor relationship statement because it judges the quality of the relationship rather than describing some aspect of the relationship. It should be marked *J*.

3.   "For the past two days you have not spoken to me once. Is something wrong with our relationship?" This is a good relationship statement because it describes how the speaker sees one aspect of the relationship. It describes the speaker's perceptions of how the two people are relating to one another. Label it *R*.

4.   "You look sick today." This is a poor relationship statement because it focuses on a person, not on a relationship. It should be marked *P*. The person may look sick, but such a statement does not describe how the two people are relating to each other. It could be reworded as a good relationship statement as follows: "For the past fifteen minutes you have been holding your head in your hands. Are you not feeling well or is what I'm saying giving you a headache?"

5.   "You really make me feel appreciated and liked." This is a good relationship statement because the speaker is describing one aspect of how the speaker and the other person relate to each other. Label it *R*.

6.   "You're angry again. You're always getting angry." This is a poor relationship statement because it speaks for the other person. It should be marked *O*. A good relationship statement would be: "You look angry. You have frequently looked angry to me during the past two days. Is there a problem about our relationship that we need to discuss?"

7.   "My older brother is going to beat you up if you don't stop doing that." This statement focuses on two other people (the older brother and the receiver). It should be marked *P*.

8.   "This job stinks!" Definitely a judgment *(J)*. To be a good relationship statement, it would have to be something like the following: "I get so angry and upset at the way you treat me that I dislike working here."

9.   "I'm concerned that when we go to lunch together we are often late for work in the afternoon." This is a relationship statement and should be marked *R*. It describes an aspect of the relationship in that the two people manage their lunches together in such a way that they end up being late for work in the afternoon.

COMPREHENSION TEST F

Test your understanding of the previous communication skills by answering true or false to the following statements. Answers are at the end of the chapter.

True   False   1. Evaluative responses encourage the sender to elaborate on her statements.

True   False   2. Paraphrasing is restating the ideas and feelings of the sender before responding.

True   False   3. Paraphrasing shows that you care about what the other person is saying.

True	False	4. Paraphrasing helps the receiver understand the sender's message.
True	False	5. In selective perception, you respond to only part of the communication.
True	False	6. Our own needs, attitudes, and expectations can bring about selective perception.
True	False	7. The way to avoid misunderstandings due to selective perception is to avoid having any expectations, needs, or opinions.
True	False	8. The more you speak for yourself, the more confused your message will be.
True	False	9. When you make good personal statements, you talk about the other person's personal life.
True	False	10. Relationship statements focus mainly on the other individual in the relationship.

UNDERSTANDING THE OTHER'S PERSPECTIVE

Meg and Marge attend the same college. Meg is very wealthy, having inherited a great deal of money from her grandparents. Marge, whose parents are very poor, earns barely enough money to pay her tuition, buy books, and live inexpensively. They both buy tickets for the state lottery in which they could win up to $5,000. Two months later, they both receive letters. Meg reads her letter and says, "Hey, I won $5,000 in that lottery. Imagine that." Marge reads her letter, starts jumping up and down and screams, "I won! I won! I won $5,000!!! I won $5,000! I won! I won!" She throws her arms around her friend, both crying and laughing at the same time. She is too excited to eat or sleep.

Why did Meg and Marge react so differently to the news that they had each won $5,000 in the state lottery?

Different people have different perspectives. You see things from your shoes, I see things from my shoes, and our perspectives will never be quite the same. Misunderstandings often occur because we assume that everyone sees things from the same perspective as we do. If we like Italian food, we assume that all our friends like Italian food. If we are interested in sports, we assume that everyone is interested in sports. If we get angry when someone laughs at our behavior, we assume that being laughed at angers everyone. If we think a boss is stupid, we are surprised when a coworker thinks the boss is brilliant. As children, we can see things only from our perspective. As we become adults, we learn that different people

have different perspectives, and we learn how to understand other people's perspectives.

You can have two different perspectives at two different times. When you are a tired clerk who wants to go home early to get ready for an important date, a customer's behavior may seem unreasonable. When you are a manager who is trying to increase sales, the same customer behavior may seem very understandable. On Monday, if a clerk overcharges you, you may laugh it off. But on Tuesday, when you have been overcharged at the last three stores you have visited, a careless clerk may make you angry. If you have been lifting 100-pound bags of cement and someone tosses you a 40-pound bag, it will seem very light. But if you have been lifting 20-pound bags, the 40-pound bag will seem very heavy. As your experiences, assumptions, career, and values change, your perspective will change.

The same message can mean two entirely different things to two different people. If you tease a classmate, she may laugh. But if you tease a prominent professor, she may get angry and throw you out of class. *Different perspectives result in the message being given different meanings.* From one perspective, a message may be interpreted as a joke. From another perspective, the same message may be interpreted as hostile insubordination.

Perspective taking is a vital skill for communicating effectively. To phrase your messages effectively, you need to take into account the perspective of the receiver. When deciding how to phrase a message, you need to consider:

1.   The receiver's perspective
2.   What the receiver already knows about the issue
3.   What further information the receiver needs and wants about the issue

By taking these factors into account, you can phrase the message so the receiver can easily understand it.

To be skilled in receiving messages accurately, you need to understand the sender's perspective. When deciding what a message means, you need to take into account:

1.   The sender's perspective
2.   The meaning of the message from the sender's perspective

By taking these factors into account, you can decide accurately what the sender wanted to communicate with the message.

There is no skill more important for effective communication than taking into consideration the other person's perspective. Try standing in someone else's shoes; it will considerably improve your communication with that person.

EXERCISE 4.3: FROM THEIR SHOES

The purpose of this exercise is to provide some practice in phrasing messages so they are appropriate to the receiver's perspective. The procedure is:

1.   Form into groups of four and read the story entitled "The Typists," which follows below. As a group, write out what Jim might say to Sally, John Adams, and Dr. Elizabeth Smith. Then read the story entitled "The Laboratory Technicians." Write out what Edythe might say to Buddy, Helen, Dr. Smith, and Mrs. Jonathan.
2.   In your group, discuss the following questions:
     a.   How do your group's answers compare with the answers of the other groups?
     b.   What did you learn about making messages appropriate to the perspective of the receiver?
     c.   How do you find out what another person's perspective is?

The Typists

Sally and Jim are typists for a small publishing firm. Sally and Jim often tease each other about who is the faster typist. Their boss, John Adams, asks Jim to type a manuscript for one of their authors, whose name is Dr. Elizabeth Smith.

Dr. Smith is a well-known authority in mathematical psychology. The manuscript is very complicated. It contains a great many mathematical equations that are hard to type. It contains a lot of psychological jargon that Jim does not understand. It has handwritten notes all over it that are impossible for him to read. Dr. Smith, for example, has written sentences filled with psychological jargon, in small and sloppy handwriting and in ink that is smeared all over the page. It takes Jim hours trying to figure out what the handwritten notes say. Since he does not know what half the words mean, he cannot be sure whether he has typed the notes correctly or not. The math included in the manuscript, furthermore, is very complicated. It all has to be double checked to make sure it is correctly typed. This has taken hours and hours of proofreading and correcting mistakes. All in all, Jim hates the manuscript. But he is working hard to finish it correctly. To top it all off, Jim is using an old typewriter that is difficult to type on. He asked his boss, John, for a new one several weeks ago, but so far John has not tried to get him one.

One morning Sally looks over at Jim, smiles, and says, "That manuscript is really taking you a long time to type. How come?" Then John walks in and asks, "Jim, I have other typing for you to do and you're still working on Dr. Smith's manuscript. Why is it taking you so long?" Then Dr. Smith phones Jim and says, "Look! I have to revise the manuscript before next month! I need a clean, typed copy immediately. Why haven't you finished it?"

If you were Jim, would you say the same thing to Sally, John, and Dr. Smith? If you phrased your answers differently, what would you take into account about the persons? In phrasing his messages to each person, Jim might take into account:

1. Who the person is
2. What his or her position in the company is
3. How much the person knows about the condition and content of the manuscript
4. What the nature of the relationship between Jim and the person is
5. How appropriate it is to be fully honest about:
    a. Jim's feelings about the manuscript
    b. The facts about why it is so hard to type

The Laboratory Technicians

Buddy and Edythe are laboratory technicians in a large hospital. They have worked with each other for just a few days and do not know each other very well. One morning their supervisor, Helen, asks them to do a rush job on a blood sample. Helen is Edythe's older sister. Helen states that Dr. Smith is very worried about the patient. The tests, therefore, have to be done perfectly. The patient's name is Mrs. Jonathan. Edythe has never met either Dr. Smith or Mrs. Jonathan.

Edythe quickly conducts a series of blood tests. The results indicate that Mrs. Jonathan has blood cancer. As she finishes writing up the results of the tests, Buddy comes over and asks, "What'd you find?" Then Helen rushes in and asks, "What were the results of the blood tests for Dr. Smith?" Dr. Smith then calls on the phone for a quick report from Edythe. Finally, later in the day, Mrs. Jonathan calls up Edythe and says, "Look! I'm the person paying the bills! I want to know the results of my blood tests! And don't tell me to ask Dr. Smith! I already did and he won't tell me!"

If you were Edythe, would you say the same thing to Buddy, Helen, Dr. Smith, and Mrs. Jonathan? If the answer is no, what would you take into account in replying to each person? You might want to take the following factors into consideration:

1. Who the person is
2. What his or her position in the hospital is
3. How much the person knows about blood tests and blood cancer
4. What the nature of the relationship between Edythe and the person is
5. How appropriate it is to be fully honest about the results of the blood tests

EXERCISE 4.4: OBSERVING COMMUNICATION BEHAVIOR

You have just been through a series of short experiences on effective and ineffective communication behavior. You may wish to sharpen your skills in recognizing such behavior. The procedure for this exercise is:

1. Pick a group to observe, or sit down in a crowded area in which a number of conversations are going on.
2. Using the observation sheets that follow, count the number of times each type of effective or ineffective communication behavior takes place.
3. Within a week's time, discuss in the group the results of your observations. What general conclusions can you draw from what the members of your group observed?

Observation Sheet for Ineffective Communication

1. The receiver fails to listen to the message:

    _____

    _____

2. The receiver listens only to part of the message in order to say what he wants to say rather than responding fully to the message:

    _____

    _____

3. The receiver distorts the message to conform with his expectations of what he thought the sender was going to say:

    _____

    _____

4. The receiver is listening in order to make judgments and evaluations of the sender, thus making the sender defensive and guarded in formulating the message:

    _____

    _____

5. The receiver understood the words of the message but not the underlying meaning:

    _____

    _____

6. The sender uses general pronouns and nouns to refer to her own feelings and ideas:

_____

_____

7. Other ineffective communication behaviors:

_____

_____

Observation Sheet for Effective Communication

1. The receiver paraphrases the sender's remarks:

_____

_____

2. The receiver checks out the meaning of the sender's remarks:

_____

_____

3. The receiver does not give evaluations or judgments about the sender's remarks:

_____

_____

4. The receiver keeps his interpretation of the sender's remarks tentative until he checks it out with the sender:

_____

_____

5. The receiver focused upon the meaning of the message, not the specific words:

_____

_____

6. The sender used personal statements:

_____

_____

7. The sender used relationship statements:

_____

_____

8. Other effective communication behaviors:

_____

_____

TOWARD IMPROVED COMMUNICATION SKILLS

The difficulties in establishing effective communication between individuals are very real. What, then, can be done to improve understanding? One thing is the development of an atmosphere of mutual confidence and trust through the use of personal and relationship statements. Secondly, the use of communication skills such as paraphrasing, negotiating meaning, and making your responses relevant to the sender's message improves understanding. You may also facilitate the development of close, personal relationships by making your messages reflect personal and relationship statements and by making your responses reflect a recognition of the other person's strengths and capabilities. Through the use of such skills, you can consciously make the most of your chances to develop close, fulfilling relationships with other people.

CHAPTER REVIEW

Test your understanding of how to increase your communication skills by answering true or false to the following statements. Answers are at the end of the chapter.

True	False	1. Interpersonal communication is a message sent with a conscious attempt to affect the receiver's behavior.
True	False	2. The factors that most interfere with communication are external, not internal.
True	False	3. In effective communication, the receiver must interpret the message the way the sender intended.
True	False	4. Sending messages effectively involves "owning" your messages.
True	False	5. If a sender is lacking in credibility, she will have trouble communicating.
True	False	6. Getting feedback from the receiver helps eliminate misunderstandings.
True	False	7. Paraphrasing involves giving your opinion of the sender's message.
True	False	8. Relationship statements describe how one person feels about how both people are relating.
True	False	9. Most people have the same perspective.
True	False	10. Different perspectives result in the same message having different meanings.

In this chapter a series of communication skills have been discussed. Indicate below which ones you have mastered and which ones you need more work on.

1. I have mastered the following:
    — Paraphrasing response
    — Negotiating for meaning response
    — Making good personal statements
    — Making good relationship statements
    — Understanding the other person's perspective
    — Recognizing when effective and ineffective communication are taking place

2. I need more work on:
    — Paraphrasing response
    — Negotiating for meaning response
    — Making good personal statements
    — Making good relationship statements
    — Understanding the other person's perspective
    — Recognizing when effective and ineffective communication are taking place

You now should have increased your communication skills, and you should now know how to send and receive messages accurately. These skills take continual practice to perfect. As you continue to practice communication skills, you need to be able to say what you feel. The next chapter will discuss how to become more aware of your feelings and more skillful in communicating them effectively.

ANSWERS

Comprehension Test A: 1. true; 2. true; 3. true; 4. false; 5. true; 6. true; 7. true; 8. true; 9. b, d, e, f, h, i j; 10. a, d, e.

Comprehension Test B: 1. true; 2. true; 3. false; 4. false; 5. false; 6. true; 7. true; 8. false; 9. false; 10. true.

Comprehension Test C: 1. true; 2. true; 3. true; 4. true; 5. false; 6. true; 7. true; 8. true; 9. true; 10. true.

Comprehension Test D: 1. c, e, f; 2. b, c, e; 3. a, b.

Comprehension Test E: 1. b; 2. b, d, e; 3. b.

Practicing personal statements: 1. 0; 2. P; 3. P; 4. N; 5. O; 6. N; 7. P.

Comprehension Test F: 1. false; 2. true; 3. true; 4. true; 5. true; 6. true; 7. false; 8. false; 9. false; 10. false.

Chapter Review: 1. true; 2. false; 3. true; 4. true; 5. true; 6. true; 7. false; 8. true; 9. false; 10. true.

5

Expressing Your Feelings Verbally

SAYING WHAT YOU FEEL

Feeling the warmth, support, acceptance, and caring of close friendships is one of the most exciting aspects of being alive. And feelings are especially wonderful when they are shared with other people. One of the most rewarding aspects of relationships is sharing personal feelings. The more you share your feelings with other people, the happier and more meaningful your life will be. Yet one of the characteristics of our society is that we are not given much training in how to express feelings in such a way that there will be little chance of misunderstanding. Years and years of our education focus on communicating ideas clearly and unambiguously, yet relatively little education is given in communicating feelings clearly and unambiguously. And although the words that describe aspects of friendships, such as "like," "love," "dislike," and "hate," are among the most frequently used in the English language, our language has relatively few words that label feeling states. Sanskrit, for example, is reputed to have over nine hundred words describing various feeling states, but English has fewer than fifty, if one excludes slang and figures of speech.

To experience emotions and express them to another person is not only a major source of joy, it is also necessary for your psychological well-being. It is natural to have feelings. The capacity to feel is as much a part of being a person as is the capacity to think and reason. A person without feelings is not a person at all; he or she is a machine. The quest of individuals who really enjoy life is to feel a greater range of emotions and to build relationships in which emotions are aroused and allowed positive expression. Feeling and expressing caring for another person, feeling and expressing love for another person, even feeling and expressing anger toward another person are all potentially highly rewarding and beautiful experiences. And it is through experiencing and sharing feelings that close friendships are built and maintained.

There is a wide variety of feelings you may have while relating to other people. Here is a partial list of the feelings you may experience:

happy	confused	cautious	proud
pleased	surprised	confident	anxious
daring	silly	glad	grieving
bored	lonely	excited	confused
satisfied	elated	delighted	overjoyed
uncomfortable	apathetic	fearful	frightened
ecstatic	hopeful	embarrassed	humiliated
angry	weary	supported	accepted
shy	scared	discontented	
loved	appreciated	sad	

Feelings are internal physiological reactions to your experiences. You may begin to tremble, sweat, or have a surge of energy. Your heart may beat faster. Tears may come. Although feelings are internal reactions, they do have outward signs. Sadness is inside you, but you cry or frown on the outside. Anger is inside you. But you may stare and shout at the person you are angry with. Feelings are always internal states, but you use overt behaviors to communicate your feelings to other people.

It is often difficult to express feelings. Whenever there is a risk of being rejected or laughed at, expressing feelings becomes very difficult. The more personal the feelings, the greater the risk you may feel. It is also sometimes difficult to control your expression of your feelings. You may cry when you don't want to, get angry when it is best not to, or even laugh at a time it disturbs others. Expressing feelings appropriately often means thinking before you communicate them.

Having feelings is a natural and joyful part of being alive and being human. Feelings provide the cement holding relations together as well as the means for deepening relationships and making them more personal. The accurate and constructive expression of feelings, furthermore, is one of the most difficult aspects of building and managing your relations with other people. The purpose of this chapter is to provide the material and experiences necessary for becoming more skillful in appropriately saying how you feel.

You can't enjoy your feelings if you aren't aware of them. You can't express feelings you refuse to acknowledge. You can't communicate feelings you refuse to accept as yours. To accept your feelings you have to be aware of them and accept them as yours. You have to "own" them. And you have to communicate effectively. That is what this chapter is about.

Feelings are internal reactions to your experiences. To be aware of your feelings you have to be aware of how you are reacting to what is currently taking place around you. There are five aspects of such internal reactions (Miller, Nunnally, and Wachman 1975):

1. You gather information about what is going on through your five senses (seeing, hearing, touching, tasting, smelling).
2. You decide what the information means by interpreting the meaning of the information you sense.
3. You have a feeling based on your interpretation.
4. You decide how you intend to express your feeling.
5. You express your feeling.

Here is an example. "I see you sitting in the library, a book open in front of you, but you are looking around the room (sensing). I think you must be looking for an excuse to stop studying so that you can go to lunch (interpreting). I feel sorry that you can't take a break from studying (feeling). I want to give you a chance to enjoy yourself for a few minutes (intending). So I ask you if you'd like to eat lunch with me (expressing)."

When we are relating to other people, we sense, interpret, feel, intend, and express all at the same time. It all happens faster than you can read a word. *Everything happens so fast that it seems as though it is only one step instead of five!* To become aware of the five steps you have to slow down the process. Being aware of, and understanding, the five aspects of experiencing and expressing a feeling give you the basis for skillfully and appropriately communicating your feelings and for changing negative feelings (such as anger, depression, guilt, hopelessness, frustration, and fear) to positive ones. Each of the five steps, therefore, is discussed below in more detail.

Sensing

The only way you can gather information is through your five senses: seeing, hearing, touching, tasting, and smelling. All information about the world and what is taking place in your life comes to you through one of the five senses. You look, listen, touch, taste, and smell to be aware of your immediate experiences. These senses give you *descriptive* information only. You hear a person's voice get louder. You see a person frown. You feel his fist hit your nose. You smell and taste the blood dripping from your nose. *Such sensory information only describes what is taking place. It does not place any meaning on what is happening.*

Interpreting: Deciding What It Means

After your senses make you aware of what is going on, you have to decide what the information means. *The information is neutral: You decide what it means.* Interpretations are yours; they take place inside you. They are not in another person's behavior or in the events that take place in your life. Different people, for example, interpret the same sensory information quite differently. One friend may interpret the fact that your voice is loud to mean that you are angry. Another friend may decide that your loud voice means you are nervous. The sensory information (your voice seems loud) they have is the same, but they interpret it in two different ways.

When you are interacting with your friends and acquaintances, or even with strangers, your interpretations of what the information gathered by your senses means depends on at least three things:

1.   The information you receive through your senses

2.   What you think is causing the other person's actions

3.   The assumptions you make about what is good or bad, what you do
      or do not need, and what causes what in the world (your assumptions
      are an important part of your perspective, which was discussed in the
      previous chapter)

The information you receive through your senses has already been
discussed, so we will now look at deciding what is causing another person's
actions. When someone's voice gets louder, you look around to see what's
causing it. If you see a huge dog with its teeth embedded in the person's
leg, you decide that pain and fear are causing his voice to get louder. If
you see someone else tickling him, you interpret the loud voice as indicating happiness. If you notice that the person has just paid $1,000 for a new
stereo, and it fell apart when he picked it up to take it home, you decide
his loud voice means he is angry.

What you decide is causing the person's actions will influence your
interpretation of the meaning of the information you sense. Let's take another example. You feel pain on your nose. You see that a fist of another
person has just landed on your nose. You then decide whether the person
intended to hit you, or whether it was an accident. If it was an accident
you will be less angry than if you decide the person did it on purpose. If
you decide the person intended to hit you, you decide whether he had just
cause (you were kicking him at the time) or whether he did not have just
cause (if not, he is a mean, nasty person). All of this happens so fast that
for the most part you are not aware that it is going on. Your interpretations
follow your gathering of information much faster than a speeding bullet!

Finally, your perspective influences your interpretations. Your assumptions especially influence what you decide the sensory information
means. If you *assume* that people are as mean and nasty as goblins, your
interpretation of someone's fist landing on your nose may be biased. You
may immediately jump to the conclusion that this is another example of
how mean and nasty people are. Or, if you *assume* that people are basically
gentle and harmless creatures, you may jump to the conclusion that the
person hit you accidentally. Your assumptions and your overall perspective
have a powerful effect on your interpretations.

First you sense, then you interpret, and finally you feel. Your interpretations determine your feelings. Every feeling you have is based on an
interpretation about the meaning of the information you sense. You can,
therefore, control what you feel. By changing your interpretations, you can
change your feelings. This does not mean that changing your feelings is
easy. Most people make interpretations so automatically that it seems difficult to change them. But it can be done if they want to work at it. Chap-

ter 7 explains how feelings such as anger, depression, resentment, fear, frustration, and guilt can be changed and controlled.

Feeling

You sense, you interpret, then you feel. Your feelings are a spontaneous reaction to your interpretations. You may hear and see an acquaintance say, "Hope you're feeling well this morning!" How you feel in response to the statement is based on what you decide it means. If you think the acquaintance is being sarcastic, you may feel angry. If you think the acquaintance is expressing liking and concern for you, you will feel warmth and appreciation. All this happens immediately and automatically. The important thing to remember is that the acquaintance's actions did not cause your feeling; your feeling was caused by your interpretation of the meaning of the person's statement.

Feelings promote an urge to take action. They prepare your body for action. If you feel angry, for example, your muscles tense, adrenalin is pumped into your bloodstream, your heart begins to beat faster, all of which prepares you for either running away or physically fighting. Feelings activate the physiological systems within your body so that they are ready for action. Because of the action-urge aspect of feelings, it takes energy to hide your feelings from yourself and others. That means the more you are aware of your feelings, accept them as yours, and express them to others, the more energy you will have for enjoying yourself and your friendships. In addition, you will be able to communicate more easily and effectively.

It is unhealthy, both physically and psychologically, to avoid expressing your feelings. Yet many people do try to avoid or ignore their feelings. Some people believe that what they are not aware of does not exist and can't hurt them. Yet the repression and denial of feelings such as anger can lead to physiological damage due to the failure to take action and reestablish a homeostatic state within one's body. Ulcers and headaches are commonly thought to result from chronically repressed anger. And the repression of feelings can lead to a self-alienation that leaves a person confused as to what motivates and causes her behavior.

Feelings will keep trying to be expressed until you do so in a way that ends them. Sadness, for example, can be expressed by crying and talking to an understanding friend. Walking around with a smile on your face will not end the sadness inside of you. When you refuse to express your feelings, they start to control you. If you are holding sadness inside, for example, you will begin to avoid anything that makes you sad. When your friends become sad you will get angry at them. Pretty soon your whole life is organized around avoiding sadness because you are afraid that otherwise your own sadness will come out.

You *do not* control feelings by holding them inside. You *do not* control feelings by pretending they really don't exist. You *do* control feelings by accepting them as being yours and expressing them. You let them happen. Don't fight them or hold them back. Be aware of them. Take responsibility for them. They are yours. Usually things will be all right if you let your feelings take their natural course. It is even helpful to try to feel them more. If you are happy, feel happier. If you are sad, feel sadder. The important thing is to allow them to exist and to be appropriately expressed. Feelings don't have to be justified, explained, or apologized for. As you become more and more aware of your feelings, you will recognize what they are telling you about yourself and the situation you are in. *You control feelings by being aware of them, accepting them, giving them direction, and expressing them appropriately.* And if you are constantly depressed, anxious, or unhappy, you can change your feelings by changing the interpretations you are making.

Feelings activate your body physically so it is ready for action. Feelings urge you to take action to express them. What is lacking is a sense of direction. Do you run? Do you fight? Do you hug? Do you move toward another person? Do you move away? Feelings get the body ready for action. But they do not give you a sense of direction. It is your intentions that give you a sense of direction.

Intending

Your senses provide you with information about what is taking place within your environment. Your interpretations give the information meaning. Your feelings are your reactions to your interpretations. Your *intentions* are your guides to action, pointing out how the feelings can be expressed. They are your immediate goals as to what you want to have happen as a result of your feeling the way you do.

Intentions give your feelings direction. A few examples of intentions are:

to reject	to love	to play	to be caring
to cooperate	to clarify	to help	to share
to avoid	to hurt	to demand	to understand
to praise	to persuade	to accept	to defend yourself
to protest	to support	to resign	to try harder

Intentions are important because they have such power over your actions. They organize your actions in expressing your feelings. They identify what you want to do to express your feelings. They guide your actions so that your feelings are terminated through expression.

Once you decide how to express your feelings, the next step is taking action and actually expressing them.

Expressing

You say it. You act it out. You smile. You frown. You laugh. You cry. You jump up and down. You run screaming out of the building. You burn this book. Your words and nonverbal actions express your sensations, interpretations, feelings, and intentions. This chapter focuses on expressing your feelings verbally in a way that is easily understood. The next chapter deals with the nonverbal expression of feelings. Chapter 7 discusses how you can control your feelings by modifying your interpretations.

COMPREHENSION TEST A

Test your understanding of the above material by answering true or false to the following statements. Answers are at the end of the chapter.

True	False	1. Feelings are external events that force a reaction from you.
True	False	2. Feelings are internal reactions to your experiences.
True	False	3. Expressing feelings is a sign of weakness.
True	False	4. Expressing feelings is a psychological necessity and a source of joy.
True	False	5. Your senses gather information about what is happening and give meaning to it.
True	False	6. You interpret the information that your senses gathered and decide what it means and whether it's good or bad.
True	False	7. Your previous assumptions will influence your interpretations of an event.
True	False	8. Your feelings are caused by the event you are responding to.
True	False	9. Controlling feelings means that you hold them inside.
True	False	10. Your intentions are your guides on how to express your feelings.

WHEN FEELINGS ARE NOT EXPRESSED

One of the most frequent sources of difficulty in building and maintaining good relationships is communicating feelings. We all have feelings about the people we interact with and the experiences we share, but many times we do not communicate these feelings effectively. Problems arise in relationships not because we have feelings but because we are not effective in communicating our feelings in ways that strengthen our relationships. When we repress, deny, distort, or disguise our feelings, or when we communicate them in an ineffective way, we are asking for trouble in our relationships.

There are several difficulties that arise when feelings are not recognized, accepted, and expressed constructively.

1. Suppressing and denying your feelings can create relationship problems. If you suppress your feelings, it can result in increased conflicts and barriers that cause deterioration in the relationship. A friend's actions may be irritating, and as the irritation is suppressed, anger and withdrawal from the relationship may result.

2. Suppressing and denying your feelings can interfere with the constructive diagnosis and resolution of relationship problems. Maintaining a relationship requires an open expression of feelings so that difficulties or conflicts can be dealt with constructively. There is a common but mistaken belief that being rational, logical, and objective requires you to suppress and ignore your feelings. Nothing is further from the truth! If you want to be effective in solving interpersonal problems, you need all the relevant information (including feelings) you can get. This means that your feelings need to be conscious, discussable, and controllable.

3. Denying your feelings can result in selective perception. When feelings are unresolved, your perceptions of events and information may be affected. If you are denying your anger, you may perceive all hostile actions but be completely blind to friendly overtures. Threatening and unpleasant facts are often distorted or not perceived. Unresolved feelings tend to increase blind spots and selective perception.

4. Suppressing your feelings can bias your judgments. It is common for people to refuse to accept a good idea because someone they dislike suggested it, or to accept a poor idea because someone they like is for it. If you are aware of your feelings and manage them constructively, you will be far more unbiased and objective in your judgments.

5. Implying a demand while expressing your feelings can create a power struggle. Many times feelings are expressed in ways that demand changes in the receiver's behavior. If someone says to you, "You make me angry when you do that," she is indirectly saying, "Stop doing it." Or if a friend says, "I like you, you are a good friend," he may be indirectly demanding that you like him. When feelings imply demands, a power struggle may result over whether or not the demands are going to be met.

6.   Other people often ask you to suppress or deny your feelings. A person may say, "Don't feel that way" whenever you express a feeling. If you say, "I feel depressed," he will say, "Cheer up!" If you say, "I'm angry," she will say, "Simmer down." If you say, "I feel great," she will say, "The roof will cave in any moment now." All these replies communicate: "Don't feel that way. Quick, change your feeling!"

COMPREHENSION TEST B

Test your understanding of expressing your feelings constructively by answering true or false to the following statements. Answers are at the end of the chapter.

True	False	1. Problems arise in relationships because we have feelings.
True	False	2. Feelings should be ignored when making rational decisions.
True	False	3. If feelings are communicated effectively, the relationship will be strengthened.
True	False	4. If feelings are ignored, an idea may be disliked because the person suggesting it is disliked.
True	False	5. Blind spots happen when facts are ignored or distorted on account of unresolved unpleasant feelings about them.
True	False	6. Unresolved feelings will tend to increase blind spots.
True	False	7. Expressing feelings may imply a demand for the other person to do something.
True	False	8. People often respond to expressions of feelings by telling others to deny them.
True	False	9. If someone tells you that he is sad, you should say something to make him happy.
True	False	10. If someone tells you that your actions make her unhappy, she may be asking you to change.

EXPRESSING YOUR FEELINGS VERBALLY

There are two ways of communicating feelings: verbally and nonverbally. If you want to communicate clearly, your verbal and your nonverbal expression of feelings must agree or be congruent. Many of the communication difficulties experienced in relationships spring from giving contradictory messages to others by indicating one kind of feeling with words, another with actions, and still another with nonverbal expressions. This chapter focuses on the verbal expression of feelings. The next chapter focuses on the nonverbal expression of feelings. The congruence between the verbal and nonverbal expression of feelings is emphasized in both chapters.

Communicating your feelings depends on your being aware of your feelings, accepting them, and being skillfull in expressing them constructively. When you are unaware or unaccepting of your feelings, or when you lack skills in expressing them, your feelings may be communicated indirectly through:

1. *Labels:* "You are rude, hostile, and self-centered" versus "When you interrupt me I get angry."

2. *Commands:* "Shut up!" versus "I'm annoyed at what you just said."

3. *Questions:* "Are you always this crazy?" versus "You are acting strangely, and I feel worried."

4. *Accusations:* "You do not care about me!" versus "When you do not pay attention to me I feel left out."

5. *Sarcasm:* "I'm glad you are early!" versus "You are late; it has delayed our work, and that irritates me."

6. *Approval:* "You are wonderful!" versus "I like you."

7. *Disapproval:* "You are terrible!" versus "I do not like you."
8. *Name Calling:* "You are a creep!" versus "You are embarrassing me."

Such indirect ways of expressing feelings are common. But they are ineffective because they do not give a clear message to the receiver. And the receiver often will feel rejected and "put down" by the remarks. We are taught how to describe our *ideas* clearly and correctly. But we are rarely taught how to describe our *feelings* clearly and correctly. We express our feelings, but we do not usually name and describe them. Here are four ways you can describe a feeling.

1. Identify or name it: "I feel angry." "I feel embarrassed." "I like you."
2. Use sensory descriptions that capture how you feel: "I feel stepped on." "I feel like I'm on cloud nine." "I feel like I've just been run over by a truck." Because we do not have enough names or labels to describe all our feelings, we make up ways to describe them.
3. Report what kind of action the feeling urges you to do: "I feel like hugging you." "I feel like slapping your face." "I feel like walking on your face."
4. Use figures of speech as descriptions of feelings: "I feel like a stepped-on toad." "I feel like a pebble on the beach."

You describe your feelings by identifying them. A description of a feeling must include:

1. A personal statement—refer to "I," "me," "my," or "mine."
2. A feeling name, simile, action urge, or figure of speech.

Anything you say can convey feelings. Even the comment, "It's a warm day," can be said so that it expresses resentment or irritation. To build and maintain a friendship or any relationship, you must be concerned with communicating your feelings clearly and accurately, especially the feelings of warmth, affection, and caring. If you convey your feelings by commands, questions, accusations, or judgments, you will tend to confuse the person with whom you are interacting. When you want to express your feelings, your ability to describe them is essential for effective communication.

When you describe your feelings, expect at least two results. First, describing your feelings to another person often helps you to become more aware of what it is you actually do feel. Many times we have feelings that seem ambiguous or unclear to us. Explaining them to another person often clarifies our feelings to ourselves as well as to the other person. Second, describing your feelings often begins a dialogue that will improve your relationship. If other people are to respond appropriately to your feelings, they must know what the feelings are. Even if the feelings are negative, it is often worthwhile to express them. Negative feelings are signals that something may be going wrong in the relationship, and you and the other person need to examine what is going on in the relationship and figure out how it may be improved. By reporting your feelings, you provide information that is necessary if you and the other person are to understand and improve your relationship. When discussing your relationship with another person, describing your feelings conveys maximum information about what you feel in a more constructive way than giving commands, asking questions, making accusations, or offering judgments.

COMPREHENSION TEST C

Test your understanding of expressing feelings by answering true or false to the following statements. Answers are at the end of the chapter.

True	False	1. Indirect methods of communicating feelings are often quite effective.
True	False	2. Indirect methods of communicating feelings do not give a clear message to the receiver.
True	False	3. Eight indirect ways to communicate feelings are labels, commands, questions, accusations, sarcasm, approval, disapproval, and name calling.
True	False	4. Describing your feelings can help you become aware of your feelings.
True	False	5. Describing your feelings can begin a dialogue that will improve your relationship.
True	False	6. You should describe only positive feelings if you want to maintain relationships.
True	False	7. A feeling description must include a personal statement and the name of a feeling.
True	False	8. "I think you stink!" is a good feeling description.
True	False	9. Feeling descriptions can be figures of speech or sensory descriptions.
True	False	10. "I feel like a low-down toad" is a good feeling description.

EXERCISE 5.1: DESCRIBING YOUR FEELINGS

The objectives of this exercise are to help you recognize when you are displaying feelings without describing them, to explain how you may express your feelings verbally in a way that communicates them effectively, and to give you a chance to practice the latter. In the list below, each of the ten items consists of two or three statements. One statement is a description of a feeling; the others are expressions that do not describe the feeling involved. The procedure for the exercise is:

1. Divide into groups of three.

2. Work individually. In item 1 put a *D* before the sentence that describes the sender's feelings. Put a *No* before the sentence that conveys feeling but does not describe what it is. Mark the answers for item 1 only; do not go on to item 2 yet.

3. Compare your answers to item 1 with those of the other two members of your triad. Discuss the reasons for any differences.

4. Turn to the answers that follow the list and read the answer for item 1. Discuss the answer in your triad until you all understand the point.

5. Repeat steps 2, 3, and 4 for item 2. Then continue the same procedure for each item until you have completed all ten.

1. ___ a. Stop driving this fast! Slow down right now!
   ___ b. Your driving this fast frightens me.
2. ___ a. Do you have to stand on my foot?
   ___ b. You are so mean and vicious you don't care if you cripple me for life!
   ___ c. I am annoyed at you for resting your 240-pound body on my foot.
3. ___ a. I feel ecstatic about winning the Reader's Digest Sweepstakes!
   ___ b. This is a wonderful day!
4. ___ a. You're such a helpful person.
   ___ b. I really respect your ideas; you're so well informed.
5. ___ a. Everyone here likes to dance with you.
   ___ b. When I dance with you I feel graceful and relaxed.
   ___ c. We all feel you're a great dancer.
6. ___ a. If you don't start cleaning up after yourself, I'm moving out!
   ___ b. Did you ever see such a messy kitchen in your life?
   ___ c. I am afraid you will never do your share of the housework.
7. ___ a. This is a very interesting book.
   ___ b. I feel this is not a very helpful book.
   ___ c. I get very excited when I read this book.
8. ___ a. I don't feel competent enough to contribute anything of worth to this group.
   ___ b. I'm not competent enough to contribute anything worthwhile to this group.
9. ___ a. I'm a born loser; no one will ever like me!
   ___ b. Sue is a rotten creep! She laughed when I told her my score on the test!
   ___ c. I'm depressed because I flunked that test.

10. ____ **a.** I feel warm and comfortable in my group.

____ **b.** Someone in my group always seems to be near when I need company.

____ **c.** I feel everyone cares that I'm a part of this group.

Answers

1. **a.** No Commands like these communicate strong feelings, but they do not name the feeling that underlies the commands.

b. D This statement both expresses and names a feeling. The person communicates the feeling by describing himself as frightened.

2. **a.** No A feeling is implied through a question, but the specific feeling underlying the question is not described.

b. No This statement communicates considerable feeling through an accusation, but it is not clear whether the accusation is based on anger, hurt, fear, or some other feeling.

c. D The person describes the feeling as annoyance. Note that the speaker also "owns" the feeling by using the personal pronoun "I."

3. **a.** D The speaker describes herself as feeling ecstatic.

b. No This statement communicates positive feelings without describing what they are. The speaker appears to be commenting on the weather when in fact the statement is an expression of how the speaker feels. We cannot tell whether the speaker is feeling proud, happy, caring, accepted, supported, or relieved.

4. **a.** No The speaker makes a value judgment communicating positive feelings about the other person, but the speaker does not describe the feelings. Does the speaker admire the other person or like the other person, or is the speaker only grateful?

b. D The speaker describes the positive feelings as respect.

5. **a.** No This statement does name a feeling (likes) but the speaker is talking for everyone and does not make clear that the feeling is personal. A description of a feeling must contain "I," "me," "my," or "mine" to make clear that the feelings are within the speaker. Does it seem more friendly for a person to say, "I like you," or "Everybody likes you"?

b. D The speaker communicates clearly and specifically the feeling the speaker has when dancing with the other person.

c. No First, the speaker does not speak for herself, but rather hides behind the phrase "we feel." Second, "You're a great dancer" is a value judgment and does not name a feeling. Note that merely placing the word *feel* in front of a statement does not make the statement a description of feeling. People often say *feel* when they mean *think* or *believe.*

6. **a.** No This statement communicates general and ambiguous negative feelings about the person's behavior. It refers to the condition of the apartment or house and the speaker's future behavior, but not to the speaker's inner feelings.

b. No The speaker is trying to communicate a negative feeling through a rhetorical question and a value judgment. Although it is clear the feeling is negative, the specific feeling is not described.

c. D The speaker describes fear as the negative feeling connected with the other person's housework.

Note: Notice that in *a* and *b* the feelings could easily have been interpreted as anger. Many times the expression of anger results from an underlying fear. Yet when the receiver tries to respond, she may understand that the other person is angry without comprehending that the basic feeling to be responded to is a feeling of fear.

7. a. No The speaker communicates a positive value judgment that conveys feelings, but the specific feelings are not described.

b. No The speaker uses the words "I feel" but does not then describe or name a feeling. Instead, the speaker gives a negative value judgment. What the speaker actually meant was "I believe" or "I think" the book is not very good. People commonly use the word *feel* when they mean *think* or *believe*. Consider the difference between, "I feel you don't like me" and "I believe (think) you don't like me."

c. D The speaker describes a feeling of excitement while reading this book.

Note: Many times people who say they are unaware of what they feel— or who say they don't have any feelings about something—state value judgments about recognizing that this is the way their positive or negative feelings get expressed. Many times useless arguments can be avoided if we are careful to describe our feelings instead of expressing them through value judgments. For example, if Joe says the book is interesting and Fred says it is boring, they may argue about which it "really" is. If Joe, however, says he was excited by the book and Fred says he was frustrated by it, no argument should follow. Each person's feelings are what they are. Of course, discussing what it means for Joe and Fred to feel as they do may provide helpful information about each person and about the book.

8. a. D Speaker communicates a feeling of incompetence.

b. No Warning! This statement is potentially hazardous to your health! Although it sounds much the same as the previous statement, it states that the speaker actually is incompetent—not that the speaker currently feels incompetent. The speaker has passed a negative value judgment on himself and labeled himself as incompetent.

Note: Many people confuse *feeling* with *being*. A person may feel incompetent yet behave very competently or a person may feel competent and perform very incompetently. A person may feel hopeless about a situation that turns out not to be hopeless once his behavior is given an appropriate focus. *A sign of emotional maturity is that a person does not confuse feelings with the reality of the situation.* An emotionally mature person knows he can perform competently, even though he feels incompetent. He does not let his feelings keep him from doing his best because he knows the difference between feelings and performance and knows that the two do not always match.

9. **a.** No   The speaker has evaluated herself—passed a negative value judgment on herself by labeling herself a born loser.

   b. No   This statement also communicates a negative value judgment, but against another person rather than of oneself. Although the statement contains strong feelings, the feelings are not specifically named or described.

   c. D   The speaker states she feels depressed. Statements *a* and *c* highlight the important difference between passing judgment on yourself and describing your feelings.

   Note: Feelings are constantly changing and are by no means written in concrete once they occur. To say that you are now depressed does not imply that you will or must always feel the same. If you label yourself as a born loser, however, you imply a permanence to a feeling of depression by defining it as a trait rather than as a temporary affective response. You can *feel* anger without being an *angry person.* You can *feel* shy without being a *shy person.* Many people try to avoid new situations and activities by labeling themselves. "I'm not artistic," "I'm not a good public speaker," "I can't participate in groups" are examples. If we could recognize what our feelings are beneath such statements, maybe we would be more willing to risk doing things we are somewhat fearful of.

10. **a.** D   The speaker communicates a feeling by describing it and taking ownership of it.

   b. No   The speaker communicates a positive feeling but does not take direct ownership of it and does not say whether the feeling is happiness, gratefulness, supportiveness, or what.

   c. No   Instead of "I feel" the speaker should have said "I believe." The last part of the statement really tells what the speaker believes the others feel about her. It does not tell what the speaker feels. Expressions *a* and *c* relate to each other as follows: "Because I believe that everyone cares whether I am part of this group, I feel warm and comfortable."

EXERCISE 5.2: AMBIGUITY OF EXPRESSION OF FEELINGS

The objective of this exercise is to increase your awareness of the ambiguity or unclearness in expressing feelings in ways that are not descriptive. Given below are a series of statements. Each statement presents an interpersonal situation. The procedure for the exercise is:

1. Divide into groups of three.
2. For each situation below write descriptions of *two different* feelings that might have given rise to the expression of feelings in the statement.
3. Compare your answers with the answers of the other members of your trio. Discuss them until you understand each other's answers.
4. In the group as a whole, discuss the results of ambiguity in expressing feelings in interpersonal relationships.
      a. What happens when persons make ambiguous statements of feeling? How do other persons respond? How do they feel?
      b. Why would you state feelings ambiguously? In what circumstances

would you be ambiguous rather than descriptive? What would be the probable consequence?

1. A girl asks her boyfriend, "Why can't you ever be any place on time?" What might the girl have said that would have described her feelings openly?

2. You notice that a person in the group who was talking a lot has suddenly become silent. What might the person have said that would have described his feelings openly?

3. During a group meeting, you hear John tell Bill, "Bill, you're talking too much." What might John have said that would have described his feelings openly?

4. Sally abruptly changed the subject after Ann made a comment. What might Sally have said that would have described her feelings openly?

5. A boy told his girl friend, "You shouldn't have brought me such an expensive gift." What might the boy have said that would have described his feelings openly?

6. You hear a passenger say to a taxi driver, "Do we have to drive this fast?" What might the passenger have said that would have described his feelings openly?

7. Sam says to Jane, "You're really wonderful." What might Sam have said that would have described his feelings openly?

CHECKING YOUR PERCEPTION OF ANOTHER'S FEELINGS

Feelings are internal reactions, and we can tell what people are feeling only from what they tell us and from their overt actions. Overt actions include such things as smiles, frowns, shouts, whispers, tears, and laughter. When other people describe their feelings to us, we can usually accept their feelings to be what they say they are. But if other people express their feelings indirectly (such as through sarcasm) or nonverbally (such as through a frown), we often need to clarify how they actually feel. A basic rule in interpersonal communication is that before you respond to a person's feelings, you need to check to make sure you really know what the other person actually feels.

The best way to check out whether or not you accurately understand how a person is feeling is through a perception check. A *perception check* has three parts:

1. You describe what you think the other person's feelings are.

2. You ask whether or not your perception is accurate.

3. You refrain from expressing approval or disapproval of the feelings.

"You look sad. Are you?" is an example of a perception check. It describes how you think the person is feeling, then it asks the person to agree with or correct your perception, and it does both without making a value judgment about the feeling. A perception check communicates the message, "I want to understand your feeling; is this the way you feel?" It is an invitation for other people to describe their feelings more directly. And it shows you care enough about the person to want to understand how the person feels. Perception checking will help you avoid actions you later regret because they are based on false assumptions about what the other person is feeling.

Checking out our impressions of how others are feeling is an important communication skill. Our impressions are often biased by our own fears, expectations, and present feelings. If we are afraid of anger and expect other people to be angry, then we may think they are angry when in fact they are not. If we feel guilty, we may think other people are about to reject us. We frequently misperceive how other people are feeling, and it is therefore essential that we check out our perceptions before taking action.

EXERCISE 5.3: IS THIS THE WAY YOU FEEL?

The purpose of this exercise is to provide an opportunity to increase your understanding of perception checking by indicating which of the statements given below are perception checks and which are other types of statements. The procedure is:

1. Working by yourself, read each of the statements below. On a separate sheet of paper write your answers.

    Put a *PC* for each perception check.
    Put a *J* for each statement that makes a judgment about the other person.
    Put an *O* for each statement that speaks for the other person rather than for yourself.
    Put a *Q* for each question that does not include a description of your perceptions of the other person's feelings.

2. Form groups of four. Review the answers of each member for each statement. Discuss any disagreements until all members agree on the answer. Answers are at the end of the chapter.

3. Go around the group and have members check out their perceptions of how other members are feeling.

Statements

1. ____ Are you angry with me?
2. ____ You look as if you are upset about what Sally said. Are you?
3. ____ Why are you mad at me?

4. _____ You look as if you feel put down by my statement. That's stupid!
5. _____ What is it about your boss that makes you resent her so much?
6. _____ Are your feelings hurt again?
7. _____ You look unhappy. Are you?
8. _____ Am I right that you feel disappointed that nobody commented on your suggestion?
9. _____ Why on earth would you get upset about that? That's pretty crazy!
10. _____ I get the impression you are pretty happy with my work. Are you?
11. _____ Are you feeling rejected?
12. _____ If you are dumb enough to get angry about that, the hell with you!
13. _____ You're always happy!
14. _____ I'm not sure whether your expression means that I'm confusing you or hurting your feelings. Which one is it?
15. _____ Half the time you're laughing. The other half of the time you're staring off into space. What's going on?

CHAPTER REVIEW

Test your understanding of how to express your feelings verbally by answering true or false to the following statements. Answers are at the end of the chapter.

True   False   1. You become aware of your feelings by being aware of how you are reacting to what is happening around you.

True   False   2. You express your feelings after you have gone through the process of sensing, interpreting, feeling, and intending.

True   False   3. The best way to express your feelings is to describe how the other person feels.

True   False   4. How you feel about a situation reflects how the situation really is.

True   False   5. "Everyone likes you!" is an example of a good feeling description.

True   False   6. A perception check is done to make sure a person really understands how you feel.

True   False   7. In a perception check, you describe what you think the other person's feelings are and ask whether you are right, without showing approval or disapproval.

True   False   8. A perception check will help you understand the other person's message.

True   False   9. We often receive an inaccurate impression of someone else's feelings because of our fears and angers.

True   False   10. "You look happy! Is that the way you feel?" is an example of a good perception check.

Indicate below which skills you have mastered and which you still need more work on.

1.   I have mastered the following:
    ＿＿＿ Being aware of my feelings
    ＿＿＿ Describing my feelings to others in a direct way
    ＿＿＿ Using a perception check when it is needed
    ＿＿＿ Avoiding the indirect expression of feelings through commands, questions, accusations, and so on

2.   I need more work on the following:
    ＿＿＿ Being aware of my feelings
    ＿＿＿ Describing my feelings to others in a direct way
    ＿＿＿ Using a perception check when it is needed
    ＿＿＿ Avoiding the indirect expression of feelings through commands, questions, accusations, and so on.

By now, you should know how to get in touch with your feelings and express them verbally in constructive ways. You should also know how to check your perception of another person's feelings. The next chapter will help you learn the skills of constructively expressing your feelings nonverbally.

ANSWERS

Comprehension Test A: 1. false; 2. true; 3. false; 4. true; 5. false; 6. true; 7. true; 8. false; 9. false; 10. true.

Comprehension Test B: 1. false; 2. false; 3. true; 4. true; 5. true; 6. true; 7. true; 8. false; 9. true; 10. true.

Comprehension Test C: 1. false; 2. true; 3. true; 4. true; 5. true; 6. false; 7. true; 8. false; 9. true; 10. true.

Is This the Way You Feel?: 1. Q; 2. PC; 3. O; 4. J; 5. O; 6. Q; 7. PC; 8. PC; 9. J; 10. PC; 11. Q; 12. J; 13. O; 14. PC; 15. PC.

Chapter Review: 1. true; 2. true; 3. false; 4. false; 5. false; 6. false; 7. true; 8. true; 9. true; 10. true.

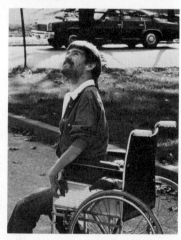

6

Expressing Your Feelings Nonverbally

INTRODUCTION

When we talk we rarely trust the words alone to convey our messages. We shift our weight, stand close to the other person or far away, wave our arms, smile or frown, speak loudly or softly, touch or don't touch, or use other nonverbal behaviors to emphasize or clarify what our words mean. We communicate by the way we sit or stand, straighten our clothing, place our hands, manipulate a glass, and so forth. Consciously and unconsciously we use nonverbal behaviors to communicate our feelings, liking, and preferences as well as to reinforce the meaning of our words.

Many people have great difficulties in communicating clearly and accurately to other individuals how they feel, despite the fact that awareness, acceptance, and expression of feelings are crucial for psychological health and for building and maintaining fulfilling relationships. Expressing warmth and liking is especially important for establishing and keeping friendships. The previous chapter focused on constructive ways of expressing feelings verbally. This chapter focuses on the skills necessary for effective nonverbal expression of feelings. The objectives of this chapter are to:

1. Remind you of the importance of the congruence between your verbal and nonverbal messages in communicating your feelings to another person clearly and accurately

2.   Increase your awareness of how you communicate feelings to others
3.   Provide skill practice in expressing feelings nonverbally

NONVERBAL COMMUNICATION

Actions speak louder than words. Because nonverbal messages tend to be less conscious we tend to believe them even more than the words people say. In communicating effectively with other individuals it may be more important to have a mastery of nonverbal communication than fluency with words. In a normal two-person conversation, the verbal components carry less than 35 percent of the social meaning of the situation, while more than 65 percent is carried by nonverbal messages (McCroskey, Larson, and Knapp 1971). That may seem surprising to you, but we communicate by our manner of dress, physique, posture, body tension, facial expression, degree of eye contact, hand and body movements, tone of voice, continuities in speech (such as rate, duration, nonfluencies, and pauses), spatial distance, and touch, as well as by words. In order to communicate effectively with other people, therefore, you must be as concerned with the nonverbal messages you are sending as with the verbal ones, if not more so. It is the nonverbal messages that most clearly and powerfully communicate liking and disliking, acceptance and rejection, and interest and boredom.

In comparison with verbal language, however, nonverbal behavior is very limited. Usually nonverbal messages are used to communicate feelings, likings, and preferences, and they customarily either reinforce or contradict messages that are communicated verbally. Feelings, in particular, are communicated more by nonverbal messages than by the words a person uses. Facial expressions and tone of voice are especially important in communicating feelings. Smiles, for example, communicate friendliness, cooperativeness, and acceptance of other individuals. There appears to be more eye contact between people who like each other than between people who do not like each other. Emotional meanings are communicated quite accurately through voice tone and inflection.

The problem is that it is often difficult to know for sure what another person really feels. People often say one thing but then do another. Someone can seem to like you but never say so. A person can say he or she likes you, but somehow you do not feel the statement is sincere. Feelings are often misunderstood and misinterpreted for two major reasons: (1) the ambiguity of nonverbal messages and (2) the frequent contradictions between verbal and nonverbal messages.

Since nonverbal messages are inevitably ambiguous, the receiver cannot be sure about what the sender is feeling. For one thing, the same feeling can be expressed nonverbally in several different ways. Anger, for example, can be expressed by jumping up and down or by a frozen still-ness. Happiness can be expressed through laughter or tears. Any single nonverbal message, furthermore, can arise from a variety of feelings. A blush may show embarrassment, pleasure, nervousness, or even anger. Crying can be caused by sadness, happiness, excitement, grief, pain, or confusion. Also there are wide differences among social groups as to the meaning of many nonverbal messages. Standing close to the receiver may be a sign of warmth to a person from one cultural background and a sign of aggressiveness and hostility to a person from another cultural back-ground. In understanding nonverbal messages, the receiver must interpret the sender's actions. As these actions increase in ambiguity, the chance for misinterpretation increases.

It is often difficult to make accurate judgments about the feelings of other people because of the different degrees of feelings or contradictory kinds of feelings being expressed simultaneously through verbal and non-verbal messages. We have all been in situations in which we have received or sent conflicting messages on verbal and nonverbal channels. The parent who screams, "I WANT IT QUIET AROUND THIS HOUSE," or the teacher who says, "I've always got plenty of time to talk to a student," are examples. Sometimes a person may say, "I like you," but communicate nonverbally, "Don't come close to me," by using a cold tone of voice, looking worried, and backing away. When receiving such conflicting mes-sages through two different channels, we tend to believe the messages that we perceive to be harder to fake. This is often the nonverbal channel. You are, therefore, more apt to believe the nonverbal communication than the verbal one. Such contradictory communications are known as double binds and can make the receiver anxious and suspicious.

When communicating your feelings, it pays to take special care that your verbal and nonverbal messages are congruent. It is when your verbal and nonverbal messages are redundant and reinforce and complement each other that you will be most successful in effectively communicating what you feel. Especially when communicating liking and acceptance, avoid stoop shoulderedness and downcast eyes (signs of depression and disap-pointment) and keep your posture erect with your head held high (signs of self-acceptance and well-being). Keep good eye contact because it com-municates that you are open to communication, involvement, and feed-back. People tend to avoid eye contact when they want to hide their feel-ings, when they are tense, when they are interacting with someone they dislike, or when they are attempting to cut off social contact.

Nonverbal messages, then, are more powerful in communicating feelings than are verbal messages, but are also more ambiguous and diffi-cult to interpret accurately. To communicate your feelings clearly and ac-curately to another person, you need to be skillful in both the verbal and nonverbal ways of expressing feelings. Above all, you need to make your verbal and nonverbal messages congruent with each other. The following exercises will help you become more aware of the ambiguity of nonverbal messages and of how you presently communicate feelings nonverbally, and they will help you become more skillful in the use of nonverbal cues to communicate feelings.

EXERCISE 6.1: COMMUNICATION WITHOUT WORDS

The objective of this exercise is to increase your awareness of the ambiguity of expressing feelings in nonverbal or in behavioral ways. Given below are a series of situations. Each involves the expression of feelings through certain nonverbal behaviors. The procedure for the exercise is:

1.   Divide into groups of three.
2.   For each situation describe *two different* feelings (within the person named) that might have given rise to such a nonverbal expression of feelings.
3.   Compare your answers with the answers of the other members of your trio. Discuss until you understand each other's answers.
4.   In the group as a whole, share your feelings and reactions to the exercise. What did you learn? How would you react if someone in the group behaved similarly to the people in the situations described? Are there any times when the nonverbal expression of feelings is more effective than the verbal description of feelings?

1.   Helen, who had been talking a lot in the group, suddenly became silent. Describe two feelings that might have caused Helen to do this.
2.   Without expression, Dale suddenly changed the subject of the group's discussion. What are two different feelings that might have been responsible for Dale's changing the subject?
3.   Whenever Keith made a comment in the group, he watched the leader's face. What are two different feelings that might have led Keith to watch the leader so intently?
4.   While the group discussion was going on, Betty became more and more tense and restless. Finally, she got up abruptly and left the room without saying a word. Describe two different feelings that might have caused Betty to leave.
5.   Roger was describing in a serious manner a fight he and a friend had had earlier. In the middle of his discussion, Dale began to laugh. Describe two different feelings that might have caused Dale to laugh.

EXERCISE 6.2: INTERPRETING OTHERS' NONVERBAL CUES

The objectives of this exercise are (1) to demonstrate the ambiguity of nonverbal cues in communicating feelings and (2) to illustrate how many different feeling reactions the same nonverbal cues can give. For this exercise you need from five to ten pictures cut out of magazines. Each picture should have at least one person in it who is expressing a feeling. The procedure for the exercise is:

1. Number the pictures. Pass each picture around the group.
2. Each person answers the following questions about each picture:
   a. How do the individuals in the picture feel?
   b. How does this picture make you feel?
3. The group then shares their answers for each picture.
   a. How similar were your interpretations of what the individuals in the pictures felt?
   b. How similar were the feelings you had in response to the pictures?
   c. If you have dissimilar answers, what makes the pictures so ambiguous?
   d. Could different people interpret your own nonverbal cues in as many different ways as the group interpreted the nonverbal cues of the individuals in the pictures?

EXERCISE 6.3: HOW DO YOU EXPRESS YOUR FEELINGS?

The objective of this exercise is to increase your self-awareness of the ways in which you express your feelings. Given below are descriptions of feelings you may have experienced. For each of these you are to report two different ways that you express such feelings. The first answer should be something you would say that would express your feelings. The second answer should report how you might express such feelings by actions and without using words. The procedure for this exercise is:

1. Divide into groups of three.
2. Write out your answers to the various situations.
3. Compare your answers with the answers of the other members of your trio. Discuss until you understand each other's answers. Then discuss:
   a. What did I learn about the way I usually express my feelings?
   b. In what ways would it be helpful for me to change the ways I usually express my feelings?
   c. In what ways would it be helpful for each of you to change the ways you usually express feelings?
4. In the group as a whole, share your feelings and reactions to the exercise. Then list as many principles for constructively expressing feelings as you can think of.

1. When you feel bored with what is going on in a discussion, how do you usually express your feeling?
   Using words: _____
   Without using words: _____
2. When you feel very annoyed with another person with whom you want to build a better relationship, how do you usually express your feelings?
   Using words: _____
   Without using words: _____

3.   When another person says or does something to you that hurts your feelings deeply, how do you usually express your feelings?
Using words: _____
Without using words: _____

4.   An acquaintance asks you to do something that you are afraid you cannot do well. You also want to hide the fact that you feel inadequate. How do you express your feelings?
Using words: _____
Without using words: _____

5.   You feel affection and fondness for someone else but at the same time can't be sure the other person feels the same way about you. How do you usually express your feelings?
Using words: _____
Without using words: _____

6.   Your close friend is leaving town for a long time, and you feel alone and lonely. How would you usually express your feelings?
Using words: _____
Without using words: _____

EXERCISE 6.4: USING NONVERBAL CUES TO EXPRESS WARMTH AND COLDNESS

The objective of this exercise is to increase your skills in the use of nonverbal cues to express warmth. In order to increase your awareness of the nonverbal cues that express warmth, you will be asked to role play the expression of coldness as well as the expression of warmth. Some of the nonverbal cues that can indicate either warmth or coldness are listed in the table below.

Nonverbal cue	Warmth	Coldness
Tone of voice	Soft	Hard
Facial expression	Smiling, interested	Pokerfaced, frowning, disinterested
Posture	Lean toward other; relaxed	Lean away from other; tense
Eye contact	Look into other's eyes	Avoid looking into other's eyes
Touching	Touch other softly	Avoid touching other
Gestures	Open, welcoming	Closed, guarding oneself, and keeping other away
Spatial distance	Close	Distant

The procedure for the exercise is:

1. Divide into pairs. Designate one person *A* and the other *B*.
2. Person *A* makes three statements about his childhood in a warm way. Then Person *A* makes three statements about his childhood in a cold way.
3. Person *B* gives Person *A* feedback of how successfully he role played the nonverbal expression of warmth and coldness.
4. Reverse roles and repeat steps 2 and 3.
5. Find a new partner. Repeat steps 2 and 3 with your new partner. This time discuss the characteristics of a person you want as a friend.
6. Find a new partner. Repeat steps 2 and 3 with your new partner. This time discuss what you could do to improve your relationship with your partner.
7. Discuss the exercise in the group as a whole.
    a. Did you find it easy to role play warmth and coldness? Why or why not?
    b. How well did each of you master the skills of expressing warmth and coldness nonverbally?
    c. Are there other ways to express warmth nonverbally?
    d. What were your reactions and feelings to the exercise?
8. Go around the group and give each other feedback concerning the typical nonverbal messages you send in the group. How would you describe each other's nonverbal behavior? What is most distinctive about each other's non-verbal behavior? If you were to suggest one way for each person to change his nonverbal behavior, what would it be?

Expressing warmth is a vital skill for building and maintaining fulfilling re-lationships. More than any other behavior, warmth communicates liking, con-cern, and acceptance of another person. You should practice the nonverbal expression of warmth until you are sure that you can communicate it effectively when you want to.

EXERCISE 6.5: ACTIONS SPEAK LOUDER THAN WORDS

The following exercise will give you a chance to practice nonverbal communi-cation of feelings. You may not use words and sounds during this exercise, but must communicate only by nonverbal means, such as facial expressions, eye contact, gestures, posture, and touch. The procedure for the exercise is:

1. Form groups of six. Sit on the floor in a circle. Do not use a table. Deal out a deck of ordinary playing cards until everyone has the same number of cards and there are at least three cards left in the draw-deck. The draw-deck is placed face down in the center of the circle.
2. The winner of the game is the person who gets rid of all her cards first. You get rid of your cards by correctly identifying the feelings expressed by other group members and by accurately communicating feelings to the other group members.
3. Group members take turns expressing one feeling. To begin, the person on the dealer's left selects a card from her own hand and lays it face down in front of her. She is now the expresser. The remaining group members are to identify the feeling she expresses. Then she expresses nonverbally the feeling on the card. The feeling each card represents is listed in item 9. The other people check their hands to see if they have a card that matches the feeling that was expressed. If so, they place the card(s) face down in front of them. If not, they pass.

4. When all the cards are down for the first round, they are all turned face up at the same time. If one or more of the receivers have matched the expresser's card, the expresser puts her card and all the matching cards face down on the bottom of the draw-deck.

5. Any group member who put down a wrong card must return it to his hand and draw an additional penalty card from the top of the draw-deck. You draw the same number of penalty cards from the draw-deck as the number of cards you put down in front of you.

6. If no other group member matched the expresser's card, then the expresser failed to communicate and she returns her card to her hand and draws a penalty card from the draw-deck. In this case the other people return their cards to their hands but *do not* draw penalty cards.

7. When you have two or three cards representing the same feeling, you must play all the cards if you play one of them. If you have several queens, for example, you must play all of them if you play queens at all. So, as expresser or receiver, you may get rid of two or three cards. Or you may have to draw two or three penalty cards.

8. The expresser may use any nonverbal or unspoken behavior she wishes in order to communicate accurately the feeling she is portraying. No words may be spoken or sounds made. You may wish to use your hands, your head, your whole body, and you may involve other group members by touching them or engaging them in a nonverbal interchange.

9. Each card represents a different feeling:

2 = contentment	9 = anger
3 = shyness	10 = hope
4 = indifference	Jack = happiness
5 = fear	Queen = joy
6 = frustration	King = warmth
7 = loneliness	Ace = love
8 = sorrow	Joker = admiration

10. Discuss the following questions:
   a. Was it difficult or easy to express feelings nonverbally? Why or why not?
   b. Was it difficult or easy to interpret the nonverbal expressions? Why or why not?
   c. What nonverbal messages were most and least understandable?
   d. What did I learn about myself from this exercise?

EXERCISE 6.6: RECOGNIZING CUES FOR AFFECTION OR HOSTILITY

The following exercise is aimed at providing you with an opportunity to see if you can tell the difference between messages indicating affection and messages indicating hostility. Listed below are twenty messages. In the spaces provided, write an A if you think the message indicates affection and an H if you think the message indicates hostility. Then check your answers with the answers at the end of the chapter. Discuss with group members any that you missed until you are sure you understand them.

_____ **1.** Looks directly at the other person and gives undivided attention.

_____ **2.** Greets the person in a cold, formal manner.

_____ **3.** Engages in friendly humor.

_____ **4.** Yawns or shows other signs of boredom.

_____ **5.** Has a relaxed posture and does not appear tense or nervous.

_____ **6.** Sits close to the other person.

_____ **7.** Interrupts repeatedly.

_____ **8.** Leans toward the other person as an expression of interest.

_____ **9.** Sits relatively far away.

_____**10.** Responds directly and openly to the other person's request to know one's opinions, values, attitudes, and feelings.

_____**11.** Exhibits a cold, nonreceptive facial expression.

_____**12.** Uses the other person's vocabulary in explaining things.

_____**13.** Makes encouraging, reassuring remarks to the other person.

_____**14.** Lays traps for the other person (e.g., "A minute ago you said . . . and now you are contradicting yourself!").

_____**15.** Makes casual physical contact with the other person as an expression of liking (e.g., pat on the back, touch on the arm).

_____**16.** Says, "That stupid remark is about what I would expect from someone like you."

_____**17.** Shows consideration for the physical comfort of the other person by taking the person's coat, offering a more comfortable chair, adjusting the window, and so forth.

_____**18.** Sneers and appears amused when the other person is sharing personal feelings.

_____ **19.** Hedges or rebuffs the other person when asked a "personal" question.

_____ **20.** During the conversation looks repeatedly at the clock, out the window, away from the other person, or at papers on the desk.

IMPORTANCE OF MAKING YOUR VERBAL AND NONVERBAL MESSAGES CONGRUENT

There is no way to emphasize too much the importance of making congruent your verbal and nonverbal messages for communicating feelings. If you wish to express warmth, your words, your facial expression, tone of voice, posture, and so on must all communicate warmth. Contradictory messages will only indicate to the other person that you are untrustworthy and will create anxiety about the relationship. Some psychologists have stated that receiving contradictory verbal and nonverbal messages for a long period of time from someone you love can result in mental illness. For a person to believe that your expression of feelings is real and genuine, your verbal and nonverbal must be congruent.

CHAPTER REVIEW

Test your understanding of the nonverbal expression of feelings by answering true or false to the following statements. The answers are at the end of the chapter.

True   False   1. It is possible to communicate verbally without giving nonverbal clues.

True   False   2. The verbal message is more believable than the nonverbal message.

True   False   3. In comparison with nonverbal actions, the verbal language is very limited.

True   False   4. Direct eye contact indicates dislike for the other person.

True   False   5. Feelings are misunderstood partly because the verbal and nonverbal messages are often incongruent.

True   False   6. Feelings are misunderstood partly because the nonverbal messages are often unclear.

True   False   7. Leaning away from another person is an expression of coldness.

True   False   8. Contradictions between verbal and nonverbal messages will tell the receiver that the sender is untrustworthy.

True   False   9. Contradictions between verbal and nonverbal messages will make the receiver suspicious.

True   False   10. Continued contradictory messages from a loved one can cause mental illness.

Indicate below the skills you have mastered and the ones you need more work on.

1.   I have mastered the following:
      ____Being aware of how I express my feelings nonverbally
      ____Using nonverbal cues to express my feelings accurately
      ____Being congruent in the way my verbal and nonverbal messages express feelings
      ____Using nonverbal cues to express warmth

2.   I need more work on:
      ____Being aware of how I express feelings nonverbally
      ____Using nonverbal cues to express my feelings accurately
      ____Being congruent in the way my verbal and nonverbal messages express feelings
      ____Using nonverbal cues to express warmth

You should now understand from this chapter, the importance of having your nonverbal messages agree with your verbal messages. Also, you should have developed skill in interpreting and expressing different feelings nonverbally. This skill will be helpful in the next chapter, which deals with how to listen and respond to others in a helpful way.

ANSWERS

Recognizing Cues for Affection or Hostility: 1. A; 2. H; 3. A; 4. H; 5. A; 6. A; 7. H; 8. A; 9. H; 10. A; 11. H; 12. A; 13. A; 14. H; 15. A; 16. H; 17. A; 18. H; 19. H; 20. H.

Chapter Review: 1. false; 2. false; 3. false; 4. false; 5. true; 6. true; 7. true; 8. true; 9. true; 10. true.

7

Helpful

Listening and Responding

RESPONDING TO ANOTHER PERSON'S PROBLEMS

When someone is talking to you about something deeply distressing or of a real concern to her, how should you listen and respond in order to be helpful? How do you answer in ways that will both help the person solve her problem or clarify her feelings and at the same time help build a closer relationship between that person and yourself?

Perhaps the most important thing to remember is that you cannot solve other people's problems for them. No matter how sure you are of what the right thing to do is or how much insight you think you have into their problems, the other people must come to their own decisions about what they should do and achieve their own insights into the situation and themselves. So how do you listen and respond to ensure that other people will make their own decisions and gain their own insights?

In listening and responding to other people's messages, there are two basic things that determine the effectiveness of your help:

1. Your intentions and attitudes as you listen and give your response

2. The actual phrasing of your response

The exercises that follow deal with both of these. Your intentions are the most important single factor in helping other people to solve their problems. The appropriate phrasing of your response involves considerable skill, but skill alone is not enough. It is only when the skills in phrasing responses reflect your underlying attitudes of acceptance, respect, interest, liking, and desire to help that your response will be truly helpful. Your response is helpful when it helps the other person explore a problem, clarify feelings, gain insight into a distressing situation, or make a difficult decision. In order to examine the intentions or attitudes with which you can respond to someone asking for help with a problem or a concern, we will go through the following exercise.

EXERCISE 7.1: LISTENING AND RESPONSE ALTERNATIVES

The objectives of this exercise are to (1) identify your response style, (2) understand the different types of responses you can use in a situation where the sender has a problem he wants help with, and (3) determine when each type of response may be most effective in helping other people with their problems and in building a closer relationship between other people and yourself. Each of the response alternatives used in this exercise communicates underlying intentions and attitudes. The procedure is:

1. Using Answer Sheet A, and working by yourself, complete the questionnaire on Listening and Response Alternatives. Specific instructions are on the Answer Sheet.
2. Using Answer Sheet B, and working by yourself, identify the underlying intent of each response given in the questionnaire. Specific instructions are on the Answer Sheet.
3. Using the Scoring Key on page 294, score Answer Sheet A. Write the number of times you used each type of response in the appropriate spaces on the Answer Sheet.
4. Read the next section, which is on intentions underlying the responses. Then divide into groups of three and score Answer Sheet B, discussing each response until everyone understands it.
5. Combine two triads into a group of six. On Table 7.1 (p. 156), mark the frequency with which each member of the group used each type of response.
6. Use the questions on page 156 to discuss with your group the results summarized in Table 7.1.

Answer Sheet A: Identifying Personal Responses

Read the twelve statements in the questionnaire and circle on this Answer Sheet the response that best represents what you would say to the speaker if you were trying to form a close relationship with him and to help him solve his problems.

1.	a : b : c : d : e				7.	a : b : c : d : e		
2.	a : b : c : d : e				8.	a : b : c : d : e		
3.	a : b : c : d : e				9.	a : b : c : d : e		
4.	a : b : c : d : e				10.	a : b : c : d : e		
5.	a : b : c : d : e				11.	a : b : c : d : e		
6.	a : b : c : d : e				12.	a : b : c : d : e		

Response	Frequency
E	____
I	____
S	____
P	____
U	____

Answer Sheet B: Identifying the Intent of a Response

Study pages 150–155, on which the five basic intentions underlying the responses to the problems presented in the questionnaire are discussed. Then go back through the questionnaire and classify the responses to each problem according to the five categories. Read each of the twelve problem statements and identify the intent underlying each of the alternative responses by marking a *P* for probing, *I* for interpretative, *E* for evaluative, *S* for supportive, and *U* for understanding.

Item	1	2	3	4	5
1.					
2.					
3.					
4.					
5.					
6.					
7.					
8.					
9.					
10.					
11.					
12.					

Questionnaire on Listening and Response Alternatives

In this exercise, statements are made by several people about situations they face. Little or no information is presented about the nature of the person speaking. Following each statement is a series of five possible responses you might make in trying to help the person solve his or her problem. See Answer Sheet A for specific directions on how to complete this exercise.

1. **David.** "I'm determined to be a success, and I know I can do it if I just work hard enough. I may have to work eighteen hours a day and stay chained to my typewriter, but if that's what it takes, I'll do it. My home life and my family may suffer, but it will be worth it in the end. I will be a success, and that's all that matters."

   a. You seem to be a person who wants badly to succeed at your job. That is understandable, but it may stem from your insecurity about your own competence and ability.

   b. I guess we all, at some time or other, go through a period where we want to achieve success. Lots of people worry about whether their family will suffer while they work so hard. I'm sure everything will turn out all right for you and your family.

   c. I think you are right. Hard works always pays off. Keep at it!

   d. You see yourself as a very ambitious person. Yet you're unsure about whether you want your family to suffer because of the long hours you believe you will have to work in order to be successful.

   e. Can you tell me a little more about why success is important to you? What will you do when you've achieved this success? Will you be happy? Will it give you all that you want out of life?

2. **Roger.** "I never seem to have enough time to do the things I enjoy. Just as I'm ready to go enjoy a nice game of golf or tennis, my brother reminds me of some writing I need to do, or my wife saddles me with household chores. It's getting harder and harder to have the fun out of life that I expect to have. It's depressing!"

   a. Wanting to have fun is OK, but don't you think you should do some work too? I certainly wouldn't play golf if I thought that later I would regret not having worked. Life does have responsibilities.

   b. It's upsetting that your work and household responsibilities are increasing to the extent that you don't have time for the fun and recreation you want.

   c. Maybe your leisure activities are just a way of getting out of the unpleasant jobs you should do.

   d. I'm curious. How much time do you spend on your favorite sports?

   e. You're in a busy time of your life right now. I bet you will have more leisure time as you get older.

3. **Frank.** "I never have any luck with cars. Every car I've ever gotten has been a lemon. Not only have I paid handsomely for the cars, but just when they are out of warranty, something major goes wrong. The car I have now needs a new engine. What's wrong with me? Why should I have all the bad luck?"

   a. You're wondering if it is your fault somehow that every car you own breaks down and has to have costly repairs. All the money you have to pay for car repairs depresses and angers you.

   b. Your anger about the poor quality of the cars you have owned is being turned against yourself and experienced as depression. Aren't the companies that made the cars to blame?

c. What kind of cars do you buy? How many cars have you owned?

d. Everyone has bad luck sometimes. I'm sure the next car you own will be more reliable. It's really not your fault the cars have turned out to be lemons. No one can tell how much repair a car will need when he first buys it.

e. You're always buying foreign cars. What you need is an American car that has a good warranty.

4. **Edythe.** "My older brothers pick on me constantly. They are always telling me what to do. I get pretty tired of their always harping at me to stand up straight or checking out my dates before I go out. What's worse, they tell things about me that are embarrassing. I've complained to my mother, and she tells them to stop, but they just keep on."

a. How often do you have serious talks with your brothers? Have you tried telling them how you feel?

b. You feel angry at your brothers because they pick on you, tell you what to do, are inconsiderate of your feelings, and want to pass judgment on your choice of dates, is that it? And you also feel helpless to change the situation, don't you?

c. I think you ought to be more understanding of your brothers. After all, they would not do it if they did not care about you.

d. Relax. Older brothers often act like that for a while. It's traditional. Once they see you have grown up, they will get off your back.

e. You resent being treated like a child. Part of establishing your independence as a person is feeling angry at people who don't treat you like an adult.

5. **Helen.** "When I was younger, I used to fight my parents because I wanted to get married. Now I'm married and I keep thinking of how good it was to be single and have no responsibilities to tie me down. I can't go anywhere without a bunch of kids clinging to me. It's rough, and there's nothing I can do about it."

a. I understand how you feel. I often feel that way too. But before long your children will grow up and then you will have all the freedom you want.

b. Let's explore how you arrange your time. How often do you wish to go somewhere without your children? How often do you hire babysitters?

c. You feel resentful and trapped because being married and having children don't allow you the freedom to go places and do things when you want to.

d. You say you fought your parents to get married. Now you feel resentful about the loss of freedom. Could it be that you are really angry at your parents for not stopping you from getting married in the first place?

e. Sounds to me as if you are stuck. You will just have to put up with the situation until your children are grown.

6. **Keith.** "I'm really depressed. I have a good job and I make an adequate salary, but I'm not happy. I guess working is not all it is cracked up to be. I have some money saved. I did not do too well in school before, but

maybe I will quit work and go back to school. I don't know what I should do."

   a. How long have you felt this way? Have the feelings just started recently, or have you always felt depressed about what you were doing?

   b. In other words, you're depressed and puzzled because your job isn't fulfilling, but school wasn't either, and they are the only two alternatives you see yourself as having.

   c. Depression is often anger turned against oneself. Perhaps you're angry at yourself for not feeling fulfilled by what you are doing.

   d. If you didn't do so well in school before, you probably won't do any better now. You should be satisfied with having a good job; many people don't you know.

   e. Lots of people have trouble making up their minds. There are a lot of people who don't like their jobs and who really don't want to go back to school. You don't need to feel depressed.

7. **Dale.** "I wish I could find a way to finish college without going to classes. I register each quarter, intending to go, but I get sidetracked and end up dropping out. I've been enrolled for six years. My parents would kill me if they knew how many credits I need to graduate!"

   a. It sounds as if you're just wasting time and money. You should probably just stop trying to go to school and get a good job instead.

   b. You feel guilty because you keep letting your parents think you are trying to finish college when in fact you are doing other things. It bothers you not to meet their expectations.

   c. Possibly if you tell me a little more about how you get sidetracked and what it is that you do while being sidetracked, we can get a clearer idea about what is involved.

   d. Many people have trouble finishing college. It's not unusual. Maybe you should quit. Your parents will understand if you explain things to them.

   e. Let's see if I understand you correctly. You're upset because you can't seem to finish college even though your parents really want you to, and you're worried about how they would react if you quit going to school. Right?

8. **David.** "All this work is driving me crazy! It seems as if I spend every waking moment working. I don't have any time to relax with my friends and family. No matter how hard I work I never seem to get caught up. I have so many responsibilities. I don't know how I'm going to get everything done."

   a. Don't feel so bad. I'm sure that if you just keep at it, you'll get things done and have the leisure you need.

   b. You're obviously trying to do too much. What you need to do is cut down on your commitments so you'll have more free time.

   c. You feel frustrated and angry that your work doesn't get finished and you can't enjoy your family and friends more; you work hard, but your responsibilities always seem to increase faster than your ability to meet them.

   d. Can you tell me more about the specific nature of your responsibilities, the way you schedule your time, and how you acquire new responsibilities?

    e. How you spend your time probably reflects your true values. Perhaps you prefer your work over your family and friends. Could it be that you consider your work more important than enjoying life?

9. **Roger.** "I never seem to get anywhere on time. I don't know why. People bug me about it and sometimes they get pretty angry. I try to keep a schedule, but it never seems to work out. I have an important golf game coming up and I'm afraid I'm going to be late for it. I don't know what to do to change."

    a. In other words, you feel frustrated with yourself because you always seem to be late and somewhat worried about the way other people react to your lateness.

    b. I'm wondering if you have investigated ways of managing your schedule more effectively. How often are you late? Are there some things you are always late for and other things you are never late for?

    c. You are obviously not very organized, and of course people will be angry when you treat them with such inconsiderateness. Perhaps you should ask someone more punctual to pick you up when you have an important engagement.

    d. I really wouldn't worry. Being late is not so bad. I'm sure that no one is really angry about such a little thing as arriving late.

    e. Being late is sometimes caused by passive-aggressiveness, where you want to punish other people but also are afraid to take responsibility for your actions.

10. **Frank.** "I just never seem to have any money. I have a good-paying job, but it seems as soon as I get my pay check, it's gone. Then I have to scrimp and save the rest of the month. Now my car needs a new engine and I don't know where I'm going to get the money to pay for it."

    a. Tell me more about how you manage your money. Have you tried budgeting? What are your major expenses?

    b. You're feeling depressed on account of your chronic lack of money and your unsureness of how you are going to pay for your needed car repairs.

    c. You may be wasting money on nonessentials. I think if you tried keeping a budget, you would be able to manage much better.

    d. I'm sure the money for your new car engine will turn up. Don't worry. You have always managed in the past.

    e. Depression such as you are experiencing often comes from a feeling of being helpless to solve your problems. Once you feel that you have some control over your financial problems, you'll feel better.

11. **Edythe.** "I just hate to bring my dates home to meet my family. I don't mind my boyfriends meeting my parents, but I wish there was some way to keep my older brothers out of the act. The way they give my dates the third degree scares my dates away. It's embarrassing."

    a. Embarrassment is often caused by older siblings, especially when they view you as a little girl. We have to plan to get them to see you as an adult and start treating you as one.

    b. It sounds as if they are pretty inconsiderate. Most people have siblings who embarrass them at some point, but your brothers sound as if they are really out of line.

   c.   Just wait. I bet that soon you will meet someone who won't be scared off by your brothers.

   d.   You feel angry about the way your brothers embarrass you by questioning your boyfriends, and you want to avoid such situations while at the same time allowing your parents to meet your dates.

   e.– Just what do your brothers do to your dates? What specific questions do they ask?

12. **Frances.** "I don't know about my children. David works too hard, Roger plays too much, Frank is always broke, Edythe married someone none of us have met, Helen got married too early, Keith quit school to work and now wants to quit work to go to school, and Dale isn't close to graduating after six years of college. You do your best and look how they turn out! It's enough to make a person give up."

   a.– You are worried about your children and yet feel helpless to change them. Each child seems to have some problem and you are unsure how well their lives will turn out.

   b.   Can you explain further how you feel about your children?

   c.   Don't worry. I'm sure they will turn out all right. All parents must worry about their children some time or another.

   d.   Tell your children to straighten out. Either they listen to their mother or else they aren't worth talking to.

   e.   You have certain expectations for each of your children, and they aren't living up to what you expect. These expectations are upsetting you.

INTENTIONS UNDERLYING THE RESPONSES

When other people want to discuss a problem or concern of theirs with you, there are at least five ways in which you can listen and respond:

1. Advising and evaluating
2. Analyzing and interpreting
3. Reassuring and supporting
4. Questioning and probing
5. Paraphrasing and understanding

Each of these alternative ways of responding communicates certain intentions. All of them, at one time or another, will be helpful. None of the responses can be labeled as good or bad, effective or ineffective. All have their place in helping other people solve their problems and gain insight into their difficulties. But some of the above responses are more helpful than others in building friendships and helping people explore further their feelings and thoughts. In exploring the intentions underlying the responses in the preceding questionnaire, the person with the problem will be called the sender and the person giving the response will be the receiver.

Advising and Evaluating (E)

Giving advice and making a judgment as to the relative goodness, appropriateness, effectiveness, and rightness of what the sender is thinking and doing are among the most common responses we make when trying to help others. These responses communicate an evaluative, corrective, suggestive, or moralizing attitude or intent. The receiver implies what the sender *ought* or *might* do to solve the problem. When advice is timely and relevant, it can be helpful to another person. Most often, however, when you give advice and evaluation you build barriers that keep you from being helpful and developing a deeper friendship.

For one thing, being evaluative and giving advice can be threatening to other people and make them defensive. When people become defensive they may closed-mindedly reject your advice, resist your influence, stop exploring the problem, and be indecisive. Why? Because giving advice and passing judgment often communicate that the receiver is assuming that her judgment is superior to that of the sender's. When a person has a problem, she does not want to be made to feel inferior. For another thing, being evaluative often seems to be a way of avoiding involvement with another person's concerns and conflicts. While it is quick, fast, and easy, it also allows the receiver to generalize about the sender's problems, and this communicates that the receiver does not care to take the time to understand the sender's problems fully. In addition, advice can encourage people not to take responsibility for their own problems. Even when praise is

used to influence others, it can communicate that the sender must meet certain expectations before she is of value. Finally, advice and evaluation often tell more about the giver's values, needs, and perspectives than about the receiver's problems. Thus, if you wish to be helpful and further a relationship, you should usually avoid such phrases as, "If I were you . . . ," "One good way is . . . ," "Why don't you . . . ?" "You should . . . ," "You ought to . . . ," "The thing to do is . . . ," and "Don't you think . . . ?"

It is important to avoid giving advice and evaluation in the early stages of helping other people understand and solve their problems and difficulties. There is a place for advising and evaluating, but there are other responses that are usually more helpful.

Analyzing and Interpreting (I)

When analyzing or interpreting the sender's problems and difficulties, the receiver's intentions are to teach, to tell the sender what his or her problem means, to inform the sender how the sender really feels about the situation, or to impart some psychological knowledge to the sender. In interpreting the sender's problems, the receiver implies what the sender might or ought to think. Analyzing or interpreting attempts to point out some deep hidden reason that makes the sender do the things he or she does. It attempts to give the person some additional insight through an explanation. Through such statements as, "Ah, ha! Now I know what your problem is," or, "The reason you are upset is . . . ," the receiver tries to teach the sender the meaning of the sender's behavior and feelings.

This suggestion will often make the sender defensive and will discourage her from revealing more thoughts and feelings for fear that these will also be interpreted or analyzed. Most of us react negatively when

someone else implies that he knows more about us than we do. When the receiver tries to analyze or interpret the sender's behavior, thoughts, and feelings, the receiver may communicate "I know more about you than you know yourself." People will usually respond better when you help them think about themselves and their feelings than if you try to figure out what causes them to do the things they do. It also frees you from being an "expert" on human behavior.

Reassuring and Supporting (S)

Supportive and reassuring responses indicate that the receiver wants to reassure, be sympathetic, or reduce the intensity of the sender's feelings. When the receiver rushes in with support and reassurance, this often denies the sender's feelings. Statements such as, "It's always darkest just before the dawn," and "Things will be better tomorrow," frequently end up communicating a lack of interest or understanding. Supportive statements are, however, frequently used by people trying to help a friend, student,

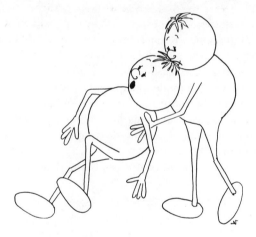

or child. It's distressing to see a friend depressed, so all too often a person will communicate, "Don't be depressed," rather than listening carefully and helping clarify the causes and potential solutions for the depression. While there are times when other people need to be reassured as to their value and worth or supported in their reactions and feelings, reassurance and support are often ways of saying, "You should not feel as you do."

Questioning and Probing (P)

Probing by asking questions indicates that the receiver wants to get further information, guide the discussion along certain lines, or bring the sender to a certain realization or conclusion the receiver has in mind. In asking a question, the receiver implies that the sender ought or might profitably develop or discuss a point further. Questioning is, however, an important skill in being helpful to people who wish to discuss their problems and concerns with you. In using questions skillfully, it is necessary to understand the difference between an open and closed question and the pitfalls of the "why" question. An *open question* encourages other people to answer at greater length and in more detail. The *closed question* usually asks for only a simple yes or no answer. An example of an open question is, "How do you feel about your job?" while an example of a closed question is, "Do you like your job?" Because open questions encourage other people to share more personal feelings and thoughts, they are usually more helpful.

When you intend to deepen a relationship or help other people understand and solve their problems, it is usually recommended that you avoid why questions. To encourage people to give a rational explanation for their behavior may not be productive because most people do not fully know the reasons they do the things they do. Being asked why can make people defensive and encourages them to justify rather than explore their actions. Why questions are also often used to indicate disapproval or to give advice. For example, the question, "Why did you yell at the teacher?" may imply the statement, "I don't think you should have yelled at the teacher." Because criticism and advice tend to be threatening, people may feel less free to examine the reasons that led them to a particular action or decision. Instead of asking people to explain or justify their actions through answering why, it may be more helpful to ask "what, where, when, how, and who" questions. These questions help other people to be more specific, precise, and revealing. For a more complete discussion of question asking, see Johnson (1979).

Asking questions skillfully is an essential part of giving help to other

people who are discussing their problems and concerns with you. But questions, while they communicate that you are interested in helping, do not necessarily communicate that you understand. It may sometimes be more effective to change questions into reflective statements that encourage the person to keep talking. An example is changing the question, "Do you like swimming?" to a reflective statement, "You really like swimming." Reflective statements, which are discussed in the next section, focus on clarifying and summarizing without interrupting the flow of communication because they don't call for an answer.

Paraphrasing and Understanding (U)

An understanding and reflecting response indicates that your intent is to understand the sender's thoughts and feelings. In effect, this response asks the sender whether you, the receiver, have understood what the sender is saying and how she is feeling. This is the same as the paraphrasing response discussed in chapter 4. There are three situations in which you will want to use the understanding response. The first is when you are not sure you have understood the sender's thoughts and feelings. Paraphrasing can begin a clarifying and summarizing process that increases the accuracy of understanding. The second is when you wish to ensure that the sender hears what he has just said. This reflection of thoughts and feelings often gives the sender a clearer understanding of himself and of the implications of his present feelings and thinking. Finally, paraphrasing reassures the sender that you are trying to understand his thoughts and feelings.

In order to be truly understanding, you may have to go beyond the words of the sender to the feelings and underlying meanings that accompany the words. It is the true meaning of the statement and the sender's feelings that you paraphrase.

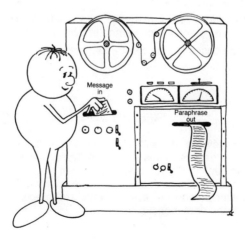

TABLE 7.1: FREQUENCY WITH WHICH THE GROUP MEMBERS USED EACH TYPE OF RESPONSE

Frequency	Evaluating	Interpreting	Supporting	Probing	Understanding	Total
0–2						
3–5						
6–8						
9–12						
Total	6	6	6	6	6	

After you have finished the procedure for scoring both answer sheets, record the frequency with which each member of the group used each type of response. This can be done by taking one member of the group, asking her how many times she used the evaluating response, placing a tally mark in the appropriate box, then asking the member how many times she used the interpreting response, and so forth. When the recording is completed, you will have a tally mark for each group member under each type of response. Then, as a group, discuss the results summarized in the above table. The following questions may be helpful:

1. What were the most frequently used responses by the members of the group?
2. How frequently did each member use each of the responses?
3. How does a person trying to explain a problem to you react when you use each type of response?
4. When is each type of response most useful in helping other people with their problems and concerns and in building a relationship with them?
5. What responses tell the most about the receiver?

EXERCISE 7.2: PRACTICING THE FIVE RESPONSES

This exercise provides you with a chance to practice each of the five types of responses. The exercise consists of two parts, one in which you are given a problem statement and you write down what you would say (assuming you wanted to respond with each of the five types of intentions), and one in which you and another person make statements and practice with each other giving the different types of responses.

Read the following paragraphs and write a response for each category. Do this by yourself.

"Sometimes I get so depressed I can hardly stand it. Here I am, twenty-five years old and still not married. It's not as if I haven't had any chances, but I've never really wanted to marry any of the guys I've dated. All my friends are married; I can't understand why I'm not. Is there something wrong with me?"

    Evaluative response

    Interpretative response

    Supportive response

    Probing response

    Understanding response

"I'm really concerned about a friend of mine named Jane. She never seems to take life seriously enough. She's dropped out of school, she gets a job, and then she quits after a week. She is using drugs and plans to move to a commune. I'm really worried that someday she'll ruin her life. I don't know what I should do."

    Evaluative response

    Interpretative response

    Supportive response

    Probing response

    Understanding response

"I need your advice about my relationship with June. She wants us to get very serious. But I don't even know if I like her. We spend a lot of time together, I have fun when I'm around her, but she's all the time pushing me not to date other girls and to see her more often than I now do. I don't like to be pushed; but I don't want to hurt her by not dating her any more. What would you do?"

    Evaluative response

    Interpretative response

    Supportive response

    Probing response

    Understanding response

1.   Divide into pairs. Discuss each other's answers and make suggestions as to how they might be improved.

2.   Think of a problem you now are having either at your job or in school. It may be a major problem or it may be a minor one. Each person in the pair

tells the other his problem. The receiver then gives an evaluative response, an interpretative response, a supportive response, a probing response, and then an understanding response.

3. Think of a problem you are having with your family. It may be either a minor or a major problem. Each person in the pair tells the other his problem. The receiver gives each of the five responses.

4. Think of a problem, either a major or a minor one, you are having with a friend. Each person in the pair tells the other his problem. The receiver gives each of the five responses.

5. In your pair, give each other the feedback concerning how well each of you can respond in the five ways discussed in this chapter. You may wish to continue practicing the different responses until you have mastered them to your satisfaction. This can be done by consciously applying them to your everyday conversations or by pairing up with a member of your group and setting specific practice times for the two of you to increase your response skills.

COMPREHENSION TEST A

Test your understanding of responding to people's problems by answering true or false to the following statements. Answers are at the end of the chapter.

True ~~False~~ 1. If you try hard enough, you can solve other people's problems for them.

~~True~~ False 2. The effectiveness of your help depends partly on your intentions and attitudes as you listen and give your response.

~~True~~ False 3. The phrasing of your response influences the effectiveness of your help.

True ~~False~~ 4. Your intentions are of minor importance in helping people solve their problems.

~~True~~ False 5. A helpful response helps other people explore a problem, clarify feelings, gain insight, or make a difficult decision.

True ~~False~~ 6. Giving advice is helpful to the sender's problems.

True ~~False~~ 7. Telling the sender the underlying meaning of her feelings will bring a grateful response.

True ~~False~~ 8. It's helpful to try and cheer up someone who's depressed.

True ~~False~~ 9. Asking "why" questions will help the sender see the problem more clearly.

True   False   10. "You really hate your job" is a good example of a reflective statement.

HELPING PEOPLE SOLVE THEIR PROBLEMS

There are many times when a friend or acquaintance will wish to discuss a problem or concern with you. People do not often get very far in understanding their experiences and deciding how to solve their problems unless they talk things over with someone else. There is nothing more helpful than discussing a problem with a friend who is an effective listener. The first rule in helping other people solve their problems and understand distressing situations is to remember that all insights, understandings, decisions, and solutions occur within the other people, not within you. No matter how convinced you are that you know what the other people should do, your goal in helping must be to assist them in reaching their own decisions and forming their own insights.

The second rule in helping others solve their problems is to differentiate between an internal frame of reference (how the other person sees and feels about the situation) and an external frame of reference (how you see and feel about the other person's situation). You are able to give help to the extent that you understand and respond to the sender's frame of reference rather than imposing your frame of reference on the problem situation. It is not what makes you angry that is important, it is what makes the other person angry. It is not how you see things that matters, it is how the other person sees things. Your ability to be helpful to another person is related directly to your ability to view the situation from the other person's perspective.

Listening and responding in ways that help you understand the other person's perspective or frame of reference is always a tentative process. Many times the other person will not fully understand or be able to communicate effectively her perspective. While you are clarifying your own understanding of the other person's perspective, you will also be helping the other person to understand herself better.

LISTENING AND RESPONDING ALTERNATIVES

The exercise on listening and responding alternatives is based on the work of Carl Rogers, a noted psychologist. Several years ago he conducted a series of studies on how individuals communicate with each other in face-to-face situations. He found that the categories of evaluative, interpretative, supportive, probing, and understanding statements encompass 80 percent of all the messages sent between individuals. The other 20 percent of the statements are incidental and of no real importance. From his observations of individuals in all sorts of different settings—businessmen, housewives, people at parties and conventions, and so on—he found that the responses were used by individuals in the following frequency: (1) evaluative was most used, (2) interpretative was next, (3) supportive was the third most common response, (4) probing the fourth, and (5) understanding the least. Finally, he found that if a person uses one category of response as much as 40 percent of the time, then other people see him as *always* responding that way. This is a process of oversimplification similar to stereotyping.

The categories of response are in themselves neither good nor bad. It is the overuse or underuse of any of the categories that may not be functional or the failure to recognize when each type of response is appropriate that interferes with helping the sender and building a better friendship. If, in answering the response alternatives questionnaire, you use only one or two of the responses, it may be that you overuse some types of responses while you underuse others. You can easily remedy that by becoming more aware of your responses and working to become proficient in using all five types of responses when they seem appropriate.

When is each response appropriate? From your own experience and from listening to the discussion of your group, you may have some good ideas. In terms of what is appropriate in the early stage of forming a friendship, two of the possible responses to be most sensitive to are the understanding and the evaluative responses. Basically, the understanding response revolves around the notion that when an individual expresses a message and that message is paraphrased in fresh words with no change of its essential meaning, the sender will expand upon or further explore the ideas, feelings, and attitudes contained in the message and achieve a recognition of previously denied meanings or feelings or move on to express a new message that is more meaningful to him. Even when the receiver has misunderstood and communicated a faulty understanding of the sender's ideas and feelings, the sender will respond in ways that will clarify the receiver's incorrect response, thus increasing the accuracy and clarity of communication between the two individuals.

It is the understanding response that is most likely to communicate to the sender that the listener is interested in the sender as a person and has an accurate understanding of the sender and of what he is saying, and it is this same response that most encourages the sender to go on and elaborate and further explore his problem. The understanding response may also be the most helpful for enabling the receiver to see the sender's problem from the sender's point of view. Many relationships or conversations are best begun by using the understanding response until a trust level is established; then the other categories of response can be more freely used. The procedures for engaging in the understanding response are rather simple (see chapter 4), and anyone who takes the time and effort can become quite skillful in their use.

As has been discussed in chapter 4, the major barrier to mutual understanding is the very natural tendency to judge, evaluate, approve, or disapprove of the messages of the sender. For this reason you should usually avoid giving evaluative responses in the early stages of a relationship or of a conversation about the sender's problems. The primary reaction to a value judgment is another value judgment (for example, "You say I'm wrong, but I think I'm right and you're wrong"), with each person looking at the issue only from his own point of view. This tendency to make evaluations is very much heightened in situations where feelings and emotions are deeply involved, as when you are discussing a personal problem. Defensiveness and feelings of being threatened are avoided when the listener responds with understanding rather than with evaluative responses. Evaluative responses, however, may be helpful when you are specifically asked to make a value judgment or when you wish to disclose your own values and attitudes.

There will be times when another person tries to discuss an issue with you that you do not understand. *Probing responses* will help you get a clear definition of the problem before you respond. They may also be helpful if you do not think the sender is seeing the full implications of some of her statements. *Supportive responses* are useful when the person needs to feel accepted or when she needs enough support to try to engage in behavior aimed at solving her problem. Finally, *interpretative responses* are sometimes useful in confronting another person with the effect of her behavior on you; this situation will be further discussed in chapter 9. Interpretation, if carried out with skill, integrity, and empathy, can be a powerful stimulus to growth. Interpretation leads to insight, and insight is a key to better psychological living. Interpretation is one form of confrontation.

COMPREHENSION TEST B

Test your understanding of effective listening and responding by answering true or false to the following statements. Answers are at the end of the chapter.

True   False   1. Give advice freely, remembering that the insights and understandings happen within the receiver, not the sender.

True   False   2. There is a difference between how you see the situation and how the sender sees it.

True   False   3. Clarifying your understanding of the other person's perspective will help the other person to understand herself better.

True   False   4. Ninety percent of all messages between two people are evaluative, interpretative, supportive, probing, and understanding.

True   False   5. The frequency of the responses from most used to least used is in this order: evaluative, interpretative, supportive, probing, and understanding.

True   False   6. If a person uses one category of response as much as 40 percent of the time, he is seen as always responding that way.

True   False   7. Giving evaluative responses early is a barrier to mutual understanding.

True   False   8. The understanding response best helps the receiver see the sender's point of view and encourages further communication.

True   False   9. Probing responses help the receiver understand what the problem is.

True   False   10. Interpretation is a form of confrontation.

PHRASING AN ACCURATE UNDERSTANDING RESPONSE

The second important aspect of listening with understanding is the phrasing you use to paraphrase the message of the sender. The phrasing of the response may vary in the following ways:

1. *Content.* Content refers to the actual words used. Interestingly enough, responses that are essentially repetitions of the sender's statements do not communicate the receiver's understanding to the sender. It seems that repeating a person's words actually gets in the way of communicating an understanding of the essential meaning of the statement. It is more effective if the receiver paraphrases the sender's message in the receiver's own words and expressions.

2. *Depth.* Depth refers to the degree to which the receiver matches the depth of the sender's message in his response. You should not respond lightly to a serious statement, and correspondingly, you should not respond seriously to a shallow statement. In general, responses that match the sender's depth of feeling or that lead the sender on to a slightly greater depth of feeling are most effective.

3. *Meaning.* In the receiver's efforts to paraphrase the sender's statements, he may find himself either adding meaning or omitting meaning. Some of the obvious ways in which meaning can be added are (1) completing a sentence or thought for the sender, (2) responding to ideas the sender has used for illustrative purposes only, and (3) interpreting the significance of a message. Perhaps the most obvious way meaning can be omitted is by responding only to the last thing the sender said.

4. *Language.* The receiver should keep the language he uses in his response simple in order to ensure accurate communication.

EXERCISE 7.3: PHRASING AN ACCURATE UNDERSTANDING RESPONSE

This exercise provides you with an opportunity to classify responses according to their wording. The procedure for the exercise is:

1. Each person should answer the questionnaire on the wording of an understanding response. The specific instructions are given on Answer Sheet A.
2. Study the categories of the understanding response given on page 166. Then categorize the responses for each item in the questionnaire as to the type of understanding response it represents. The specific instructions are given on Answer Sheet B.
3. Using the Scoring Key on page 295, score Answer Sheet B. Indicate in the appropriate space on the Answer Sheet the number of times you used each type of wording.
4. Form groups of three and score Answer Sheet B, discussing each type of wording until everyone in the triad understands it.
5. Combine two triads into a group of six. On Table 7.2 (p. 167), mark the frequency with which each member of the group used each type of wording.
6. Use the questions on page 167 to discuss the results summarized in Table 7.2

Answer Sheet A: Identifying Personal Responses

Read the nine statements in the questionnaire below and mark on this Answer Sheet the response that best represents what you would personally say to the speaker if you were trying to form a close personal relationship with him and help him solve his problems.

1.	a	:	b	:	c	:	d	6.	a	:	b	:	c	:	d
2.	a	:	b	:	c	:	d	7.	a	:	b	:	c	:	d
3.	a	:	b	:	c	:	d	8.	a	:	b	:	c	:	d
4.	a	:	b	:	c	:	d	9.	a	:	b	:	c	:	d
5.	a	:	b	:	c	:	d							

Response	Frequency
A	____
S	____
P	____
I	____

Answer Sheet B: Identifying the Phrasing of Understanding Responses

Study page 166, on which the four different phrasings of understanding responses are discussed. Then read each of the nine statements below and identify the category of each understanding response by: *I* = identical content, *P* = paraphrasing content, *S* = shallow or partial meaning, and *A* = additional meaning.

Item	1	2	3	4
1.				
2.				
3.				
4.				
5.				
6.				
7.				
8.				
9.				

Questionnaire on Accurate Understanding

In this exercise there are nine consecutive statements made by a young man who has sought help from a friend because of some things that have gone wrong in his life. Each statement is followed by four possible responses. In considering each alternative response, read it as a tentative, questioning statement that asks, "Do I understand you correctly; is this what you mean?" See Answer Sheets A and B for specific instructions on what to do with these statements.

1. "Boy, am I ever discouraged! Everything is going wrong in my life. It seems that everything I do is doomed to failure. I might as well not even try."
   a. You feel discouraged and ready to give up because of failure.
   b. Your whole life is a mess and you feel suicidal.
   c. You are feeling discouraged because things aren't working out for you, is that right?

    d. You are feeling a little unhappy right now.

2. "For instance, yesterday at work I messed up my job, and the boss made me stay until I got it right. She was really mad at me. I felt awful."

    a. Your boss was in a bad mood.

    b. You messed up at work, and the boss made you stay late, and you felt awful.

    c. You were depressed because your boss was angry at you and saw you as not doing your job correctly.

    d. You're going to get fired because you can't do your job correctly.

3. "Because I had to stay late at work, I was late for my most important class. We had an exam and I know I flunked it. I didn't even have time to finish the test. And I have to pass this class to graduate!"

    a. You are flunking out of school because you messed up at work.

    b. You think you did badly on a test.

    c. Staying late at work made you late for an important exam, which you didn't finish.

    d. You are worried about whether you will graduate after having done badly on an important exam in a required class.

4. "Then I went over to my girl friend's house, and she was out on a date with someone else. That really tore me up! I started crying. I couldn't help it."

    a. You became even more depressed because when you needed someone to give you support and sympathy, your girl friend was gone on a date with another man.

    b. You have really given up, haven't you?

    c. You are feeling discouraged.

    d. Your girl friend was out on a date with someone else, and you cried about it.

5. "At this point I don't know whether to jump off a bridge or throw myself under a train. (Pause) What do you think?"

    a. You want me to tell you whether to jump off a bridge or get run over by a train, right?

    b. There doesn't seem to be any way out.

    c. You have decided to take revenge on the world by killing yourself, is that it?

    d. You want my advice.

6. "You know, I thought Carol really liked me. I can't believe she would be so dirty as to go out behind my back. Well, women are rotten, but I thought Carol was an exception."

    a. You don't have much confidence in women, but you thought Carol was different, and now you feel let down.

    b. You thought Carol was different from other women.

    c. Now you have proven that all women are rotten.

    d. You thought Carol really liked you until she went out behind your back.

7. "I really liked my job, too. The people are great to be around and the boss is usually easygoing. (Pause) I guess I'm the rotten apple in the barrel. It can't be fun to work with someone as incompetent as I am. I guess if I don't quit, I will get fired.

    a. You don't think you will ever be able to do any job well.

    b. You feel discouraged because you don't think you are doing very well at your job, even though you like it; and you are afraid your coworkers don't like you even though you like them.

    c. You like your job and the people you work with, but you feel you are incompetent and will get fired.

    d. You're going to quit your job.

8. "My parents are really going to be happy when they find out I flunked out of school. They always told me I was aiming too high and couldn't do it. They have never had any confidence in me. (Pause) I guess that is why I don't have much confidence in myself."

    a. Your parents' and your own expectations are going to be met by your doing badly in school.

    b. Your parents will be happy about your flunking out of school because they don't have any confidence in you, which is why you don't have confidence in yourself.

    c. You think you are going to flunk out of school.

    d. Your parents really hate you, don't they?

9. "If I could just get over this slump, maybe I could make it. Things have been bad for me before, and somehow I managed to muddle through. If I can just hang on, maybe things will turn out all right."

    a. You are going through a slump, and you have been through slumps before, and maybe things will turn out all right.

    b. You want to get out of this slump.

    c. You are confident about the future.

    d. You feel some hope that if you just stay with it, things will work out for you, as they have in the past.

Types of Phrasing of an Understanding Response

After you have completed Answer Sheet A, study and discuss the following categories of the understanding response. Do not proceed until you are sure you understand each of the categories.

In the beginning of this section we discussed four aspects of an understanding response: content, depth, meaning, and language. The above questionnaire focuses upon two of these dimensions—content (either identical or paraphrased) and meaning (either partial or additional). In this questionnaire, all of the alternatives following the statements are so phrased as to appear to be attempts to communicate an understanding intent. For each statement, however, the alternatives differ in the following ways:

Identical content (I): a response in which the attempt at understanding is implemented in large part by simply repeating the same words used by the sender

Paraphrasing content (P): a response in which the attempt at understanding is implemented by rephrasing in fresh words the gist of the sender's expression without changing either the meaning or the feeling tone

Shallow or partial meaning (S): a response in which the attempt at understanding is implemented in a limited way by bringing in only a part of what the sender expressed or by undercutting or watering down the feeling tone expressed

Additional meaning (A): a response in which the attempt at understanding actually goes beyond the meaning of the sender and adds meaning not expressed by the sender.

TABLE 7.2: FREQUENCY WITH WHICH THE GROUP MEMBERS USED EACH TYPE OF RESPONSE

Frequency of response	Type of responses			
	I	P	S	A
0–1	_____	_____	_____	_____
2–3	_____	_____	_____	_____
4–5	_____	_____	_____	_____
6–7	_____	_____	_____	_____
8–9	_____	_____	_____	_____

After you have finished the procedure for scoring both answer sheets, mark the frequency with which each member of the group used each type of phrasing. In the group, discuss the results summarized in Table 7.2 and the consequences of using each type of phrasing. The following questions may be helpful:

1. What type of phrasing was most commonly used by the members of the group?
2. What would be your feelings if a person used each type of phrasing in discussing your problems and concerns?
3. How may I develop my skills in paraphrasing to ensure the most effective phrasing of my response?

EXERCISE 7.4: PRACTICING THE PHRASING OF AN UNDERSTANDING RESPONSE

The next exercise provides you with practice in the phrasing of an understanding response. The exercise has two parts, one in which you are given a problem statement and you write down what you would say, and one in which you and another person make statements and practice with each other giving an appropriately phrased understanding response. The exercise is:

1. Read the following paragraphs and write an understanding response for each one. Do this by yourself. Be sure your response matches the paragraph in content, depth, language and meaning.
    a. "I'm really upset! That stupid professor gave me a C on my research paper! I worked on it for six weeks, and it was twice as long as the paper Joe turned in, yet he got an A. That paper represented a lot of learning on my part. And he had the nerve to give me a C! What does he want anyway? Or is it that I'm just dumb?"
    b. "I need your help. There's a new girl who just moved in next door to you that I think I know. She may be a girl I dated several years ago; but I'm not sure since I haven't been able to get a close look at her. If she is the same girl I want to meet her; if she isn't the same girl, I don't want to meet her. Can you find out her name, telephone number, and where she grew up?"

2. Divide into pairs. Discuss each other's responses and make suggestions as to how they might be improved.
3. Think of a problem you are having with a friend or a member of your family. It may be a major problem or a minor problem. Each person in the pair should share his problem; the receiver gives an understanding response which is appropriate in content, depth, language, and meaning.
4. In the pairs, give each other feedback concerning the appropriateness of the content, depth, language, and meaning of the understanding responses. You may wish to continue practicing the phrasing of the understanding response until you have mastered it to your satisfaction. This can be done by consciously applying it in your everyday conversations or by pairing up with a member of your group and setting specific practice times for the two of you to increase your skills.

CHAPTER REVIEW

Test your understanding of helpful listening and responding by answering true or false to the following statements. Answers are at the end of the chapter.

True   False   1. The aim of a receiver is to help the other person come to her own understanding and solution to her problem.

True   False   2. If your underlying attitude is not one of acceptance and liking, you won't be able to make a helpful response.

True   False   3. The most helpful response to help people explore their feelings and thoughts is the probing response.

True   False   4. "How do you feel about your job?" is an example of a closed question.

True   False   5. "Do you like your teacher?" should be changed to, "You like your teacher." to become a reflective statement.

True   False   6. There is no difference between how you see and feel about a situation and how another person sees and feels about it.

True   False   7. Just repeating what the sender says is effective paraphrasing.

True   False   8. When you interpret the significance of a message, you are adding to the meaning of it.

True   False   9. You will communicate more accurately if you use simple language in your responses.

True   False   10. Responses that are slightly lighter in meaning than the sender's message are most effective.

Indicate below which skills you have mastered and which ones you need to work on further.

1. I have mastered the following:
    ____ Using the evaluative response
    ____ Using the interpretative response
    ____ Using the supportive response
    ____ Using the probing response
    ____ Using the understanding response
    ____ Matching the message in paraphrasing content
    ____ Matching the message in depth
    ____ Matching the message in meaning
    ____ Matching the message in language

2. I need more work on:
    ____ Using the evaluative response
    ____ Using the interpretative response
    ____ Using the supportive response
    ____ Using the probing response
    ____ Using the understanding response
    ____ Matching the message in paraphrasing content
    ____ Matching the message in depth
    ____ Matching the message in meaning
    ____ Matching the message in language

At this point, you should understand and be able to use appropriately evaluative, interpretative, supportive, probing, and understanding responses. You should understand how to make reflective statements and ask open questions. You should also be able to match a message in content, depth, meaning, and language. The next chapter will expand on an important factor in being able to respond helpfully to others: the acceptance of others—and of yourself.

ANSWERS

Comprehension Test A: 1. false; 2. true; 3. true; 4. false; 5. true; 6. false; 7. false; 8. false; 9. false; 10. true.

Comprehension Test B: 1. false; 2. true; 3. true; 4. false; 5. true; 6. true; 7. true; 8. true; 9. true; 10. true.

Chapter Review: 1. true; 2. true; 3. false; 4. false; 5. true; 6. false; 7. false; 8. true; 9. true; 10. false.

8

Acceptance of Self
and Others

If I am not for myself, who will be for me? But if I am only for myself, what am I?

The Talmud

ACCEPTING YOURSELF AND ACCEPTING OTHERS

In order to build and maintain relationships with other people, you must be accepting of yourself and others. The greater your self-acceptance, and the greater your acceptance of other people, the easier it is for you to maintain and deepen your relationships. This chapter focuses on the strategies and skills of accepting yourself and communicating acceptance to other people.

SELF-ACCEPTANCE

Self-acceptance is a high regard for yourself or, conversely, a lack of cynicism about yourself. It is a judgment about your self-worth, based on a process of conceptualizing and gathering information about yourself and your experiences. Self-acceptance is related to (1) your willingness to disclose your thoughts, feelings, and reactions to others; (2) your psychological health; and (3) your acceptance of other people.

There are three important ways in which self-acceptance and self-disclosure are related:

1. The greater your self-acceptance, the greater your self-disclosure.
2. The greater your self-disclosure, the greater others' acceptance of you.
3. The greater others' acceptance of you, the greater your self-acceptance.
4. And, of course, the greater your self-acceptance, the greater your self-disclosure.

In order for you to disclose your thoughts, feelings, and reactions to other people, you must first see yourself and your potential disclosures as acceptable. If you do not feel you are acceptable, you will not let other people get to know you. The more you accept and appreciate yourself, the easier it is to let other people get to know you as you really are. The more you accept and appreciate yourself, the easier it is to share your thoughts, feelings, needs, and reactions with other people. Self-confidence about your worth reduces the risks involved in self-disclosing. Self-acceptance is the key to reducing anxiety and fears about vulnerability resulting from self-disclosure. If you are afraid to let others know you, or anxious about the reactions others may have to your self-disclosures, you will not be open and disclosing, and therefore you will not be able to develop good relationships with other people.

If you are self-rejecting, you will find self-disclosure very risky. The deepest conviction of a self-rejecting person is that once he is known he will be rejected and unloved. Before a self-rejecting person can have this conviction disconfirmed and experience acceptance from other people, she must take the risk of disclosing. It is important for your self-acceptance that you be honest, genuine, and authentic in your self-disclosing. If you hide information about yourself or selectively try to create an impression, the acceptance other people give you may actually decrease your self-acceptance; you will know that it is your "mask" other people like and accept, not your "real" self. Being accepted for a "lie" leads only to self-rejection. It is only as you discover that you are loved for what you are, not for what you pretend to be or for the masks you hide behind, that you can begin to feel you are actually a person worthy of respect and love.

People are not usually accepting of individuals they do not know. Most often they are neutral or indifferent. If you do not self-disclose, you cannot be accepted by others, and your self-acceptance will not increase. One of the major sources of information about ourselves is the information we obtain from the way other people interact and react to us. To experience liking and acceptance from others, and thereby increase our self-acceptance, we must let other people honestly know us.

Your self-acceptance is built by knowing that others are accepting you. If they think you are worthwhile, then you think you are worthwhile. The acceptance of you by others plays a critical role in increasing your self-acceptance. This is especially true for those you care about and respect. One of the ways in which you become more self-accepting is to believe that other people whom you like and respect accept and value you. In this chapter we will also be focusing on how to express acceptance toward others in order for you to learn how to help them increase their self-acceptance.

No one can make you feel inferior without your consent.

Eleanor Roosevelt

Self-Acceptance and Psychological Health

Generally, a high level of self-acceptance is reflected in a high quality of personal adjustment (see Hamachek 1971). People's psychological health is closely related to the quality of their feelings about themselves. Just as people must maintain a healthy view of the world around them, so they must learn to perceive themselves in positive ways. Psychologically healthy individuals see themselves as being liked, capable, worthy, and acceptable to other people. Highly self-critical individuals are more anxious, insecure, and cynical about themselves. Carl Rogers (1951) considers self-acceptance crucial for psychological health and growth. It is not the individuals who believe that they are liked, wanted, acceptable to others, capable, and worthy who are found in prisons and mental hospitals; it is those who feel deeply inadequate, unliked, unwanted, unacceptable, and unable. Self rejecting people are usually unhappy and unable to form and maintain good relationships. In order for you to grow and develop psychologically, you must be self-accepting. And to help other people grow and develop psychologically, you must help them become more self-accepting.

I can't be right for someone else if I'm not right for me!

Self-Acceptance and Acceptance of Others

There is considerable evidence that self-acceptance and the acceptance of other people are related (see Hamachek 1971). Individuals who are self-accepting are usually more accepting of others. If you think well of yourself, you are likely to think well of other people, but if you disapprove of yourself, you are likely to disapprove of others. For example, things you try to hide from yourself about yourself are often the same things that you are very critical of in others. A person who suppresses hostility may be highly critical of people who express hostility. A person who suppresses sexual feelings may be highly critical of individuals who are more open with their sexual feelings. If you recognize and accept your feelings, you are usually more accepting of such emotional expressions in others. A frequent side effect of becoming more self-accepting is becoming more accepting of others.

Self-Acceptance and Self-Fulfilling Prophecies

Self-fulfilling prophecies occur when your expectations about how other people are going to view you are actually confirmed as a result of your actions. For example, a self-rejecting person expects to be rejected by others and will tend to reject others; as a result of his rejection of others, the other people will reciprocate by rejecting him, and the person's original expectations are then confirmed. A self-accepting person, on the other hand, will expect to be accepted by others and will tend to accept other people; they, in turn, will tend to reciprocate by being accepting, and the person's original expectations are then confirmed. Such self-fulfilling prophecies may help or hurt you in building good relationships with other people.

Deciding Whether You Are Acceptable or Unacceptable

More important than your current assessment of your worth is the process by which you make conclusions about your acceptability. Conclusions about your worth can be derived in at least five ways (Johnson 1979). The first is called *reflected self-acceptance* and involves making conclusions about yourself on the basis of how you think other people see you. If other people like you, you tend to like yourself. The second is *basic self-acceptance* and involves a belief that you are intrinsically and unconditionally acceptable. A third way to derive conclusions about your self-worth is *conditional self-acceptance*, which is based on how well you meet external standards and expectations. It is characterized by "if-then" logic. "If I meet the external standards and expectations placed on me by other people, then I am of value. If I don't then I am worthless." A fourth is *self-evaluation* and involves your estimate of how positively your attributes compare with those of your peers. And finally, in *real-ideal comparison* you may judge how your real self compares with your ideal self, that is, the correspondence between what you think you are and what you think you should be. Most people use one or more of these procedures for making judgments about their self-worth. It is important that you learn not only to accept yourself but also learn a constructive method of judging your self-worth from the information that is available to you about yourself. Usually, an unconditional, basic self-acceptance is viewed as the most constructive way to determine your self-acceptance.

COMPREHENSION TEST A

Test your understanding of self-acceptance by answering true or false to the following statements. Answers are at the end of the chapter.

True   False   1. Self-acceptance is a high regard for yourself and a lack of cynicism about yourself.

True   False   2. Self-acceptance leads to self-disclosure, which leads to acceptance by others, which leads back to self-acceptance.

True   False   3. If you are self-rejecting, you can still easily be self-disclosing.

True   False   4. It is not necessary to be honest and genuine when self-disclosing.

True   False   5. You can be just as confirmed by other people's acceptance of what they think you are as by their acceptance of what you really are.

True   False   6. If you expect to be accepted, you probably will be rejected.

True   False   7. While reflected self-acceptance is accepting yourself because others accept you, basic self-acceptance is believing that you are unconditionally acceptable.

True   False   8. While conditional self-acceptance is comparing how you match up to your friends, self-evaluation is living up to the standards of other people.

True   False   9. Real-ideal comparison is comparing how you are to how you think you should be.

True   False   10. The most constructive way to determine your self-acceptance is by basic self-acceptance.

EXERCISE 8.1: HOW SELF-ACCEPTING ARE YOU?

How do you tell if you are self-accepting? One way is to list all the assets you have. If you can list two-hundred to three-hundred assets, then you are very self-accepting. Another way is to see if you can plan how to use your assets when you get into a stressful or problem situation. Finally, you can measure yourself against the following checklist, which summarizes much of the research conducted on self-accepting people (Hamachek 1971). Write "yes" if the item fits you, write "no" if it does not.

— I strongly believe in certain values and principles. I am willing to defend them, even in the face of strong group opposition. I feel personally secure enough to change them if new experiences and new evidence suggest I am in error.

— I am capable of acting on my own best judgment. I do this without feeling overly guilty or regretting my actions, even if other people disapprove of what I have done.

— I do not spend a lot of time worrying about what is coming tomorrow, what has happened to me in the past, or what is taking place in the present.

— I am confident in my ability to deal with problems, even in the face of failure and setbacks.

— I feel equal to other people as a person. I do not feel superior or inferior. I feel equal even when there are differences in specific abilities, family backgrounds, job prestige, or amount of money earned.

— I take for granted that I am a person of interest and value to others, at least to the people I associate with.

— I can accept praise without the pretense of false modesty; I can accept compliments without feeling guilty.

— I am inclined to resist the efforts of others to dominate me.

— I am able to accept the idea and admit to others that I am capable of feeling a wide range of impulses and desires. These range from being angry to being loving, from being sad to being happy, from feeling deep resentment to feeling deep acceptance.

— I am able to genuinely enjoy myself in a wide variety of activities. These include work, play, loafing, companionship, and creative self-expression.

— I am sensitive to the needs of others, to accepted social customs, and particularly to the idea that I cannot enjoy myself at the expense of others.

EXERCISE 8.2: STRENGTH-BUILDING

Accepting and appreciating yourself is related to being aware of your strengths and assets. We all have many strengths. We all have strengths we are not using fully. We all can develop new strengths. A *strength* is any skill, ability, talent, or personal quality that helps you be effective and productive. You increase your self-acceptance as you become more aware of your strengths and develop new ones. The more you see yourself as having real skills, abilities, talents, and other personal strengths, the more you will value and accept yourself.

In this exercise you will concentrate on identifying your strengths and determining how they can be used most productively to build personal relationships. The objectives of this exercise are to increase your self-acceptance through the increased awareness of your strengths and to increase your awareness of how your strengths can be used to develop fulfilling relationships with other individuals. In this exercise you will be asked to discuss your strengths

openly with the other group members. This is no place for modesty; an inferiority complex or unwillingness to be open about your positive attributes is not a strength. You are not being asked to brag, only to be realistic and open about the strengths that you possess. The procedure for the exercise is:

1. Think of all the things that you do well, all the things which you are proud of having done, all the things for which you feel a sense of accomplishment. List all your positive accomplishments, your successes, of the past. Be specific.

2. Divide into pairs and share your past accomplishments with each other. Then, with the help of your partner, examine your past successes to identify the strengths you utilized to achieve them.

3. In the group as a whole, each person should share the full list of his strengths. Then ask the group, "What additional strengths do you see in my life?" The group then adds to your list other qualities, skills, characteristics that you have overlooked or undervalued. The feedback should be specific; that is, if one member tells another he has a strength, he must back his feedback up with some evidence of behavior that demonstrates the strength.

4. After every group member has shared her strengths and received feedback on what further strengths others see in her life, each member should then ask the group, "What might be keeping me from utilizing all my strengths?" The group then explores the ways you can free yourself from factors that limit utilizing your strengths.

5. Think about your past successes and your strengths. Think about how your strengths may be utilized to improve the number or quality of your close relationships. Then set a goal for the next week concerning how you may improve either the number or the quality of your close relationships. Plan how utilizing your strengths will help you accomplish this goal.

EXERCISE 8.3: GAINING ACCEPTANCE NONVERBALLY

Sometimes other people do not just give you acceptance; you have to earn it. We often spend a great deal of time and energy trying to gain the acceptance of individuals we like and admire. This exercise gives you an opportunity to experience gaining acceptance from the group nonverbally. The procedure for the exercise is:

1. One member volunteers to be an outsider. The other members of the group form a tight circle by locking arms and pressing close to each other's sides.
2. The outsider has to break into the group by forcing his way to the center of the circle. This is quite an active exercise. You should, therefore, be careful not to hurt anyone by becoming too rough. Anyone with a physical handicap or injury should not take part in this exercise.
3. After everyone who wishes to has been an outsider, discuss the experience. The discussion may center upon:
   a. How did you react to being an outsider? What did you learn about yourself from the experience?
   b. How did you react to trying to keep the outsiders from gaining entry into the group? What did you learn about yourself from the experience?

EXERCISE 8.4: EXPRESSING ACCEPTANCE NONVERBALLY

The purpose of this exercise is for you to have an opportunity to experience fully the acceptance felt toward you by others. At the same time, the members of the group are given an opportunity to express acceptance nonverbally. The procedure for the exercise is:

1. One member volunteers to stand in the center of a circle made up by the other members of the group. She is to shut her eyes and be silent.
2. The other members of the group are all to approach her and express their positive feelings nonverbally in whatever way they wish. This may take the form of hugging, stroking, massaging, lifting, or whatever each person feels.
3. After everyone who wishes to has been in the center of the circle, the group may wish to discuss the experience. The discussion may center on the following two areas:
   a. How did it feel to receive so much acceptance and affection? What were the reactions of each person in the center. Was it a tense situation for you or was it an enjoyable one? Why do you react as you do? What did you learn about yourself?
   b. How did it feel to give so much acceptance and affection to other members of the group? What are your reactions to such giving? Why do you react this way? What did you learn about yourself from this experience?

ACCEPTANCE OF OTHER INDIVIDUALS

Communicating acceptance of the other person is vital to developing and maintaining close personal relationships. The mutual communication of acceptance leads to feelings of *psychological safety*, that is, to a belief that no matter what you do or what you disclose about yourself, the other person in the relationship will react in an accepting and nonevaluative way. In order to build close, satisfying relationships other people must feel you accept them unconditionally and nonevaluatively.

There are two major skills involved in communicating acceptance to another individual. The first is *paraphrasing* or listening with understanding to the other person. When you listen with understanding, you come to understand the other person's thoughts, feelings, and reactions from his point of view. You also communicate that you sincerely wish to understand him in a nonevaluative way. You cannot accept what you do not know or understand. Through paraphrasing what the other person is saying, you communicate interest, caring, and acceptance. The second skill in communicating acceptance to another person is the *expressing of warmth and liking*. The expression of warmth and liking is vital to building a climate of psychological safety in the relationship and a feeling on the part of the other person that you accept him as a person. There is almost universal recognition that a degree of warmth in interpersonal relationships is absolutely essential for psychological growth. Without the communication of positive regard, you cannot communicate acceptance to another person.

There are two types of acceptance you may communicate to the other person: antecedent acceptance and consequent acceptance. Encouraging the other person to take risks in self-disclosure or to build a closer relationship is *antecedent acceptance*. Expressing acceptance to the other person following her risk taking in self-disclosure or attempts to build a closer relationship is *consequent acceptance*. The primary means of expressing antecedent acceptance is to communicate unconditional warmth and liking. *Unconditional warmth* is communicating to the other person that you have a deep and genuine regard for him as a person, which allows him complete freedom in expressing the ways in which he is different from other individuals. In other words, unconditional warmth allows the other person to be who and what he or she is.

This unconditional warmth does not mean that you will approve of everything the other person does. Approval is quite different from accepting someone as a person you care for. A sign of true friendship is often a willingness to tell the other person when you disapprove of his behavior while still communicating that you accept him as a person. There is a marked difference between disapproval and rejection. We usually do not want our friends to approve of all our behavior no matter what we do, as we all behave in ways that we disapprove of later. Another way of ensuring antecedent acceptance is by building a high level of trust in the relationship. Ensuring that the other person trusts you to respond with acceptance and support to her risk taking in self-disclosure, despite the fact that you may not approve of all her behavior, is another primary means of expressing antecedent acceptance.

If the communication of antecedent acceptance is crucial for encouraging an individual to take the risks necessary to build a closer, more fulfilling relationship, then the communication of consequent acceptance keeps the relationship building and growing. Consequent acceptance reinforces the other person's behavior and increases the frequency with which the other person engages in behaviors that increase the quality of the relationship. Consequent acceptance is a reinforcement for positive behavior, such as self-disclosure and the expression of feelings, and as such, it will be discussed at greater length later in this chapter. For the present, it should be noted that the response of listening with understanding and the expression of warmth and liking are both ways of immediately reinforcing the other person's behavior.

In addition to the skills of listening with understanding and expressing warmth and liking, the tacit ways in which your behavior indicates acceptance of the other person are important in expressing antecedent and consequent acceptance. Being available when the other person needs help, going out of your way to give the other person support or help, asking the other person to help when you need it, spending time with the other person are all ways in which your behavior *tacitly communicates acceptance*. Such tacit communication is an important aspect of building close, satisfying relationships.

FAILURES IN ACCEPTANCE

There are three ways you may fail to indicate any real acceptance for another person. The first is to give cliché or ritualistic acceptance. Our language is filled with socially appropriate clichés expressive of acceptance, for example: "I know how you feel." "Is there anything I can do?" "You must feel awful." "You're so strong and wonderful." The difference between a statement that expresses genuine acceptance and a cliché is the *amount of feeling and sincerity* expressed in the statement and whether the statement opens up a discussion of the other person's feelings or closes off such a discussion.

The second way you may fail is to imply that you would do the same thing for anyone—that it doesn't depend on the quality of your relationship. Cheap acceptance, which you hand out to anyone and everyone, does not communicate any real acceptance of the other person. Giving cheap acceptance is similar to being a Red Cross worker who rushes to give aid to everyone she sees. Meaningful acceptance is based upon your relationship with the other person and should reflect either the present quality of the relationship or the desire to build a closer relationship.

Finally, the greatest failure to communicate acceptance is caused by silence. When you interact with another person, silence is often taken as a sign of indifference and unwillingness to commit yourself to the relationship. Certainly, silence does not communicate either antecedent or consequent acceptance to the other person, and it may communicate consequent rejection.

COMPREHENSION TEST B

Test your understanding of acceptance of others by marking the following statements true or false. Answers are at the end of the chapter.

True   False   1. To build close relationships with other people, they must feel that you accept them unconditionally and nonevaluatively.

True   False   2. The two skills that communicate acceptance are paraphrasing and expressing patience and tolerance.

True   False   3. Antecedent acceptance is communicating acceptance before a person self-discloses, while consequent acceptance is communicating acceptance after she self-discloses.

True   False   4. If you accept someone unconditionally, you must approve of everything he does; there is no difference between disapproval and rejection.

True   False   5. Antecedent acceptance encourages a person to self-disclose, while consequent acceptance rewards a person for self-disclosing.

True   False   6. Asking a person to help you when you need it is a way of communicating acceptance.

True   False   7. "I know how you feel" is a good example of a warm, accepting statement.

True   False   8. You will fail to indicate acceptance if you use clichés.

True   False   9. You should show acceptance to everyone.

True   False   10. If you are silent in an interaction, you will probably communicate rejection.

EXERCISE 8.5: EXPRESSING ACCEPTANCE VERBALLY

The purpose of this exercise is to give you an opportunity to practice communicating acceptance to another person. The skills involved in expressing acceptance are listening with understanding and expressing warmth. In this exercise you will conduct a discussion in which you practice listening with understanding and the expression of warmth. The procedure is:

1. Divide into trios. Two people will engage in a discussion; one person will observe. The role of the discussants is to express acceptance to each other. The role of the observer is to give the two discussants feedback concerning how successfully they communicated acceptance to each other. An observation sheet is provided below for the observer's use.

2. The two discussants spend ten minutes discussing how their current close friendships were initiated and developed. Or they may discuss any topic that is of real interest to the two of them; do not spend more than one minute, however, on the selection of a topic to discuss. During the discussion the two participants should be practicing both listening and understanding and expressing warmth. To listen with understanding is to paraphase the other person's expressed feelings and ideas in your own words without any indication of approval or disapproval; this involves listening for meaning as well as listening to the other's words. To express warmth is to describe your feelings and to use the nonverbal cues of facial expression, tone of voice, posture, and so on in your dicussion with your partner.

OBSERVATION SHEET: EXPRESSING ACCEPTANCE VERBALLY

Listening with understanding	Person 1	Person 2
Paraphrased other's feelings and ideas in own words	_____	_____
Did not indicate approve or disapproval	_____	_____
Depth of response was appropriate	_____	_____
Did not add or subtract meaning	_____	_____
Did not change the feeling tone	_____	_____
Negotiated for meaning	_____	_____
Language was understandable and appropriate	_____	_____
Did a perception check for other's feelings	_____	_____
Expressing warmth	Person 1	Person 2
Direct description of own feelings	_____	_____
Tone of voice	_____	_____
Facial expression	_____	_____
Posture	_____	_____
Eye contact	_____	_____
Touching	_____	_____
Gestures	_____	_____
Spatial distance	_____	_____
Congruence between verbal and nonverbal expressions of feelings	_____	_____

3.   At the end of the ten-minute discussion, the observer and the two discussants give the two discussants feedback about how well they expressed acceptance to each other. Be specific.

4.   Next, the trio switches roles so that one of the former discussants is now the observer, and the other two members conduct a discussion. Follow the instructions given in step 2. This time discuss what your greatest fears and hopes are about initiating friendships.

5.   Conduct a feedback session according to the instructions given in step 3.

6.   Switch roles once more and conduct a discussion on why you need friends. Follow the instructions given in steps 2 and 3.

EXERCISE 8.6: LEVEL OF ACCEPTANCE IN YOUR GROUP

What is the level of acceptance in your group? You may wish to get everyone's opinion by completing the following questionnaire and summarizing the results. The purpose of this exercise is to provide a way in which the level of acceptance in your group may be assessed and discussed. The procedure is:

1.   Each member of the group fills out the questionnaire below. Questionnaires should be unsigned so that no one's responses can be identified.

2.   The results are tabulated in the Summary Table that follows the questionnaire.

3.   Discuss the conclusions that can be drawn from the results.

4.   What is contributing to the present high or low level of acceptance in the group?

5.   How may the level of acceptance in the group be increased?

Questionnaire: Level of Acceptance

Think about the ways in which the members of your group normally behave toward you. In the parentheses in front of the items below, place the number corresponding to your perceptions of the group as a whole, using the following scale:

> 5 = They *always* behave this way.
>
> 4 = They *typically* behave this way.
>
> 3 = They *usually* behave this way.
>
> 2 = They *seldom* behave this way.
>
> 1 = They *rarely* behave this way.
>
> 0 = They *never* behave this way.

My fellow group members:

1.   (___) ....are completely honest with me.

2.   ....(___) ....understand what I am trying to communicate.

3.*   ....(___) ....interrupt and ignore my comments.

4.   ....(___) accept me just the way I am.

5. (____) ....tell me when I bother them.

6.* ....(____) ....don't understand things I say or do.

7. ....(____) ....are interested in me.

8. ....(____) make it easy for me to be myself.

9.* (____) ....don't tell me things that would hurt my feelings.

10. ....(____) ....understand who I really am.

11. ....(____) ....include me in what they are doing.

12.* ....(____) evaluate whether I am acceptable or unacceptable.

13. (____) ....are completely open with me.

14. ....(____) ....immediately know when something is bothering me.

15. ....(____) ....value me as a person, apart from my skills or status.

16. ....(____) accept my differences or peculiarities.

(____) Authenticity with me

(____) Understanding of me

(____) Valuing of me

(____) Accepting of me

Add the total number of points in each column. Items with starred (*) numbers are reversed in the scoring—subtract from 5 the rating given to each before adding the totals for each column.

SUMMARY TABLE: LEVEL OF ACCEPTANCE

Score	Authenticity	Understanding	Valuing	Accepting
0–4	_____	_____	_____	_____
5–8	_____	_____	_____	_____
9–12	_____	_____	_____	_____
13–16	_____	_____	_____	_____
17–20	_____	_____	_____	_____

COMPREHENSION TEST C

How well do you remember the material discussed so far in this chapter? You may wish to match the elements of the two columns below to review the content presented on self-acceptance and acceptance of others. Answers are at the end of the chapter.

_____ 1. Self-acceptance

a. Any skill, talent, ability, or personal trait that helps you to function more productively

_____ 2. Self-fulling prophecy

_____ 3. Psychological safety

_____ 4. Antecedent acceptance

_____ 5. Unconditional warmth

_____ 6. Failure to accept other person

_____ 7. Consequent acceptance

_____ 8. Expressing acceptance to another person

_____ 9. Personal strength

_____ 10. Listening with understanding

b. Clichés, Red-Crossing, and silence

c. Encouraging self-disclosure from another person

d. A high regard for yourself

e. A deep and genuine regard for another person, which allows him to be who he is

f. Expressing acceptance to another person following her risking self-disclosure

g. An expectation that comes true because it influenced the situation

h. Attempting to view the ideas and feelings of another person from his point of view

i. Feeling that other people will react to you in accepting and non-evaluative ways

j. Listening with understanding and expressing warmth and liking

REINFORCING OTHERS' INTERPERSONAL SKILLS

Relationships are built because they are reinforcing to the two people involved. And the interpersonal skills necessary for building and maintaining fulfilling relationships do not appear magically when a person reaches a certain age. They are learned according to learning principles that include reinforcement theory. Many people with whom you may become involved are lonely because they have not learned the skills needed for the development of fulfilling relationships. Reinforcement theory is one of the tools you may use to help them increase their skills. When using reinforcement theory, the attitude you adopt toward the other individual is of great importance. Reinforcement principles can be used to manipulate and control other people, and they can be used to help others increase their interpersonal skills and thereby increase their feelings of happiness and their sense of fulfillment. In this chapter the use of reinforcement theory to help others accomplish their goals is emphasized. The use of reinforcement theory to manipulate and control others does not produce growth and should be guarded against.

Reinforcement theory is based on the simple rule that behavior is influenced by its consequences. If you say hello to a person you are just getting to know and receive a warm smile and a hello back, you are likely to repeat the behavior in the future. If you receive a blank look and silence, however, you will be less likely to repeat the behavior in the future. When we engage in a particular behavior, it is to create the consequences we want. If those desired consequences do not result, we tend not to repeat the behavior but rather to switch to a new behavior that may be more effective in the future. This means that through the control of consequences you may increase, decrease, or keep constant the frequency of another person's behavior. The procedure for the use of reinforcement theory in influencing the behavior of other individuals is: (1) specify an objective (pinpoint a behavior), (2) arrange a consequence, and (3) observe for a change in the frequency of the response.

The use of reinforcement theory begins when you pinpoint a behavior whose frequency you want to increase, stabilize, or decrease. It is important that the behavior is observable and countable. Thus you may decide that your objective is to increase the number of times John paraphrases George's remarks when they are discussing their personal relationship or to decrease the number of times Sally frowns at Jane. To change the frequency of the behavior you have pinpointed, you must control the consequences of the targeted behavior. There are two major types of consequences that you may use: (1) strengthening consequences, such as warmth, acceptance, or praise, and (2) weakening consequences, such as coolness and ignoring. To increase the frequency of someone else's behavior, it is important that you give a strengthening consequence immediately and consistently. There are two approaches to decreasing the frequency of another person's behavior. The first is to give a weakening consequence immediately and consistently. The second is to increase the frequency of an incompatible behavior. Increasing the frequency of an incompatible behavior is usually preferred in this situation. If, for example, a friend talks too much when he first meets another person, you can frown at him and tell him immediately and consistently to shut up, or you can reinforce him by making probing statements to draw him out and by listening attentively to what he has to say. If you want to maintain the frequency of another person's behavior, it is important that you give a strengthening consequence immediately and inconsistently.

How do you tell what is a strengthening consequence for another individual? The expression of acceptance and warmth and the appropriate use of praise are commonly accepted as strengthening consequences. There are times when paraphrasing and negotiating for meaning communicate interest and concern and are thereby strengthening consequences. Ignoring the behavior of the other person is commonly accepted as a weakening response. By observing the other person and asking her what it is that she values, it is possible to find out what consequences the other person thinks are strengthening and weakening. It is important to remember that there are large individual differences; what is strengthening for you may not be strengthening for another person.

The conscientious reader will profit a great deal by keeping records of the number of times the person she is building a relationship with engages in the pinpointed behavior. A critical factor in specifying behavioral objectives clearly is to be able to count the number of times the other person engages in the behavior in order to determine whether your behavior is having the intended effect on the other person's actions.

In helping other people learn more effective interpersonal skills, it is often helpful to model or demonstrate the skill and then reinforce the other person for engaging in it. Nothing teaches like a good example. Learning new behaviors by imitating others is a major means of acquiring new skills. By engaging in the needed skills you can encourage others to do likewise, and then you can reinforce them for doing so.

COMPREHENSION TEST D

Test your understanding of reinforcing others' interpersonal skills by answering true or false to the following statements. Answers are at the end of the chapter.

True   False   1. Reinforcement theory is based on the rule that behavior is influenced by previous action.

True   False   2. People repeat behaviors that result in desired consequences.

True   False   3. The procedure for reinforcement theory, in order, is (1) specify an objective, (2) observe for a change in response frequency, then (3) arrange a consequence.

True   False   4. To increase the frequency of a behavior, you must give a strengthening consequence, such as warmth, acceptance, or praise, and you must give it immediately and consistently.

True   False   5. To decrease the frequency of a behavior, you can give a weakening consequence (coolness, ignoring) immediately and consistently or you can decrease the frequency of an incompatible behavior.

True   False   6. What is a strengthening consequence for you will be a strengthening consequence for another person.

True   False   7. If you keep records of the number of times the person engages in the pinpointed behavior, you can tell whether you are changing that behavior.

True   False   8. One good way to bring change in another is to be a good example.

True   False   9. An example of a good behavior target is to increase the number of times Roger says to Frances, "I like you."

True   False   10. An example of a good behavior target is to increase the number of books David writes by buying more of them.

EXERCISE 8.7: REINFORCING ANOTHER PERSON'S STRENGTHS

The objective of this exercise is to give you practice in reinforcing another person for behaving in ways that demonstrate one of his basic strengths or attempt to overcome a barrier to expressing his strengths. The procedure is:

1. Think of a person you know (1) whose relationship skills you could help improve, (2) who lacks the self-confidence to use his relationship skills, or (3) to whom you would like to express more support. On a sheet of paper, describe this person's basic strengths.

2. What are the barriers that keep this person from expressing his strengths in interpersonal situations? List them on a sheet of paper. Examples of possible barriers are a lack of self-confidence, fear of rejection, fear that friends will think he is foolish, wanting to be overly nice, or lack of self-acceptance.

3. What possible strengthening consequences could you give this person? Examples of possible strengthening consequences are expressing warmth, acceptance, encouragement, understanding, self-disclosure about your positive reactions to his behavior, and many of the other behaviors that

have been discussed in this book. List the behaviors you could engage in that are possible strengthening consequences.

4. Reviewing what you have listed in steps 1, 2, and 3, write out a series of behavioral objectives for your interactions with the person for the next week. Such a list should include a statement that describes the countable behavior on the part of the other person, indicates the desired change in the countable behavior, and specifies countable behavior by you to provide a strengthening consequence. An example of such a behavioral objective is: Increase the number of times John initiates a conversation by expressing warmth toward him immediately after he does so in my presence.

5. Review your objectives. It is important that they are not attempts to manipulate the other person but rather expressions of support for behaviors you feel will help the person express his strengths or eliminate barriers to showing his strengths. Your objectives should reflect a sincere attempt to be supportive, not an attempt to remake the other person. On the basis of your review, rewrite any objectives that may seem more manipulative than supportive.

6. In the group as a whole, discuss the objectives your have listed. Review what you wrote on steps 1, 2, and 3 in order to provide background for the objectives written in step 4. Help each other increase the specificity and concreteness of your objectives. Suggest new ideas for strengthening consequences for each other; help each other write new objectives that may be more effective in helping the other person.

7. During the next week, keep the record sheet that follows. Bring the sheet back to the group meeting and discuss the results. Is there any relationship between the number of strengthening consequences you engaged in and the number of times the other person engaged in behaviors that demonstrated his strengths or attempts to overcome barriers to the expression of his strengths?

Record Sheet: Reinforcing Another Person's Strengths

	Number of Times Other Person Engaged in Behavior to Be Increased	Number of Times I Engaged in a Strengthening Consequence
Day One		
Day Two		
Day Three		
Day Four		
Day Five		
Day Six		
Day Seven		

EXERCISE 8.8: REINFORCING YOUR OWN STRENGTHS

In addition to reinforcing another person's strengths, you can set up situations in which your own behavior gets reinforced. Through such reinforcement systems you may maximize your strengths and facilitate the development of your interpersonal skills. The process is the same as reinforcing another person's behavior; when your behavior is followed by a strengthening consequence, you will tend to repeat the behavior. The more immediately the strengthening consequence follows your behavior, the more likely you will be to repeat the behavior in the future. If you consistently receive a strengthening consequence immediately after engaging in the behavior, you will increase the number of times you engage in the behavior at a rapid rate. To maintain the frequency of your behavior, it is better to receive strengthening consequences immediately, but inconsistently. When you have important goals you are trying to accomplish, it is often helpful to find ways of receiving reinforcers for engaging in the behavior that will help you accomplish your goal.

In this book we discuss a variety of interpersonal skills that will increase the quality of your relationship if put to use. But in order to apply what is learned you need to have some personal goals about building better relationships and to apply the skills in a systematic way and build systems to receive reinforcement for engaging in the skills. Such a process involves being aware of, and building upon, your present strengths and skills. This does not mean you cannot develop new strengths; indeed, the purpose of this book is to help you develop new strengths in interpersonal skills. But developing new strengths is helped by being aware and using your present strengths.

The objective of this exercise is to give you an opportunity to use reinforcement theory to increase the number or quality of your strengths in relating to other people. The procedure for the exercise is:

1. Using the skills presented in the previous chapters of this book, set a goal for increasing the quality of your relationship with one or more people.

2. What specific behaviors will you have to engage in to accomplish your goal? What specific behaviors will indicate that the goal is accomplished?

3. What personal strengths will you utilize to accomplish your goal?

4. What are the barriers to your using your strengths to accomplish your goal?

5. Review what you have written for steps 1, 2, 3, and 4. Set a series of behavioral objectives for yourself. Make sure that they are countable and have direction.

6. In the group as a whole, review each person's objectives. Set aside some time during the next several group meetings to review each member's progress toward accomplishing her objectives. All possible support should be given to the members of the group who make progress toward achieving their objectives. It is the support and praise of the group that will serve as the major strengthening consequence for engaging in the behavior that helps to accomplish your objectives.

Summary Questionnaire: Reinforcing Your Own Strengths

1. My long-term objectives for building better relationships are:

_____

_____

_____

_____

2.   My short-term objectives for building better relationships are:

_____

_____

_____

_____

3.   The strengths and skills I will use to accomplish my objectives are:

_____

_____

_____

_____

4.   The way in which I will know when my objectives are accomplished is:

_____

_____

_____

_____

5.   The system of reinforcement for the behavior I engage in to accomplish my objectives is:

_____

_____

_____

_____

CHAPTER REVIEW

Test your understanding of accepting yourself and others by answering true or false to the following statements. Answers are at the end of the chapter.

True   False   1. Self-acceptance means that you regard yourself highly and are aware of your strengths.

True   False   2. Because self-acceptance gives you the confidence to be self-disclosing, it leads to your being accepted by others, which further increases your self-acceptance.

True   False   3. It is not necessary psychologically to be self-accepting.

True   False   4. The more self-accepting you are, the less you will be accepting of others.

True   False   5. The best feeling about your self-worth is an unconditional basic self-acceptance.

True   False   6. If you paraphrase and express warmth and liking, you will be able to convince other people that you accept them.

True   False   7. If you are to accept another person, you must approve of the things she does.

True   False   8. You use reinforcement to help improve other people's interpersonal skills.

True   False   9. You reinforce by picking a skill, arranging a consequence, and observing to see if the skill is used more often.

True   False   10. Reinforcement works only if you want to encourage behavior, not if you want to discourage behavior.

Indicate which skills you have mastered and which skills you still need more work on.

1. I have mastered the following:
   _____ Awareness of my strengths
   _____ Sharing of my strengths
   _____ Using my strengths to build relationships
   _____ Expressing acceptance nonverbally
   _____ Expressing acceptance verbally
   _____ Reinforcing another person's strengths
   _____ Reinforcing my own strengths

2. I need more work on:
   _____ Awareness of my strengths
   _____ Sharing of my strengths
   _____ Using my strengths to build relationships
   _____ Expressing acceptance nonverbally
   _____ Expressing acceptance verbally
   _____ Reinforcing another person's strengths
   _____ Reinforcing my own strengths

In this chapter you learned how to accept yourself and others, how to express acceptance verbally and nonverbally, and how to reinforce the strengths of yourself and others. In Chapter 9, you will learn what to do when you have conflicts in a relationship.

ANSWERS

Comprehension Test A: 1. true; 2. true; 3. false; 4. false; 5. false; 6. false; 7. true; 8. false; 9. true; 10. true.

Comprehension Test B: 1. true; 2. false; 3. true; 4. false; 5. true; 6. true; 7. false; 8. true; 9. false; 10. true.

Comprehension Test C: 1. d; 2. g; 3. i; 4. c; 5. e; 6. b; 7. f; 8. j; 9. a; 10. h.

Comprehension Test D: 1. false; 2. true; 3. false; 4. true; 5. false; 6. false; 7. true; 8. true; 9. true; 10. ask David.

Chapter Review: 1. true; 2. true; 3. false; 4. false; 5. true; 6. true; 7. false; 8. true; 9. true; 10. false.

9

Resolving Interpersonal Conflicts

INTRODUCTION

Every relationship contains elements of conflict, disagreement, and opposed interests. An *interpersonal conflict* exists whenever an action by one person prevents, obstructs, or interferes with the actions of another person. There can be conflicts between what people want to accomplish, the ways in which they wish to pursue their goals, their personal needs, and the expectations they hold for each other's behavior. It is inevitable that you will become involved in conflicts whenever you have a relationship with another person. The number of conflicts will vary from relationship to relationship, but even in the most friendly and congenial relationships conflicts will appear from time to time.

Despite the inevitability of interpersonal conflicts, there seems to be a general feeling in our society that conflicts are bad and should be avoided. Many people believe that a good relationship is one in which there are no conflicts. Many discussions of conflict cast it in the role of causing divorces, separations, psychological distress, social disorder, and even violence. Yet a lack of conflict may signal apathy and noninvolvement, not a healthy relationship. There is a growing recognition that it is the failure to handle conflicts in constructive ways that leads to the destruction of relationships, not the mere occurrence of conflicts.

Conflicts, when skillfully managed, can be of great value to you and your relationships. Some examples of the potentially constructive nature of conflicts are:

1. Conflicts make us more aware of problems within our relationships that need to be solved. Conflicts increase our awareness of what the problems are, who is involved, and how they can be solved.

2. Conflicts encourage change. There are times when things need to change, when new skills need to be learned, when old habits need to be modified.

3. Conflicts energize and increase motivation to deal with problems. Awareness of conflict can trigger physical reactions that provide a great deal of physical energy and an intensity of psychological focus, resulting in high motivation to resolve the conflict and the energy to put one's plans into action.

4. Conflicts make life more interesting. Being in a conflict often sparks curiosity and stimulates interest. Arguments about politics, sports, work, and societal problems make interpersonal interaction more intriguing and less boring. When other people disagree with your ideas, it may interest you in finding out more about the issue.

5. Better decisions are generally made when there is disagreement about what the decision should be among the people responsible for the decision. Disagreement often causes the decision to be thought through more carefully.

6. Conflicts reduce the day-to-day irritations of relating to someone. A good argument may do a lot to resolve the small tensions of interacting with other people.

7. Conflicts help you understand what you are like as a person. What makes you angry, what frightens you, what is important to you, and how you tend to manage conflicts are all highlighted when you are in conflict with someone. From being aware of what you are willing to argue about and how you act in conflicts, you can learn a great deal about yourself.

8. Conflicts can be fun when they are not taken too seriously. Many people seek out conflicts through such activities as competitive sports and games, movies, plays, books, and teasing. They do so because they enjoy being involved in such conflict situations.

9. Conflicts can deepen and enrich a relationship, strengthening each person's conviction that the relationship can hold up under stress, communicating the commitments and values of each person that the other must take into account, and generally keeping the relationship

clear of irritations and resentments so that positive feelings can be experienced fully.

Conflict is a pervasive and inevitable part of your relationships and can lead to your growth and development as an individual and the growth and development of your relationships with others. Because of this, it becomes important for you to learn the skills involved in handling conflicts constructively. If you put the emphasis on avoiding conflicts, resolving them prematurely, or stifling any discussion of differences, serious difficulties will arise within your relationships. Unless a relationship is able to withstand the stress involved in a conflict, it is not likely to last very long. The objectives of this chapter, therefore, are:

1. To communicate how conflicts may be managed in constructive ways
2. To provide some practice and experiences in constructively managing interpersonal conflicts

HOW TO TELL WHETHER CONFLICTS ARE CONSTRUCTIVE OR DESTRUCTIVE

There are four things to look for in deciding whether a conflict has been constructive or destructive:

1. If the relationship is stronger, with the two of you better able to interact or work with each other, the conflict has been constructive.
2. If the two of you like and trust each other more, the conflict has been constructive.
3. If both you and the other person are satisfied with the results of the conflict, the conflict has been constructive.
4. If both you and the other person, have improved your ability to resolve future conflicts with each other, the conflict has been constructive.

STRATEGIES FOR MANAGING CONFLICTS

Conflicts always occur, and you can profit from them if you have the necessary skills. It is important, therefore, that you master the skills necessary for resolving conflicts constructively. The first step for doing so is to become more aware of your most frequently used strategies for managing conflicts. Given below is a series of exercises aimed at clarifying your feelings and actions when you become involved in conflicts.

EXERCISE 9.1: MY PAST CONFLICT BEHAVIOR

Think back over the interpersonal conflicts you have been involved in during the past few years. These conflicts may be with friends, parents, brothers and sisters, girlfriends or boyfriends, husbands or wives, teachers or students, or with your boss or subordinates. On a separate sheet of paper list the five major conflicts you can remember from your past and the strategies you used and the feelings you had in resolving them.

EXERCISE 9.2: DISAGREEING

We all have different opinions about many issues. Because we have different opinions, we often get into disagreements and arguments. How we act and feel during arguments is an important aspect of our conflict strategies. If you participate actively in this exercise, you will become more aware of how you act and feel during disagreements. You will also be able to give feedback to other participants about their actions during the disagreements. The procedure is:

1. Form groups of six. Each member reads "The Fallout Shelter."
2. Working as a group, decide on the six people who are to go into the fallout shelter. You have twenty minutes to make the decision. During the discussion, argue strongly for your ideas and opinions. The future of the human species may depend on your group's decision. Make sure your group makes a good decision by arguing strongly for your opinions. Agree with the other group members only if they convince you that their ideas are better than yours.
3. Working individually, answer the following questions:
   a. What were my feelings when I disagreed with someone?
   b. What were my feelings when someone disagreed with me?
   c. How did I act when I wanted to convince someone to change her ideas?
   d. How did I act when someone was trying to convince me to change my ideas?
   e. How would my conflict strategies during the group discussion be described?
4. Draw straws to see who is going to be first. Then go around the group in a clockwise direction. Focusing on the member who is first, describe briefly how you saw his or her actions during the group discussion. Use the rules for constructive feedback given on pages 23–25. Make sure everyone in the group receives feedback before the exercise is over.

The Fallout Shelter

Your group is in charge of experimental stations in the far outposts of civilization. You work in an important government agency in Washington, D.C. Suddenly World War III breaks out. Nuclear bombs begin dropping. Places all across the world are being destroyed. People are getting into the available fallout shelters. Your group receives a desperate call from one of your experimental stations. They ask for your help. There are ten people at this station. But their fallout shelter only holds six. They cannot decide which six people should enter the fallout shelter. They have agreed that they will obey your group's decision as to which six people will go into the fallout shelter. Your group has only superficial information about the ten people. Your group has twenty minutes to make the decision. Your group realizes that the six people chosen may be the only six left to start the human species over again. Your group's decision, therefore, is very important. If your group does not make the decision within the twenty minutes allowed, all ten people will die. Here is what you know about the ten people:

> Bookkeeper, male, thirty-one years old
>
> His wife, six months pregnant
>
> Second-year medical student, male, militant black American
>
> Famous historian-author, forty-two years old, male
>
> Hollywood actress who is a singer and dancer
>
> Biochemist, female
>
> Rabbi, 54 years old, male
>
> Olympic athlete, all sports, male
>
> College student, female
>
> Policeman with gun (they cannot be separated)

Disagreeing: What's It Like?

While your group was deciding who was to enter the bomb shelter and who was not, there were some disagreements. It's impossible not to disagree, at least a little. Some members of your group may have been silent during the whole discussion. Some may have agreed very quickly to what most of the other members wanted. Others may have tried to overpower everyone else in order to get their opinions accepted. You may have noticed some members trying to seek compromises that everyone could agree to. Or you may have seen that one or more members kept trying to find out what made the most sense. They would keep going over the reasons why one person should be saved or not saved.

There are many ways to disagree. Some disagreements are so slight that they are never noticed. Other disagreements result in spirited arguments that can be heard for miles. The purpose of the bomb-shelter lesson was to help you become more aware of how you feel and act during a disagreement. Did you learn anything new about yourself?

For a discussion of the specific skills needed to manage disagreements constructively see the chapters on controversy in D. W. Johnson and F. Johnson (1975) and D. W. Johnson (1979).

EXERCISE 9.3: DIVIDING OUR MONEY

Some conflicts begin because there is only so much of something several people want, and no one can have as much as he or she would like. Salaries, promotions, office space, supplies, and even food are often the sources of such conflicts. Where there is only so much money and several people have definite plans about how it should be used, not everyone has his plans adopted by the total group. This exercise focuses on such a conflict. It requires three people to divide some money two ways. If you participate actively in this lesson, you will become more aware of how you manage such conflicts. You will also be able to give other participants feedback on how they act during such conflicts. The specific procedure is:

1. Divide into groups of three. Each person contributes twenty-five cents to the group; the seventy-five cents is placed in a pool.
2. The triad decides how to divide the money between two people. Only two people can receive money. The group has fifteen minutes to make this decision. The group cannot use any sort of "chance" procedure such as drawing straws or flipping a coin to decide which two people get what amounts of money. Side agreements—for instance, to buy a soda for the person left out—are not allowed. It is all right for one person to end up with all the money. A clear decision must be reached as to how the money is to be divided between not more than two people.
3. The purpose of this exercise is to get as much money for yourself as you can. Try to convince the other two members of your triad that you should receive all the money. Tell them you are broke, poor, smarter than they are, or more deserving of the money. Tell them you will put it to better use or will give it to charity. If the other two people make an agreement to divide the money between themselves, offer one of them a better deal. For example, if they agree to split the money fifty-fifty, tell one person that you will let her have fifty cents and will take only twenty-five cents if she agrees to split the money with you.
4. The majority rules. Whenever two people make a firm agreement to split the money a certain way, the decision is made. Be sure, however, to give the third person a chance to offer one of the two a better deal.
5. As soon as a decision is made, write your answers to these questions. Work by yourself.
   a. What were my feelings during the decision making?
   b. How did I act during the decision making? What are the ways I handled the situation? Did I give up? Did I try to persuade others to my point of view? Did I try to take the money by force?
   c. How would my conflict strategies be described during the decision making?
6. In your group of three, give each other feedback describing how you saw each other's actions during the decision making. Use the rules for constructive feedback. Make sure all members of your triad receive feedback.
7. Combine into a group of six and discuss the following questions.
   a. What were the feelings present in each triad during the decision making?
   b. How did members act in each triad during the decision making?
   c. What conflict styles were present in each triad during the decision making?
   d. What did we learn about conflict from the lesson?

Negotiating: What's It Like?

The dividing-our-money exercise was set up so you would have to negotiate. What's it like to negotiate? Did you:

_____ Stay silent during the whole thing and let the other two people divide the money?

_____ Try to force the other two people to let you have at least half the money?

_____ Try to give the money away to the two other people to make sure they didn't feel bad or get angry?

_____ Seek a compromise where somehow everyone would get his or her money back, even if it meant violating the rules for the lesson?

_____ Try to think of a reason that would make it logical for two of the people to divide the money?

Different people negotiate in different ways. The purpose of the divide-our-money exercise was to help you become more aware of how you feel and act during negotiations. Did you learn anything new about yourself?

EXERCISE 9.4: MY CONFLICT STRATEGIES

Different people learn different ways of managing conflicts. The strategies you use to manage conflicts may be quite different from those used by your friends and acquaintances. This exercise gives you an opportunity to increase your awareness of what conflict strategies you use and how they compare with the strategies used by other people. The procedure is:

1. Form into groups of six. Make sure you know the other members of the group. Do not join a group of strangers.

2. Working by yourself, complete the questionnaire, "How I Act in Conflicts."

3. Working by yourself, read the next section, "Conflict Strategies: What Are You Like?" Then take out five slips of paper. Write the names of the other five members of your group on the slips of paper. On each slip of paper write one name.

4. On each slip of paper write the conflict strategy that most fits the actions of the person named.

5. After all group members are finished, pass out your slips of paper to the persons whose names are on them. You should end up with five slips of paper, each containing a description of your conflict style as seen by the other group members. Each member of your group should end up with five slips of paper describing his or her conflict strategy.

6. Score your questionnaire. Rank the five conflict strategies from the ones you use most to the ones you use least. This will give you an indication of how you see your own conflict strategy. The second most frequently used strategy represents your back-up strategy to be used if your first one fails.

7. Draw names to see who is first. Then proceed around the group in a clockwise direction. The first person describes the results of his questionnaire. This is his view of his own conflict strategies. Then the person reads each of the five slips of paper on which are written the views of the group members about his conflict strategy. Then the person asks the group to give specific examples of how they have seen him act in conflicts. The group members should use the rules for constructive feedback. Repeat this procedure for every member of the group.

8. In your group, discuss the strengths and weaknesses of each of the conflict strategies.

How I Act in Conflicts

The proverbs listed below can be thought of as descriptions of some of the different strategies for resolving conflicts. Proverbs state traditional wisdom. These proverbs reflect traditional wisdom for resolving conflicts. Read each of the proverbs carefully. Using the scale given below indicate how typical each proverb is of your actions in a conflict.

5 = Very typical of the way I act in a conflict
4 = Frequently typical of the way I act in a conflict
3 = Sometimes typical of the way I act in a conflict
2 = Seldom typical of the way I act in a conflict
1 = Never typical of the way I act in a conflict

_____ 1. It is easier to refrain than to retreat from a quarrel.
_____ 2. If you cannot make a person think as you do, make him or her do as you think.
_____ 3. Soft words win hard hearts.
_____ 4. You scratch my back, I'll scratch yours.
_____ 5. Come now and let us reason together.
_____ 6. When two quarrel, the person who keeps silent first is the most praiseworthy.
_____ 7. Might overcomes right.
_____ 8. Smooth words make smooth ways.
_____ 9. Better half a loaf than no bread at all.
_____10. Truth lies in knowledge, not in majority opinion.
_____11. He who fights and runs away lives to fight another day.
_____12. He hath conquered well that hath made his enemies flee.
_____13. Kill your enemies with kindness.
_____14. A fair exchange brings no quarrel.
_____15. No person has the final answer but every person has a piece to contribute.
_____16. Stay away from people who disagree with you.
_____17. Fields are won by those who believe in winning.
_____18. Kind words are worth much and cost little.
_____19. Tit for tat is fair play.
_____20. Only the person who is willing to give up his or her monopoly on truth can ever profit from the truths that others hold.

_____**21.** Avoid quarrelsome people as they will only make your life miserable.

_____**22.** A person who will not flee will make others flee.

_____**23.** Soft words ensure harmony.

_____**24.** One gift for another makes good friends.

_____**25.** Bring your conflicts into the open and face them directly; only then will the best solution be discovered.

_____**26.** The best way of handling conflicts is to avoid them.

_____**27.** Put your foot down where you mean to stand.

_____**28.** Gentleness will triumph over anger.

_____**29.** Getting part of what you want is better than not getting anything at all.

_____**30.** Frankness, honesty, and trust will move mountains.

_____**31.** There is nothing so important you have to fight for it.

_____**32.** There are two kinds of people in the world, the winners and the losers.

_____**33.** When one hits you with a stone, hit him or her with a piece of cotton.

_____**34.** When both people give in halfway, a fair settlement is achieved.

_____**35.** By digging and digging, the truth is discovered.

CONFLICT STRATEGIES: WHAT ARE YOU LIKE?

Different people use different strategies for managing conflicts. These strategies are learned, usually in childhood, and they seem to function automatically. Usually we are not aware of how we act in conflict situations. We just do whatever seems to come naturally. But we do have a personal strategy, and because it was learned, we can always change it by learning new and more effective ways of managing conflicts.

When you become engaged in a conflict, there are two major concerns you have to take into account:

1. Achieving your personal goals—you are in conflict because you have a goal that conflicts with another person's goal. Your goal may be highly important to you, or it may be of little importance.

2. Keeping a good relationship with the other person—you may need to be able to interact effectively with the other person in the future. The relationship may be very important to you, or it may be of little importance.

How important your personal goals are to you and how important the relationship is to you affects how you act in a conflict. Given these two concerns, five styles of managing conflicts can be identified:

High
Importance

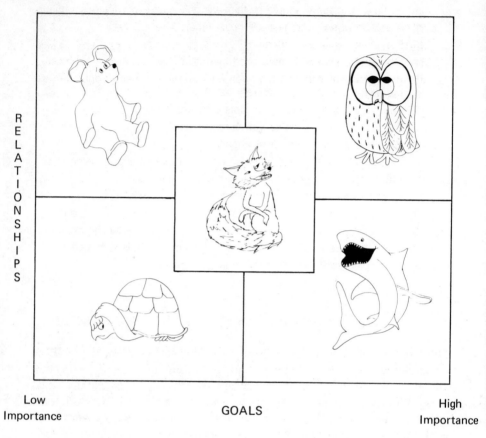

R
E
L
A
T
I
O
N
S
H
I
P
S

Low
Importance

GOALS

High
Importance

1.   *The Turtle* (Withdrawing). Turtles withdraw into their shells to avoid conflicts. They give up their personal goals and relationships. They stay away from the issues over which the conflict is taking place and from the people they are in conflict with. Turtles believe it is hopeless to try to resolve conflicts. They feel helpless. They believe it is easier to withdraw (physically and psychologically) from a conflict than to face it.

2.   *The Shark* (Forcing). Sharks try to overpower opponents by forcing them to accept their solution to the conflict. Their goals are highly important to them, and the relationship is of minor importance. They seek to achieve their goals at all costs. They are not concerned with the needs of other people. They do not care if other people like or accept them. Sharks assume that conflicts are settled by one person

winning and one person losing. They want to be the winner. Winning gives sharks a sense of pride and achievement. Losing gives them a sense of weakness, inadequacy, and failure. They try to win by attacking, overpowering, overwhelming, and intimidating other people.

3.   *The Teddy Bear* (Smoothing). To Teddy Bears, the relationship is of great importance, while their own goals are of little importance. Teddy Bears want to be accepted and liked by other people. They think that conflict should be avoided in favor of harmony and believe that conflicts cannot be discussed without damaging relationships. They are afraid that if the conflict continues, someone will get hurt,

and that would ruin the relationship. They give up their goals to preserve the relationship. Teddy Bears say, "I'll give up my goals, and let you have what you want, in order for you to like me." Teddy Bears try to smooth over the conflict in fear of harming the relationship.

4. *The Fox* (Compromising). Foxes are moderately concerned with their own goals and about their relationships with other people. Foxes seek a compromise. They give up part of their goals and persuade

the other person in a conflict to give up part of his goals. They seek a solution to conflicts where both sides gain something—the middle ground between two extreme positions. They are willing to sacrifice part of their goals and relationships in order to find agreement for the common good.

5. *The Owl* (Confronting). Owls highly value their own goals and relationships. They view conflicts as problems to be solved and seek a solution that achieves both their own goals and the goals of the other

person in the conflict. Owls see conflicts as improving relationships by reducing tension between two people. They try to begin a discussion that identifies the conflict as a problem. By seeking solutions that satisfy both themselves and the other person, owls maintain the relationship. Owls are not satisfied until a solution is found that achieves their own goals and the other person's goals. And they are not satisfied until the tensions and negative feelings have been fully resolved.

Scoring: How I Act in Conflicts

Withdrawing	Forcing	Smoothing	Compromising	Confronting
___ 1.	___ 2.	___ 3.	___ 4.	___ 5.
___ 6.	___ 7.	___ 8.	___ 9.	___ 10.
___ 11.	___ 12.	___ 13.	___ 14.	___ 15.
___ 16.	___ 17.	___ 18.	___ 19.	___ 20.
___ 21.	___ 22.	___ 23.	___ 24.	___ 25.
___ 26.	___ 27.	___ 28.	___ 29.	___ 30.
___ 31.	___ 32.	___ 33.	___ 34.	___ 35.
___ Total	___ Total	___ Total	___ Total	___ Total

The higher the total score for each conflict strategy, the more frequently you tend to use that strategy. The lower the total score for each conflict strategy, the less frequently you tend to use that strategy.

EXERCISE 9.5: NONVERBAL CONFLICT

Before you begin these exercises, please review the discussion of nonverbal exercises in chapter 3. The following nonverbal exercises dealing with various aspects of conflicts may be helpful in clarifying your feelings about conflict and your style of managing conflicts:

1. *Pushing and shoving:* Lock fingers with another person, with arms extended over your heads. Push against each other, trying to drive the other to the wall.

2. *Thumb wrestling:* Lock fingers with another person with your thumbs straight up. Tap your thumbs together three times and then try to pin the other's thumb so that the other cannot move it.

3. *Slapping hands:* Person *A* puts her hands out, palms down. Person *B* ex-

tends his hands, palms up, under Person *A*'s hands. The object of the exercise is for Person *B* to try to slap the hands of Person *A* by quickly moving his hands from the bottom to the top. As soon as Person *B* makes a move, Person *A* tries to pull her hands out of the way before Person *B* can slap them.

4. *Pushing down to the floor and helping up:* In pairs, one person tries to push the other person down to the floor. No wrestling, but the person being pushed may resist if he wants to. After the person is pushed down to the floor, then the pusher has to help the pushed person up. The person being helped up may still resist if he wants to.

5. *Unwrapping:* A member who is having internal conflicts is asked to make herself into a tight ball. Another person is chosen by her to "unwrap" her, or to open her up completely. The member may struggle against being unwrapped, or she may submit. Other members of the group may join in, some trying to keep the person wrapped and others trying to unwrap her. Or everyone in the group may pair up and take turns being unwrapped and unwrapping.

DIMENSIONS OF CONFLICT SITUATIONS

In order to manage conflicts constructively, you must be aware of several important dimensions of conflicts. Among other things, you must have an accurate perception of the conflict and communicate clearly with the opponent. You must also build a climate of trust and know how to structure cooperative resolutions to the conflict.

Accurate Perception of Your Own and Another's Behavior

In conflict situations, there are often perceptual distortions about your own and the other person's behavior, motivations, and position. Many of these distortions in perception are so common that they can be found in almost any conflict situation, whether it is between two people, two groups, or two countries. They include:

1. *Mirror image:* It is not uncommon for both you and the other person to feel that you are an innocent victim who represents truth and justice and who is being attacked maliciously by an evil enemy. In most conflicts, both people are firmly convinced that they are right and the other person wrong, that they want a "just" solution but the other person does not.

2. *Mote-beam mechanism:* Often in conflict situations each person clearly sees all the underhanded and vicious acts of the other person while being completely blind to identical acts engaged in himself. In most

conflicts both people repress all awareness of the mean things they do to the other but become quite indignant about the mean things the other person does to them.

3. *Double standard:* Even if both people are aware of identical acts engaged in by themselves and the other person, there is a strong tendency to feel that what is legitimate for you to do is illegitimate for the other person to do.

4. *Polarized thinking:* It is common in conflict situations for both people to have an oversimplified view of the conflict in which everything they do is good and everything the other person does is bad.

These misunderstandings escalate the conflict and make it more difficult to resolve it constructively. As long as you and the other person are each convinced that you are right and the other person is wrong, as long as you perceive every underhanded thing the other person does but ignore every underhanded thing you do, and as long as you apply a double standard to the behavior of yourself and the other person and think about the conflict in polarized, oversimplified ways, the conflict is bound to be destructive to your relationship.

In any conflict situation, you and the other person will usually have mixed feelings about each other. On the one hand you will feel hostile and wish that the other person would agree with your position; on the other hand, you will still feel affection for the other person and want to be agreeable to him. When selective perception or distortions in perception operate, it is very easy to fall into a trap where you see only the hostile feelings of the other person and fail to see the positive feelings. This can very easily result in a *self-fulfilling prophecy* in which (1) you assume that the other's feelings are entirely hostile, (2) you take defensive action by either attacking the other person before he can attack you or cutting off contact with the other person, (3) your action intensifies the other person's hostility and decreases his positive feelings toward you, and (4) your original, but false, assumption is confirmed. Self-fulfilling prophecies are very common in conflict situations, and whenever you become involved in a conflict you should be careful not to fall into their traps.

EXERCISE 9.6: OLD LADY/YOUNG GIRL

The objective of this exercise is to show how two people with different frames of reference can perceive the same event in two different ways. The procedure is:

1. Divide into two groups with an equal number of members in each group.

2. Each group receives a picture. The pictures are to be found in the Appendix at the end of this book. One group receives picture *A* and the other group receives picture *B*. Each group is asked to write out a description of the person in the picture, including such things as sex, clothing, hair style, and age.

3. Each member of the first group is paired with a member of the second group. Each pair is given a copy of picture *C*. The two individuals are then asked to negotiate a common description of the person in the picture, including such things as sex, clothing, hairstyle, and age.

4. Conduct a discussion in the group as a whole concerning the results of the negotiations. Did you all see picture *C* the same way? Once you perceived the picture in one way, was it difficult to see it another way? In conflict situations, what influence do your background, previous experience, expectation, and frame of reference have upon how you see your behavior and the behavior of the other person?

5. Review the section on selective perception in chapter 4. How does the information in that section apply to this situation? How does it apply to most conflict situations?

ENSURING ACCURATE COMMUNICATION

Effective and continued communication is of vital importance in the constructive resolution of conflicts. It is quite common, however, for individuals in a conflict to refuse to communicate with each other when given the opportunity to do so, and when required to communicate they often communicate lies and threats as well as promises and trustworthy statements. Only when communication is aimed at creating an agreement fair to all parties involved is it helpful in resolving a conflict constructively. This means that in communicating with a person you are in conflict with, it is important to keep communication channels open, to communicate promises and trustworthy statements aimed at creating an agreement that is fair to the other person as well as yourself. Sometimes you will find that the other person is not at the moment interested in resolving the conflict. When this is true it is important to include the following elements in your communications to the other person:

1. What your behavior to resolve the conflict is going to be

2. Your expectation as to the other person's response

3. What you will do if the other person does not behave in the expected way

4.   How friendly, cooperative relationships will be restored after your reaction to the other's violation of your expectations

In communicating with the other person in a conflict situation, several of the skills emphasized in this book are very helpful. They are:

1.   Understanding response

2.   Use of personal and relationship statements in being open about your position, motivations, and feelings

3.   Providing useful, nonevaluative feedback to the other person through constructive confrontations

4.   Communicating acceptance of the other as a person, even when you disagree with his behavior

In addition, it is important to avoid the use of evaluative responses, threats, lies, indications that you want to "win," and attempts to manipulate the other person; all of these increase the other person's defensiveness, which increases his tendency to misperceive the situation and cut off communication.

EXERCISE 9.7: ROLE REVERSAL

The primary means of ensuring accurate perception of the conflict situation and of being able to communicate effectively with the other person is to gain as much insight as possible on how the other person perceives the conflict situation. This may be done through a procedure called role reversal. *Role reversal* may be defined as a procedure where one or both of two people in a conflict present the viewpoint of the other. That is, given that A and B are in a conflict, A presents B's point of view or B presents A's point of view, or both. The specific behaviors involved in role reversal are (1) the understanding response while (2) expressing warmth. A variety of research studies have demonstrated that the use of role reversal can eliminate misunderstandings and reduce distortions of the other person's point of view (Johnson 1971).

Whenever you are in a conflict with another person it is valuable to engage in role reversal in order to clarify each other's position and feelings. This exercise gives you an opportunity to practice role reversal. The procedure is:

1.   Pick a current topic of interest on which there are differences of opinion in the group. Then divide the group in half, with each subgroup representing one side of the issue.

2.   Each subgroup meets separately for fifteen minutes to prepare to represent their side of the issue in negotiations with members of the other subgroup.

3. Each person in the subgroup is paired with a person from the other subgroup; each pair thus consists of persons representing opposite sides of the issue.

4. In the pair, designate the persons A and B. Person A then is given up to five minutes to present her side of the issue. Person B then reverses his role by presenting Person A's position as if he were Person A.

5. Person B is then given up to five minutes to present his side of the issue. Person A role reverses.

6. The pair is then given fifteen minutes to arrive at a joint agreement on the issue being discussed. During the fifteen minutes they must obey the following rule: *Before either can reply to a statement made by the other, she must accurately and warmly paraphrase the other's statement to the other's satisfaction.*

7. In the whole group discuss the impact of role reversal on your understanding and appreciation of the other side of the issue. Did role reversal help to reach an agreement? Did it affect how you felt about each other during the negotiations. Did you feel it contributed to reaching a mutually satisfying agreement?

BUILDING A CLIMATE OF TRUST

In dealing constructively with conflicts, it is important to build a climate of trust. There are two major ways to build a climate of trust in dealing with a conflict. The first is to indicate that you trust the other person by making yourself vulnerable through attempts to resolve the conflict constructively. The second is to make sure you never exploit the other person's vulnerability. See chapter 3 for an elaboration of building trust.

Structuring Cooperative Solutions

Perhaps the surest way of resolving a conflict constructively is to involve yourself and the other person in a situation where you have to cooperate with each other to achieve mutually desired goals. Cooperative interaction means that you and the other person will engage in joint action to accomplish a goal you both want. Two people who both wish to build a sand castle and help each other do so are in cooperative interaction. The members of a football team take cooperative action to win a game. A teacher and a student planning an assignment to maximize the student's learning are in cooperative interaction. Two people who wish to deepen their relationship and thus spend time on a joint activity are in cooperative interaction. Any time that you and another person have the same goal and help each other accomplish it, you are in cooperative interaction.

Cooperative interaction has very powerful, positive effects upon the relationship between two people. Cooperation produces increased liking for one another, increased trust, and a willingness to listen to and be influenced by each other. Friendships are based largely upon cooperation. The development of a fulfilling friendship rests upon the ability of two people to define mutual goals (even if the goal is to fall in love) and then to cooperate in obtaining them. In a conflict situation, the primary way to ensure a constructive resolution is to work out a cooperative solution to the conflict. Certainly any solution to a conflict should include the necessity for cooperative interaction between yourself and the other person.

CHAPTER REVIEW

Test your understanding of resolving interpersonal conflicts by taking the following quiz. Answers are at the end of the chapter.

True	False	1. If you have a really good relationship with someone, you'll not have conflicts.
True	False	2. You should avoid conflicts whenever possible.
True	False	3. Conflicts can give you energy and make your life more interesting.
True	False	4. Conflicts can help you understand yourself better and can deepen a relationship.
True	False	5. A conflict has been constructive if both people are satisfied with the results and the relationship is stronger.
True	False	6. The two major concerns you should take into account during a conflict are achieving your personal goals and keeping a good relationship with the other person.
True	False	7. You can build a climate of trust by making yourself vulnerable and by not exploiting the other person's vulnerability.
True	False	8. A cooperative interaction helps resolve conflict by increasing interaction and thus taking your mind off the conflict.

9. Match the following conflict-management styles with their definitions:

_____ The Teddy Bear   a. Solution must satisfy both parties.

_____ The Fox   b. Smooth over conflict so relationship won't be harmed.

_____ The Turtle   c. Seek a middle ground between the two extremes.

_____ The Owl   d. Withdraw rather than face conflicts.

_____ The Shark   e. Win conflict by overcoming the other person.

10. Match the following misperceptions with their definitions:

_____ Mirror image   a. Everything I do is good; everything you do is bad.

_____ Mote-beam mechanism   b. What is legitimate for me to do is illegitimate for you to do.

_____ Double standard   c. I see the mean, underhanded things you do to me, but I don't see the mean, underhanded things I do to you.

_____ Polarized thinking   d. I think I'm right and you're wrong; you think you're right and I'm wrong.

_____ Self-fulfilling prophecy   e. I expected you to be hostile. I see only your hostile feelings and not your positive ones. I then take defensive action, which causes you to be more hostile.

What skills have you mastered, and what skills do you need more work on?

1. I have mastered the following:
_____ An awareness of how I tend to manage conflicts
_____ How to get an accurate perception of the conflict
_____ How to communicate my expectations in a conflict
_____ How to view the conflict from the other person's perspective

2. I need more work on:
_____ An awareness of how I tend to manage conflicts
_____ How to get an accurate perception of the conflict

_____   How to communicate my expectations in a conflict
_____   How to view the conflict from the other person's perspective

In this chapter, you learned that conflicts, when handled constructively, are beneficial to a relationship. You identified your strategies for managing a conflict. You learned some of the perception problems that distort a relationship and how to make sure you have accurate communication in a conflict. You also learned how to ensure that you understand the other person's perspective in viewing the conflict. In the next chapter, you will learn how to define conflicts in ways that maximize the likelihood of a constructive resolution.

ANSWERS

Chapter Review: 1. false; 2. false; 3. true; 4. true; 5. true; 6. true; 7. true; 8. false; 9. b, c, d, a, e; 10. d, c, b, a, e.

10

Defining Conflicts
Constructively

In any relationship there are times when problems arise. These problems may be conflicts, periods of irritation, or changes in the relationship that make you unsure of where it is going. This chapter focuses on a way to analyze interpersonal problems and conflicts to help solve them. The key to constructive conflict resolution is in how the conflict is originally defined. A programmed approach to learning how to define conflicts constructively is presented in this chapter.

EXERCISE 10.1: LEARNING TO DEFINE CONFLICTS

Many people involved in conflicts do not worry about definitions. Why define a conflict when you know you are right and your opponent is wrong? But the lack of a clear and constructive definition often makes conflicts difficult to resolve. How a conflict is defined affects how easily it can be resolved, how well it is understood, what solutions are proposed, and how participants feel about each other. A major skill in making conflicts constructive is defining them properly.

There are two steps in defining a conflict. The first is to define the conflict by yourself. The second is to agree with the other person on a joint definition. This chapter focuses only on the first step, how you define a conflict by yourself. Your definition of a conflict will affect how you act and feel in trying to resolve it. With a poor definition, you will feel miserable and act in ways that will make the conflict worse. With a constructive definition, you will feel confident and effective, and you will act in ways that resolve the conflict. It is important that you be able to define conflicts in a skillful way.

Think of conflicts you are now having with other people. The conflicts may be with parents, friends, teachers, fellow employees, or employers. Choose one of the more important conflicts. Be sure the conflict is one that fits the following rules:

1. It is important to you.
2. It creates intense feelings, such as anger, resentment, fear, frustration, anxiety, or concern.
3. It is possible to resolve it.

You will now be given several directions about the way you define this conflict. As you respond to these directions, you will be going through the stages of defining a conflict skillfully. The procedure is:

1. Write down a simple definition of the conflict.
2. Read a discussion about what you have written.

Each time you rewrite your definition of the conflict, you will learn something valuable about defining a conflict skillfully.

Write a brief description of the conflict as it looks to you now. Don't worry about how clear the description is. Don't worry about how well you have written it. Just write it off the top of your head. "If I were to define the conflict, I would say . . ."

Now that you have defined the conflict, you can look to see what stage your definition is in. If you defined the conflict as being caused by a "sick," "mean," or "stupid" person, you are thinking in Stage 1. If you have described the other person's actions toward you, you are thinking in Stage 2.

STAGE 1	*STAGE 2*
I work with this sick, mean, stupid nut! He puts everyone down and pretends he is better than they are!	A person I work with criticizes my work. He tells me he makes fewer mistakes than I do. But he makes twice as many as I do!

Defining a conflict is like lacing your shoes. If you start out wrong, the whole thing gets messed up. If you label the other person in negative ways, he will be defensive and hostile. Labeling creates mistrust, misunderstandings, and resentment. Stage 1 thinking makes it harder to resolve a conflict. A rule to remember when defining a conflict is: *Do not label, accuse, or insult the other person! Describe the other person's actions toward you!* Conflicts must be defined as being over actions and issues, not personalities.

Look at what you wrote to describe the conflict. Are you thinking in Stage 1 or Stage 2? Now rewrite your definition of the conflict, making it as accusatory, insulting, and labeling as you can. Finally, rewrite your definition of the conflict again, making it as descriptive as you can.

"If I were to define the conflict, this time trying to describe the other person's actions toward me, I would say . . ."

Reread your definition. If you described the other person's actions as part of a "win-lose" competition, you are thinking in Stage 2. Whenever you are trying to prove who is right and who is wrong or who is superior and who is inferior, you are in a win-lose competition. If you described the other person's actions as part of a mutual problem to be solved, you are thinking in Stage 3.

STAGE 2	*STAGE 3*
A person I work with criticizes my work. He tells me he makes fewer mistakes than I do. But he makes twice as many mistakes as I do!	A person I work with criticizes my work. It isn't a matter of who is best. We need to help each other, not compete to see who is superior.

Never let yourself get caught in a win-lose conflict with a friend. In the long run, nothing good will result. Future cooperation is always hurt by win-lose conflicts. You may feel great at first if you win. But the person who loses will feel resentful. She will tend to cut off communication and will try to get back at the winner. She will dislike the winner. A win-lose definition of a conflict promotes distrust, dislike, deception, rivalry, threats, and attempts to undermine each other's work. Trying to prove that you are better than a friend will only make working an unpleasant experience.

Make sure you always try to define a conflict as a mutual problem to be solved. This will increase communication, trust, liking for each other, and cooperation with each other. No one loses when two people sit down to solve a mutual problem!

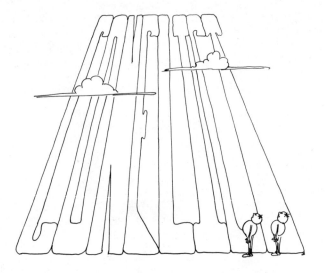

Are you thinking in Stage 2 or Stage 3? Now rewrite your definition of the conflict, making it as win-lose oriented as possible (I'm right, the other person is wrong, I'm superior, the other person is inferior). Finally, rewrite your definition of the conflict again, making it as problem oriented as possible.

"If I were to define the conflict as a mutual problem that needs to be resolved, I would say . . ."

Reread your definition. If you defined the conflict as a mutual problem to be solved, but described the other person's actions generally or vaguely, you are thinking in Stage 3. If you described the other person's actions in the most specific way possible, you are thinking in Stage 4.

STAGE 3	*STAGE 4*
A person I work with criticizes my work. It isn't a matter of who is best. We need to help each other, not compete to see who is superior.	When I make a mistake, the person I work with tells me about it in a cold tone of voice. It isn't a matter of who is best. We need to help each other, not compete to see who is superior.

Think small! The more limited the definition of the conflict, the easier it is to resolve. The larger and vaguer the description of the other person's actions, the harder it is to resolve the conflict. When it comes to resolving conflicts, *small is easy, large is hard!* In this example, the "criticizes" is more vague and general than "tells me when I make a mistake." The smaller and more specific the description of the other person's actions, the easier it will be to find a way to resolve the conflict.

Are you thinking in Stage 3 or Stage 4? Now rewrite your definition of the conflict, making it as general and vague as possible. Finally, rewrite your definition of the conflict again, making the definition as limited and specific as possible.

"If I were to define the conflict, this time trying to give as specific a description of the other person's actions as I can, I would say . . ."

Reread your definition. If you described the other person's actions in the most specific way possible but did *not* describe your feelings and reactions, you are thinking in Stage 4. If you also described your feelings and reactions, you are thinking in Stage 5.

STAGE 4

When I make a mistake, the person I work with tells me about it in a cold tone of voice. It isn't a matter of who is best. We need to help each other, not compete to see who is superior.

STAGE 5

When I make a mistake, the person I work with tells me about it in a cold tone of voice. This makes me mad. I resent his doing it. It isn't a matter of who is best. We need to help each other, not compete to see who is superior.

Do not expect your friends to be mind readers. The only way they can know how you are feeling and reacting is if you tell them. What they do not know about, they cannot be blamed for. There is a tendency in conflicts to hide feelings and reactions. You often do not want the other person to know how upset you really are. But if the conflict is to be resolved, you need to share your feelings and reactions. This helps the other person understand how her actions are affecting you. You may wish to review the material on describing your feelings (p. 120) and feedback (pp. 23–25).

Are you thinking in Stage 4 or Stage 5? Now rewrite your definition of the conflict, making it as devoid of feelings and reactions as you can. Finally, rewrite your definition of the conflict again, including a description of your feelings about and reactions to the other person's behavior.

"Focusing on describing my feelings about, and reactions to, the other person's actions, I would define the conflict as . . ."

Reread your definition. If you described your feelings but did not describe how your actions help create and continue the conflict, you are thinking in Stage

5. If you also described how your actions help create and continue the conflict, you are thinking in Stage 6.

STAGE 5	STAGE 6
When I make a mistake, the person I work with tells me about it in a cold tone of voice. This makes me mad. I resent her doing it. It isn't a matter of who is best. We need to help each other, not compete to see who is superior.	When I make a mistake, the person I work with tells me about it in a cold tone of voice. This makes me mad. I resent her doing it. I've never told her how I feel. I've never asked her to stop or do it differently. It isn't a matter of who is best. We need to help each other, not compete to see who is superior.

Who needs to change? You, me, or both of us? In a conflict, you may want the other person to change. But the easiest thing to change is your own actions. If you wish to resolve a conflict, you must begin with deciding how to change your actions. It would be nice if everyone else changed so we would never have to. But you do not have control over the actions of others. They do. What you do have control over is your own actions. *You can change your actions much more easily than you can change another person's actions! Knowing how your actions help create and continue the conflict is essential for planning how to resolve it! And neglecting to do something constructive helps create and continue the conflict just as much as doing something destructive!*

Look at your definition. Are you thinking in Stage 5 or Stage 6? Now rewrite your definition, focusing only on the changes the other person needs to make. Finally, rewrite your definition of the conflict again, including a description of your actions that help create or continue the conflict.

"Focusing on how I help create and continue the conflict by the things I am doing or I am neglecting to do, I would define the conflict as . . ."

You now have a clearer, more useful way of looking at a conflict. The more you follow the rules for defining conflicts, the more skillful you will be in resolving them. The less you follow the rules, the more likely it will be that conflicts will be destructive and harmful. The rules may be summarized as follows:

1. Describe the other person's actions; don't label, accuse, or insult. Make sure the conflict is over issues and actions, not personalities.
2. Define the conflict as a mutual problem to be solved, not as a win-lose struggle.
3. Define the conflict in the smallest and most specific way possible.
4. Describe your feelings about, and reactions to, the other person's actions.
5. Describe *your* actions (what you are doing and neglecting to do) that help create and continue the conflict.

The steps in defining conflicts constructively may be summarized as follows:

1. Examine the list of the interpersonal skills discussed in this book (pp. 286–289). On a separate sheet of paper, list the skills that will be helpful in resolving the conflict between you and the other person.

2. On a separate sheet of paper, list the assets you have that you can use in resolving the conflict.

3. Think about the specific changes in your actions that may be helpful in resolving the conflict. Think about the skills and assets you have to help you resolve the conflict. Think about your definition of the conflict. Then list on a separate sheet of paper the specific actions you will take to resolve the conflict between you and the other person.

4. Remember, the constructive resolution of conflict begins with *your* actions, *your* feelings, *your* skills and assets, *your* willingness to change, and *your* ability to define the conflict in a helpful way.

EXERCISE 10.2: FURTHER PRACTICE IN DEFINING CONFLICTS

The purpose of this exercise is to give you further practice in defining conflicts constructively. The procedure is:

1. Find a partner. Pick a conflict one of you is currently engaged in that meets the criteria of being important, creating intense feelings, and being possible to resolve.

2. As a pair, define the conflict, labeling the opponent in as negative a way as possible, and then define the conflict in a way that describes the opponent's behavior. Review the material in this chapter on labeling versus describing.

3. As a pair, define the conflict as a win-lose situation, and then define the conflict as a mutual problem to be resolved. Review the material in this chapter on win-lose versus problem-solving definitions.

4. As a pair, define the conflict in as general a way as possible, and then define the conflict in as limited and specific a way as possible. Review the material in this chapter on general versus specific definitions of conflicts.

5. As a pair, define the conflict in a way that does not mention your feelings and reactions, and then define the conflict in a way that includes your feelings and reactions. Review the material in this chapter on including your feelings and reactions as part of the definition of a conflict.

6. As a pair, define the conflict in a way that demands change only on the part of the opponent, and then define the conflict in a way that includes a description of what you are doing to create and continue the conflict. Review the material in this chapter on mutual responsibility for change.

7. As a pair, identify the correct stage of defining a conflict for each of the following statements. Be sure to discuss the characteristics of each statement that place it in one stage rather than another. Answers are at the end of the chapter.

___ When I have my friends in our room, my roomate calls me "stupid" and "slob." It is not a matter of who is smarter or neater. We need to support each other, not tear each other down.

___ My roommate is mean, vicious, and demented and is always joking around and calling me names in front of my friends. But he's far more stupid and messy than I am!

___ My roommate is always joking around and calling me names in front of my friends. It is not a matter of who is smarter and neater. We need to support each other, not tear each other down.

___ When I have my friends in our room, my roommate calls me "stupid" and "slob." This embarrasses me and makes me feel inhibited and shy. He does this because I refuse to stop throwing my dirty clothes on his bed and to stop playing my stereo and talking on the phone during our agreed-upon study hour. It is not a matter of who is smarter or neater. We need to support each other, not tear each other down.

___ My roommate is always joking around and calling me names in front of my friends. But he is far more stupid and messy than I am!

___ When I have my friends in our room, my roommate calls me "stupid" and "slob." This embarrasses me and makes me feel inhibited and shy. It is not a matter of who is smarter or neater. We need to support each other, not tear each other down.

8. Discuss the following two statements, indicating why you do or do not agree with them.

___ When a conflict is defined in a way that labels the opponent negatively, is win-lose and general, and blames the opponent for the conflict, considerable distress and destructive escalation of the conflict are likely to result.

___ When a conflict is defined as describing the opponent's behavior, as a specific and limited problem to be solved, as including your feelings and your behaviors that contribute to the conflict, constructive resolution of the conflict is likely to result.

CHAPTER REVIEW

Test your understanding of defining conflicts by answering true or false to the following statements. Answers are at the end of the chapter.

True   False   1. Defining the conflict yourself is the first step to defining a conflict.

True   False   2. The second step in defining a conflict is to agree with the other person on a joint definition.

True   False   3. How you define a conflict has little to do with how you go about resolving it.

True   False   4. Make sure the conflict is over personalities, not issues.

True   False   5. If you define the conflict as a mutual problem rather than a win-lose situation, then you will win and the other person will lose.

True   False   6. Defining the conflict in limited and specific terms will make it easier to resolve.

True   False   7. Explaining your feelings and reactions will help the other person understand how her actions are affecting you.

True   False   8. It is easier to change the other person's actions than to change your own.

True   False   9. "You make me feel small and insignificant when you listen to my suggestions and then reject them without discussion" is a good example of defining a conflict.

True   False   10. "You are a superior snot who puts everyone down and refuses to listen to good advice" is a good example of defining a conflict.

Which skills have you mastered and which ones do you need further work on?

1.   I have mastered the following:
_____   Describing actions and issues in a conflict, not personalities
_____   Describing the conflict as a mutual problem
_____   Describing the conflict specifically
_____   Describing my reactions to, and feelings about, the other person's actions
_____   Describing actions of mine that help create and continue the conflict

2.   I need more work on:
_____   Describing actions and issues in a conflict, not personalities
_____   Describing the conflict as a mutual problem
_____   Describing the conflict specifically
_____   Describing my reactions to, and feelings about, the other person's actions
_____   Describing actions of mine that help create and continue the conflict

After studying this chapter, you should be able to define conflicts in a descriptive and specific way. Next, you will find out how to negotiate with the other person a joint definition of the conflict, as a way to help solve interpersonal problems.

ANSWERS

Stages in Defining a Conflict (Exercise 10.2): 4, 1, 3, 6, 2, 5.

Chapter Review: 1. true; 2. true; 3. false; 4. false; 5. false; 6. true; 7. true; 8. false; 9. true; 10. false.

PHOTO BY JACK WAIT

11

Confrontation
and Negotiation

INTRODUCTION

In building and maintaining a close relationship, it is of utmost importance that you be honest with the other person. Friendships are built by building trust and expressing support and acceptance, but inevitably there are times when you become angry with the other person, find yourself in conflict with the other person, or believe that the other person is behaving in a way that is self-destructive, destructive to you, or destructive to other people. At this point you need to reflect on the meaning of friendship and the meaning of being committed to another person. Which is the true friend: a person who ignores the destructive behavior of another person, or one who risks rejection by confronting the other person with the consequences of his behavior in order to help the person avoid making the same mistake over and over again? If you are someone's friend, do you ignore her interpersonal mistakes, or do you confront her in a way that helps her learn not to make the same mistake in the future? If you are someone's friend, do you ignore conflicts in the relationship or do you sit down and negotiate solutions that take into account both your goals and hers? In this chapter you will examine the skills involved in confronting other people constructively with the consequences of their behavior and negotiating mutually beneficial solutions to conflicts.

In confronting another person and negotiating a resolution to a conflict, there is a series of steps one usually goes through. Those steps are:

1. Confront the opposition.
2. Jointly define the conflict.
3. Communicate any changes of positions and feelings.
4. Communicate cooperative intentions.
5. Take the other person's perspective accurately and fully.
6. Coordinate your motivation and the other's to negotiate in good faith.
7. Reach an agreement.

Each of these steps is discussed in this chapter.

STEP 1 IN RESOLVING A CONFLICT: CONFRONTATION

The first step in seeking a constructive resolution of a conflict is to confront the other person. A *confrontation* is the direct expression of one's view of the conflict and one's feelings about it while inviting the other person to do the same. Confrontations involve clarifying and exploring the issues, the nature and strength of the underlying needs of the participants, and their current feelings. It is a deliberate attempt to begin a direct and problem-solving discussion about the conflict with the other person.

The decision to confront another person is based on two major factors:

1. How high the quality of the relationship is. Generally, the stronger the relationship, the more powerful the confrontation may be.

2. How able you think the person being confronted is to act on the confrontation. If a person's anxiety level is high or his motivation or ability to change is low, don't confront. If the confrontation will not be utilized as an invitation for self-examination, it should not take place.

Thus, if you think the relationship is not strong enough or that the other person is not able to respond constructively, do not confront. It is a mistake to assume that you can *always* confront a friend or acquaintance and discuss a conflict. It is also a mistake to assume that you can *never* confront. Whether you decide to open your mouth or button your lips depends on the other person and the situation.

Usually you will want to confront when you are involved in a conflict. If you wish to resolve the conflict, a confrontation will usually be necessary. If you wish to help the other person grow and develop, a confrontation will usually be necessary. If you wish to achieve your goals or to maintain an effective relationship, a confrontation will usually be necessary. When you confront another person, the following guidelines may be helpful:

1. *Do not "hit-and-run." Confront only when there is time to define the conflict jointly and schedule a negotiating session.* A confrontation is the beginning of a negotiating process, not an end in itself. Thus, confrontations are not to be confused with hit-and-run events in which one person gives his views of, and feelings about, a conflict and then disappears before the other person can respond. Hit-and-run tactics tend to escalate conflicts in negative directions and build resentment and anger in the victims. An important aspect of confrontations is timing. Always be sure that enough time exists to discuss the conflict before confronting another person.

2. *Communicate openly your perceptions of, and feelings about, the issues involved in the conflict, and try to do so in minimally threatening ways.* Communicate your definition of the conflict, following the guidelines given in chapter 10. Adapt the strength of the wording of the confrontation to the level of defensiveness of the other person. Perhaps the most difficult aspect of confrontation is the open expression of feelings. Yet if emotions are not directly expressed verbally, they will be expressed in deeds or misdeeds later. Feelings such as anger and resentment are especially difficult for many people to express constructively during confrontations. Unexpressed anger can be turned inward and become apathy, depression, and guilt, or it can be displaced onto other people and situations. When anger is directly

and skillfully expressed, it leads to more constructive resolution of conflicts than does either not expressing existing anger or indirectly expressing anger. The major guideline for communicating anger constructively is to *focus the anger on the issues and the other person's behavior, not on the other person's character or personality*. As is discussed in chapter 12, when anger is skillfully expressed by both participants in a conflict, it can communicate positively what issues need to be resolved, where commitments are, and where the motivation to resolve the conflict is focused. Remember, focus your anger on issues and conditions that can be changed with reasonable amounts of effort and time, not on the other person. Besides anger, you will also want to express warmth and commitment to the relationship because expressing such feelings lead to better solutions and better maintenance of the relationship than not communicating these feelings does.

3.   *Comprehend fully the other person's views of, and feelings about, the conflict*. The listening skills, such as paraphrasing and negotiating meaning, are vital for effective confrontations. See chapter 4 for a full discussion.

4.   *Do not demand change (unless you are God)*. It is a mistake to demand that the other person change his behavior. Such actions move the conflict resolution procedure from confrontation to forcing. The purpose of the confrontation is to begin negotiating a way to relate more effectively and to resolve a conflict, not to force the other person to change. You may request and negotiate changes in the other's actions, but do not *demand* them.

A confrontation originates from a desire on the part of the person who is confronting to involve herself more deeply with the person being confronted. Confrontation is a way of expressing concern for another person and a wish to increase the mutual involvement in the relationship. You do not confront people with whom you do not intend to increase your involvement.

Besides demonstrating a desire to deepen the relationship, confrontations also communicate a willingness to help the other person increase his interpersonal effectiveness. As was discussed in chapter 2, the effectiveness of our behavior depends in large part on the feedback we receive from other people. Receiving feedback from other people not only provides us with an opportunity to increase our self-awareness, it also helps us determine the consequences of our behavior. The ability to receive feedback is part of the functioning of any healthy, effective individual. It is our capacity for receiving feedback that enables us continually to adjust our behavior and reactions so as to achieve the maximum possible fulfillment in our interpersonal relationships. It is through confronting us with the consequences of our behavior that other people help us grow and develop and increase our interpersonal effectiveness. If we cannot obtain information on the consequences of our behavior, we cannot modify our behavior to make it more effective.

To be effective, a confrontation must be conducted in a way that helps the other person examine the consequences of her behavior rather than causing her to defend her actions. The skills and steps involved in confrontation are (1) the communication of your observation of the other's behavior, (2) your reaction, (3) your interpretation of what the actions mean, (4) a desire to increase your understanding of the other person's behavior in order to increase your involvement, and (5) an understanding of how to minimize the other person's defensiveness. More specifically, the skills involve:

1. The use of personal statements. Personal statements are discussed in chapter 4. The hallmark of a personal statement is the use of the pronouns *I*, *me*, and *my*.

2. The use of relationship statements. Relationship statements are discussed in chapter 4. Relationship statements are those in which you express what you think or feel about the person with whom you are relating.

3. The use of behavior descriptions. Behavior descriptions are discussed in chapter 2. A behavior description is a statement describing the visible behavior of the other person.

4. Direct description of your feelings. This is described in chapter 5. A description of your feelings must be a personal statement and specify some kind of feeling by name, action urge, simile, or other figure of speech.

5. Understanding response. This is described in chapters 4 and 7. It involves paraphrasing the statements made by the other person.

6. Interpretative response. This is described in chapter 7 as well as in the present chapter. To be most helpful an interpretative response should have all the characteristics described on pages 150–155.

7. A perception check of the other person's feelings. This is discussed in chapter 5. In a perception check you state what you perceive to be the feeling of the other person in order to verify that your perception is correct.

8. Constructive feedback skills. These are discussed in chapter 2.

Test your understanding of confrontation by answering true or false to the following statements. Answers are at the end of the chapter.

True   False   1. A true friend is one who ignores your negative behaviors and concentrates on your positive traits.

True   False   2. A confrontation is telling another person how you see and feel about a conflict while asking her to do the same.

True   False   3. The stronger the relationship, the less powerful the confrontation will be.

True   False   4. If your relationship is weak or if the other person isn't able to respond constructively, don't confront.

True   False   5. A confrontation will usually be necessary if there is a conflict, if you want to help the other person grow and develop, or if you wish to keep an effective relationship with him.

True   False   6. Always be sure there is enough time to discuss the conflict before confronting another person.

True   False   7. It is OK to express anger about the other person's personality and character, but not on the issues or the other person's behavior.

True   False   8. When confronting, make sure the other person realizes your concern for him and for your relationship with him.

True   False   9. "You must change!" is an example of a good confronting statement.

True   False   10. "You are rotten for not inviting me to your party, and I hate you for it! Good-bye!" is an example of a hit-and-run confrontation.

How to Respond to a Confrontation

When another person confronts you, there are several guidelines to keep in mind in order to ensure that the confrontation develops into a constructive resolution of the conflict. The guidelines are:

1.   Check to make sure you understand the other person's position.

2.   Check to make sure you understand how the other person feels.

3. Paraphrase the other person's position and feelings.

4. Describe your position and feelings.

EXERCISE 11.1: CONFRONTING THE OPPOSITION

To resolve a conflict constructively, you and the other person have to discuss the conflict and negotiate a solution. For such a discussion to begin, one person must confront the other. Not all conflicts, however, can be successfully negotiated, and there may be times when it is advisable not to confront the opposition. The purpose of this exercise is to give you three specific examples of conflicts so that you can decide what you would do to make sure the conflicts are managed constructively. The procedure for the exercise is:

1. Working by yourself, read the first example of a conflict. Then rank the five alternatives from the best (1) to the worst (5) way to resolve the conflict. In deciding what is the best strategy to use, take into account the following:
    a. What are the person's goals?
    b. How important are the goals to the person?
    c. How important is the relationship to the person?
    d. What is the best way to:
        (1) improve the ability of the two people to relate to each other?
        (2) make their attitudes toward each other more positive?
        (3) reach an agreement that is satisfying to both people?
        (4) improve their ability to resolve future conflicts with each other?
    e. What is the most realistic thing to do?
2. Repeat this process for the second and third examples of conflicts.
3. Form a group of six members. In your group, rank the five alternative courses of action for the first example from the best (1) to the worst (5). Take into account the points listed in item 1.
4. Working as a group, list the interpersonal skills the person needs to discuss the conflict in a constructive way. You may wish to refer to the list of interpersonal skills on pages 286–290.
5. Repeat this procedure for the second and third examples.
6. Be prepared to report to the other groups the following:
    a. In what order did the group rank the five alternatives for each conflict example?
    b. What reasons does your group have for your ranking?
    c. What interpersonal skills are needed for a constructive discussion of the conflict?

Mr. Smith

You are a salesperson for a tire company. You work under a highly emotional sales manager, with whom you have a formal relationship. He calls you by your first name, but you call him "Mr. Smith." When he gets upset, he becomes angry and abusive. He browbeats you and your coworkers, and makes insulting remarks and judgments. These rages occur approximately once a week and last for about an hour. Most of the time, Mr. Smith is distant and inoffensive. He will tolerate no back-talk at any time. So far, you and your coworkers have suffered in silence during his outbursts. Jobs are scarce, and you have a spouse and a seven-month-old son to support. But you feel like a doormat and really do not like what Mr. Smith says when he is angry. The situation is making you irritable. Your anger at Mr. Smith is causing you to lose your temper more and more with your coworkers and family. Today he starts in again, and you have had it!

Rank the following five courses of action from 1 to 5. Put a 1 by the course of action that seems most likely to lead to beneficial results. Put a 2 by the next most constructive course of action and so forth. Be realistic!

_____   I try to avoid Mr. Smith. I am silent whenever we are together. I show a lack of interest whenever we speak. I want nothing to do with him for the time being. I try to cool down while I stay away from him. I try never to mention anything that might get him angry.

_____   I lay it on the line. I tell Mr. Smith I am fed up with his abuse. I tell him he is vicious and unfair. And I tell him he had better start controlling his feelings and statements because I'm not going to take being insulted by him any more! Whether he likes it or not he has to shape up. I'm going to make him stop or else I'll quit.

_____   I bite my tongue. I keep my feelings to myself. I hope that he will find out how his actions are hurting our department without my telling him. My anger toward him frightens me. So I force it out of my mind. I try to be friendly, and I try to do nice things for him so he won't treat me this way. If I tried to tell him how I feel, he would only be angry and abuse me more.

_____   I try to bargain with him. I tell him that if he stops abusing me I will increase my sales effort. I seek a compromise that will stop his actions. I try to think of what I can do for him that will be worth it to him to change his actions. I tell him that other people get upset with his actions. I try to persuade him to agree to stop abusing me in return for something I can do for him.

_____   I call attention to the conflict between us. I describe how I see his actions. I describe my angry and upset feelings. I try to begin a discussion in which we can look for a way to reduce (1) his rages and (2) my resentment. I try to see things from his viewpoint. I seek a solution that allows him to blow off steam without being abusive to me. I try to figure out what I'm telling myself about his actions that is causing me to feel angry and upset. I ask him how he feels about my giving him feedback.

Ralph Overtrain

You work as a computer technician repairing computers. You make service calls to the customers of your company. Ralph Overtrain is one of your closest coworkers. He does the same type of work that you do. The two of you are often assigned to work together on large repair projects. You are married and have two children. Ralph is single and often has trouble with his girl friend. For the past several weeks, he has asked you to do part of his repair work because he feels too depressed and upset to concentrate on his work. You have agreed to such requests. Your wife is sick now, and you want to take some time off to visit her in the hospital. You ask Ralph if he would do part of your repair work so you can slip away and visit your wife. He refuses, saying that he is too busy and that it is your work, so you should do it. He says he sees no reason why he should do work you are getting paid for. You get more and more angry at Ralph. You see his actions as being completely selfish and ungrateful!

Rank the following five courses of action from 1 to 5. Put a 1 by the course of action that seems most likely to lead to beneficial results. Put a 2 by the next most constructive course of action, and so forth. Be realistic!

_____ I try to avoid Ralph. I am silent whenever we are together. I show a lack of interest whenever we speak. I want nothing to do with him for the time being. I try to cool down while I stay away from him. I try never to mention anything that might make him angry or remind me of his ungratefulness.

_____ I lay it on the line. I tell Ralph that I am fed up with his ungratefulness. I tell him he is selfish and a deadbeat. And I tell him he had better start paying back the favors I have done for him because I am not going to help him if he will not help me. Whether he likes it or not, he is going to do part of my work so I can visit my wife. I'm going to make him pay his debts to me.

_____ I bite my tongue. I keep my feelings to myself. I hope he will find out his behavior is wrong without my having to tell him. My anger toward him frightens me. So I force it out of my mind and try to be friendly. I try to do nice things for him so he will be willing to do a favor for me in the future when I need him to. If I tried to tell him how I feel, he would only be angry. Then he would be less likely to do me favors when I need him to in the future.

_____ I try to bargain with him. I tell him that if he does my work this time, I will do part of his work tomorrow. I seek a compromise that will allow me to visit my wife. I try to think of what I can do for him that will be worth it to him to take part of my work today. I tell him that other people don't see him as being reasonable and friendly. I try to persuade him to agree to take part of my work today in return for something I can do for him.

_____ I call attention to the conflict between us. I describe how I see his actions. I describe my angry and upset feelings. I try to begin a discussion in which we can look for a way to be more cooperative regarding each other's needs and to reduce my anger. I try to see things from his viewpoint. I seek a solution that allows him to feel he is only doing his work while at the same time allows me to visit my wife in the hospital. I try to figure out what I'm telling myself about his actions that is causing me to feel angry and upset. I ask him how he feels about my giving him feedback.

Donna Jones

In your upper-grade class this year, you have a student, Donna Jones, who seems to dislike you and everything about school. When you are interacting with her you can feel the resentment. She never seems to do anything overtly, but other students have reported incidences of Donna's making faces behind your back and making rude remarks about you and your assignments outside of class. On the morning of the math test, Donna has just dropped her papers on the floor for the third time and is disrupting the work of the other students. You have had enough, so you approach Donna and tell her to keep her papers on her desk, as she is interrupting the work of other students. As you turn to walk away, you notice grins on the faces of several students in front of you, and out of the corner of your eye you see Donna standing up and mimicking you behind your back.

Rank the five alternatives. Be realistic!

_____ I would ignore Donna and go back to my desk. I would arrange a way to seat her away from most of the other students and try to avoid any contact with her unless absolutely necessary. I would avoid any situation that could lead to conflict and hope that she changes as a result.

_____ I would turn around and "nail her" in the act. I'd tell her that I was fed up with her attitude and that it is time to shape up or ship out. If she's not able to work well in the classroom, she may find the principal's office more to her liking. Being firm and laying it on the line will change her behavior in a hurry.

_____ I would ignore Donna for the present, as I want to win her over to my side. Later I'd engage her in friendly conversation, find out what her hobbies are and about any pets she might have, establishing friendly feelings between us. She would then try harder on the tasks and not disrupt the class by ridiculing me anymore.

_____ I would take her up to my desk immediately and make a bargain with her that if she will stop disrupting the class and try to do the work, I'll let her be recess monitor for the week (something she has wanted to do for some time). I would continue to look for ways to trade off things she wanted to do for appropriate behavior in class.

_____ I would take her up to my desk and call attention to the conflict between us by describing how I saw her behavior and telling her that it makes me angry and upset. I'd explain what the problem is from my perspective and its effect on the other students and discuss possible solutions. I would ask for her perception of the conflict and what her feelings are, and I would keep discussing the situation until we had a solution that we both liked.

EXERCISE 11.2: ROLE PLAYING THE CONFLICTS

Now that you have discussed the three examples of conflicts, it may be helpful to role play them. The purpose of this exercise is to role play the entire negotiation of a solution of the conflict between the two people. The procedure is:

1. Form groups of six. Take the first conflict, between the salesperson and Mr. Smith. One member should volunteer to play the part of each character. There are three conflict episodes, so each group member will play one role during the three role-playing episodes.
2. Spend up to ten minutes role playing the conflict. Begin with the initiation of

the strategy chosen by the group to be the most effective and continue through the entire negotiation of a solution to the conflict. The group members who are not playing a role observe in order to discuss the effectiveness of the person's actions in resolving the conflict.

3. In the group of six, discuss the role-playing episode:
   a. What were the strategies used to manage the conflict constructively?
   b. What interpersonal skills were used?
   c. What interpersonal skills were not used but might have been helpful?
   d. What changes in strategies would you make if you actually were in this situation?
4. Repeat this procedure for the second and third examples of conflicts.
5. What conclusions can your group make about managing conflicts on the basis of your role playing? Be ready to share your conclusions with the other groups.

Using Each Conflict Strategy Appropriately

Confronting another person is like going swimming in a cold lake. Some people like to test the water, stick their foot in, and enter slowly. They want to get used to the cold gradually. Other people like to take a running start and leap in. They want to get the cold shock over quickly. Whether you begin slowly or leap in, you have to confront the other person to negotiate a solution to a conflict.

Confrontation followed by negotiation is not the only way to manage conflicts. The conflict strategy you adopt will depend on how important it is to you to achieve your personal goals and maintain a good relationship with the other person. Each conflict strategy has its place. You need to be able to withdraw, force, smooth, compromise, or confront depending on your goals and the relationship. It is not a good idea to act the same way in every conflict. In some conflicts you may wish to use one strategy, and in other conflicts you may wish to use another. To be truly skilled in conflict management, you need to be competent in all five strategies and be able to vary your behavior according to the person and the situation. You do not want to be an overspecialized dinosaur who can deal with conflict in only one way.

When do you use each conflict strategy? Here are some guidelines:

1. When the goal is not important, and you do not need to keep a relationship with the other person, you may wish to withdraw. Avoiding a hostile stranger in the lunchroom or a bar may be the most effective strategy to adopt.

2. When the goal is very important to you, but the relationship is not, you may wish to force. When buying a used car or trying to get into a crowded restaurant, you may want to imitate a shark.

3. When the goal is of no importance to you, but the relationship is of

high importance, you may wish to smooth things over. When a friend feels strongly about something and you couldn't care less, being a Teddy Bear is a good idea.

4.   When both the goal and the relationship are of moderate importance, and it appears that both you and the other person cannot get what you want, then you may wish to bargain and compromise. When there is a limited amount of money, and both you and a fellow employee want a large raise, negotiating a compromise may be the best way to resolve the conflict.

5.   When both the goal and the relationship are highly important to you, you will want to confront.

In most conflicts, you will want to confront and smooth as these are the two most effective strategies. When the goal is important, confront, and when the goal is unimportant to you, smooth. Both of these strategies maintain good relationships. Compromising is usually only a good idea if you have limited time and cannot negotiate a mutually satisfying solution to the conflict. But remember, ideally you will be skilled in all five strategies and can use each, depending on the other person and the situation.

STEP 2 IN RESOLVING A CONFLICT: A COMMON DEFINITION

Once the confrontation has taken place, the next step in the discussion is to arrive at a mutually agreeable definition of the conflict. It is important that the conflict be defined in a way that does not make either you or the other person defensive. In building a mutual definition, follow the same rules you used in arriving at your definition of the conflict (see chapter 10).

1.   Describe each other's actions without labeling or insulting each other.

2.   Define the conflict as a mutual problem to be solved, not as a win-lose struggle.

3.   Define the conflict in the most limited and specific way possible.

4.   Describe your feelings and the feelings of the other person.

5.   Describe the actions of both yourself and the other person that help create and continue the conflict.

How the conflict is defined will affect the ease with which the conflict can be resolved. A careful, constructive definition will make any conflict easy to resolve.

STEP 3:
COMMUNICATING POSITIONS AND FEELINGS

Throughout negotiations, positions on the issues being negotiated and feelings about them may change. Thus, good communication skills will continually be necessary. An important aspect of communicating positions in negotiations is to understand what you are disagreeing about. If you do not know what you are disagreeing about, you will not be able to think of ways to combine ideas so that the conflict is resolved. Your ability to come up with satisfactory solutions depends on your understanding how the other person's thoughts, feelings, and needs are different from yours. Thus, in discussing a conflict you try to answer such questions as:

1. What are the disagreements and differences between myself and the other person?
2. What do we agree on?
3. What actions of the other person do I find unacceptable?
4. What actions of mine does the other person find unacceptable?
5. What are possible solutions that satisfy both myself and the other person?
6. What are the things I need to do to resolve the conflict?
7. What are the things the other person needs to do to resolve the conflict?

STEP 4:
COMMUNICATING COOPERATIVE INTENTIONS

The clear and direct expression of cooperative intentions helps to reach an agreement in problem-solving negotiations as well as to build a better relationship between you and the other person. It is a good idea, therefore, to communicate clearly your cooperative motivations and intentions during negotiations.

STEP 5:
TAKING THE OTHER'S PERSPECTIVE

Resolving conflicts constructively requires that you understand the other person's thoughts, feelings, and needs. To achieve such understanding, you use good listening skills and try to view the conflict from the other

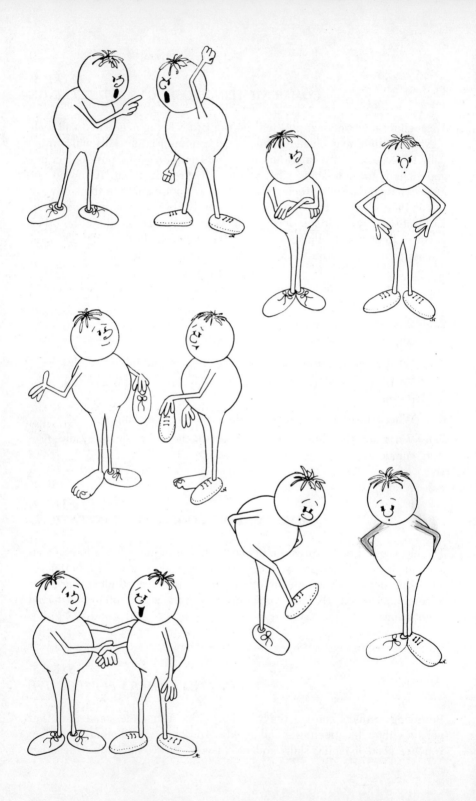

person's shoes. To understand fully the other person's position and feelings, you need to be able to view the conflict from the other person's perspective. Different people have different perspectives. No two people will see a conflict in exactly the same way. Each person will interpret the same event differently. To resolve a conflict constructively, you need to keep in mind both your own perspective and the perspective of the other person.

Role playing is an easy way to increase your understanding of another person's perspective. By trying to present the other person's position and feelings as if you were the other person, you can gain insight into the other person's perspective. When you and a friend are having a conflict, try presenting your friend's position as if you were he or she. Then have your friend present your position as if he or she were you. The more involved you get in arguing each other's positions, the more you will understand how the conflict appears from the other person's perspective, and therefore the more you will be able to find solutions that are mutually acceptable.

There is nothing more important in resolving conflicts than understanding how the other person views the conflict. Once you can view the conflict from both your own and the other person's perspective, you can find solutions that satisfy both you and the other person. You can also communicate to the other person that you really understand her position and feelings. It is usually much easier to resolve a conflict when the other person feels understood. The more skilled you are in seeing things from other people's shoes, the more skilled you will be in resolving conflicts constructively.

STEP 6:
COORDINATING THE MOTIVATION TO NEGOTIATE

There are often differences in motivation to resolve a conflict. You may wish to resolve the conflict, but your friend couldn't care less. Your friend may be very concerned about resolving the conflict, but you may want to avoid the whole thing. Today you may wish to resolve the conflict but your friend does not. Tomorrow the situation may be reversed. Usually conflicts cannot be resolved until both persons are motivated to resolve them at the same time.

The motivation to resolve a conflict is based on the perceived costs and gains of continuing the conflict for each person. The *costs* of continuing a conflict may be the loss of a friendship, enjoyment from work, salary or promotion, or family. The *gains* for continuing the conflict may be satisfaction in expressing your anger or resentment and the protection of the status quo. By protecting the status quo, you avoid the possibility that things will get worse when the conflict is resolved. Answering the following questions will often help you clarify your motivation and the motivation of the other person to resolve the conflict:

1. What do I gain from continuing the conflict?
2. What does the other person gain from continuing the conflict?
3. What do I lose from continuing the conflict?
4. What does the other person lose from continuing the conflict?

A person's motivation to resolve a conflict can be changed. By increasing the costs of continuing the conflict or by increasing the gains for resolving it, the other person's motivation to resolve it can be increased. Through changing costs and gains, you can change your own motivation to resolve the conflict and also the other person's.

STEP 7:
REACHING AN AGREEMENT

The conflict ends when you and the other person reach an agreement. All parties need to be satisfied with the agreement and committed to abiding by it. The agreement should specify:

1. The joint position being adopted.
2. The ways in which you will act differently in the future.
3. The ways in which the other person will act differently in the future.
4. The ways in which cooperation will be restored if one person slips and acts inappropriately.
5. The times the two of you will meet to discuss your relationship and to see if further steps can be taken to improve your cooperation with each other.

It is important that both you and the other person understand which actions trigger anger and resentment in the other. Criticism, put-downs, sarcasm, belittling, and other actions often trigger a conflict. If the two of you understand what *not* to do as well as what to do, the conflict will be resolved more easily.

Test your understanding of the steps for resolving a conflict by taking the following quiz. Answers are at the end of the chapter.

1. Match the conflict strategy with the best situation for using it:

____ Goal and relationship very important	**a.**	Withdraw
____ Goal and relationship moderately important	**b.**	Force
____ Goal and relationship not important	**c.**	Smooth
____ Goal important, relationship not important	**d.**	Compromise
____ Goal not important, relationship important	**e.**	Confront

True   False   **2.** It is a good idea to act the same way in every conflict.

True   False   **3.** The conflict strategy you adopt will depend on how important it is to you to maintain a good relationship with the other person and to achieve your personal goals.

True   False   **4.** The two most effective conflict strategies are confronting and compromising.

True   False   **5.** Defining the conflict carefully and constructively will make it easier to resolve.

True   False   **6.** Your ability to come up with satisfactory solutions depends on how well you understand how the other person's thoughts, feelings, and needs are different from yours.

True   False   **7.** The important thing about viewing the conflict from the other person's perspective is that you can see how to get her to agree to your point of view.

True   False   **8.** If the other person feels understood, he will not try to see your point of view.

True   False   **9.** By increasing the costs of continuing the conflict or by increasing the gains for resolving it, the motivation to resolve the conflict can be increased.

True   False   **10.** A conflict agreement should specify a joint position, future changed behaviors, and plans for dealing with behavior slips and for continuing the relationship.

EXERCISE 11.3: FEELINGS IN CONFLICTS

A basic aspect of any conflict is the feelings a person has while the conflict is taking place. Two common feelings are rejection and distrust. Many people are afraid of conflicts because they are afraid they will be rejected. And many people avoid conflicts because they do not trust the other person. The purposes of this exercise are to experience the feelings of rejection and distrust and to discuss how they influence your actions in conflicts. The procedure is:

Part 1: Rejection

1. Form into groups of four.
2. Pass out the instructions (Appendix, p. 299) to each member of your group. The group has ten minutes to select one person to be rejected and excluded from the group.
3. Combine two groups of four into a group of eight. Discuss the following questions:
    a. Did you feel rejected by the other members of your group of four?
    b. What is it like to feel rejected? What other feelings result from being rejected?
    c. How do you act when someone is rejecting you?
    d. When you are in a conflict, how can you act to minimize feelings of rejection on both your part and the part of the other person?

Part 2: Distrust

1. Form pairs.
2. Give each member of the pair an instruction sheet (Appendix, p. 300). Your pair has five minutes to interact after you have both read the instructions.
3. Combine three pairs into a group of six and discuss these questions:
    a. Did you feel distrusted by the other member of your pair?
    b. Did you distrust the other member of your pair?
    c. How do you act when someone distrusts you?
    d. What is it like to feel distrusted? What other feelings result from being distrusted?
    e. When you are in a conflict, how can you minimize the feelings of distrust on both your part and on the part of the other person?
4. Be prepared to share with other groups your conclusions about how to minimize rejection and distrust.

EXERCISE 11.4: RESOLVING CONFLICTS: A CHECKLIST

____ **1.** I clarify my goals and the degree to which I want to maintain the relationship. This helps me plan the most appropriate conflict strategy.

____ **2.** I am aware of my habitual ways of dealing with conflict, and I am on the lookout for self-defeating and ineffective patterns of behavior.

____ **3.** I have defined the conflict by myself, making sure I:
   a. described the other person's actions without labeling, accusing, or insulting the person, so that the conflict is over issues and actions, not personalities;
   b. defined the conflict as a mutual problem to be solved, not as a win-lose struggle;
   c. defined the conflict in the most limited and specific way possible;
   d. described my feelings about, and reactions to, the other person's actions; and
   e. described actions of mine (what I am doing and neglecting to do) that helps create and continue the conflict.

____ **4.** Given that I wish to both achieve my goals and maintain the relationship in good condition, I *confront* the other person, making sure that:
   a. I do not "hit-and-run" but rather confront at an appropriate time when the conflict can be fruitfully discussed;
   b. I openly communicate my perceptions of, and feelings about, the issues, focusing on the issues, not on the other person;
   c. I communicate that I fully understand the other person's views of, and feelings about, the conflict;
   d. I do not demand that the other person change.

____ **5.** I negotiate a joint definition of the conflict, making sure the joint definition meets the criteria for a constructive definition.

____ **6.** I communicate any changes in my position and feelings, making sure I understand the differences between my views of the conflict and the other person's views.

____ **7.** I communicate that I sincerely wish to resolve the conflict cooperatively so that both the other person and I will get what we want and the quality of our relationship is maintained or even strengthened.

____ **8.** I take the other person's perspective accurately and fully, making sure I understand it and that the other person knows I understand his or her perspective.

____ **9.** I coordinate motivation to negotiate in good faith by highlighting the costs of continuing the conflict and the gains for resolving it.

____ **10.** I make sure that the agreement is satisfactory to both parties and that it clearly specifies:
   a. the agreement
   b. the ways in which each person will act differently in the future
   c. the ways cooperation will be restored if one of us slips and acts inappropriately
   d. when future meetings will be held to check how well the agreement is working

Test your understanding of confrontation and negotiation by answering true or false to the following statements. Answers are at the end of the chapter.

True   False   1. Use confrontation when you want to solve a conflict, the relationship is strong, and the other person can respond constructively.

True   False   2. In confronting, you need to communicate your observation of the other person's behavior, your reaction, your interpretation, and your desire to understand the other person.

True   False   3. In confronting, it is important that you make your point and come out on top.

True   False   4. Two useful communication skills in confrontations are personal statements and the hit-and-run technique.

True   False   5. Confrontation should be used in almost all conflict situations.

True   False   6. Defining the conflict is a major part of confrontation and will help resolve the conflict.

True   False   7. Taking the other person's perspective will help you find mutually acceptable solutions to the conflict.

True   False   8. Many people avoid conflict because of fear they will be rejected.

True   False   9. You should avoid any expression of anger in a confrontation.

True   False   10. "I am upset about what you are doing and I'd like to talk to you about it" is a good confronting statement.

Indicate which skills you have mastered and which you still need work on.

1.   I have mastered the following:
    ____ Knowing when to confront
    ____ Knowing what to say when confronting
    ____ Knowing what to avoid when confronting
    ____ Knowing how to build a mutually agreeable definition of the conflict

____ Knowing how to take the other person's perspective
____ Knowing how to negotiate a solution to the conflict
____ Knowing how to follow up on negotiated agreements

2.   I need more work on:
____ Knowing when to confront
____ Knowing what to say when confronting
____ Knowing what to avoid when confronting
____ Knowing how to build a mutually agreeable definition of the conflict
____ Knowing how to take the other person's perspective
____ Knowing how to negotiate a solution to the conflict
____ Knowing how to follow up on negotiated agreements

By now, you have learned when and how to use confrontation as a way of resolving conflicts. The following chapter will follow up by giving you ways of dealing with anger and stress, helping you to manage your feelings better.

ANSWERS:

Comprehension Test A: 1. false; 2. true; 3. false; 4. true; 5. true; 6. true; 7. false; 8. true; 9. false; 10. true.

Comprehension Test B: 1. e, d, a, b, c; 2. false; 3. true; 4. false; 5. true; 6. true; 7. false; 8. false; 9. true; 10. true.

Chapter Review: 1. true; 2. true; 3. false; 4. false; 5. false; 6. true; 7. true; 8. true; 9. false; 10. true.

12

Anger, Stress, and Managing Your Feelings

WE ARE ALL CHILDREN OF NATURE

We are always under some stress, as long as we are alive. Sometimes the stress is small—when we are asleep, for instance—and sometimes the stress is large—for instance, when we are being attacked by muggers. But as long as we are alive, we are experiencing stress. Stress cannot be avoided, and our stress level is never at zero.

Besides the fact that stress is unavoidable, there are several aspects of stress that you should understand. One is that both too high and too low a stress level is damaging. If we experience too high a level of stress for too long, physiological problems such as headaches, ulcers, and muscle pains can develop. But boredom can make us just as sick as high distress. A certain amount of stress is necessary for meeting the challenges of our lives and for providing the energy required to maintain life, resist aggression, and adapt to constantly changing external influences.

Another important aspect of stress is that the human body reacts to stress in a stereotyped, physiological way. Stress results in an emergency discharge of adrenalin and corresponding changes in the hypothalamus, pituitary, and thymus. Briefly, the autonomic nervous system and the endocrine system combine to speed up cardiovascular functions and slow down gastrointestinal functions. This equips us to take physical action to restore the situation and our internal physiological state to normal. It really

doesn't matter whether we are reacting with great joy or great fear, our physiological response is the same. To understand stress fully, homeostasis must first be understood. *Homeostasis* is the ability to stay the same. The internal environment of our bodies (our temperature, pulse rate, blood pressure, and so forth) must stay fairly constant, despite changes in the external environment, or else we will become sick and even die. Stress alerts our bodies that action is needed to adapt to the external environment by changing our internal environment. The body then strives to restore homeostasis. *Stress,* therefore, can be defined as a nonspecific, general response of the body, signaling a need to perform adaptive functions so that normalcy or homeostasis can be restored.

Humans, as a species, are stress seeking. We seem to long for new experiences and new challenges. Traveling to the North Pole, climbing mountains, living in deserts, and exploring the bottom of the oceans are all activities for which we are biologically and socially ill-adapted, but we do them anyway. Humans seek out certain types of stress and enjoy it.

Emotions are always involved in stressful situations, and one of the most common emotions in stressful interpersonal situations is anger. When other people obstruct your goal accomplishment, frustrate your attempts to accomplish something, interfere with your plans, make you feel belittled and rejected, or indicate that you are of no value or importance, then you get angry and stress appears in your life. It is when other people get angry at you that anxiety, fear, and concern is felt, and stress occurs. Most of our stress originates from interaction with other people.

When other people create stress in your life and make you angry, the results can be either destructive or constructive. If the results are destructive, your anger can be expressed in a way that creates dislike, hatred, frustration, and a desire for revenge on the part of the other person, or it can be repressed and held in, creating irritability, depression, insomnia, and physiological problems, such as headaches and ulcers, for you. If the results are constructive, you will feel more energy, motivation, challenge, and excitement, and the other person will feel friendship, gratitude, goodwill, and concern. In this chapter we shall examine anger in some depth and discuss how it can be managed so that constructive rather than destructive results occur. Anger as a source of stress will be discussed first, and a set of rules for constructively expressing anger will then be outlined. Then the specific skills involved in expressing anger constructively and being assertive in expressing anger are covered. Finally, the chapter deals with managing feelings constructively, and there are a number of exercises aimed at improving your skills in expressing anger and managing your feelings.

ANGER AS A SOURCE OF STRESS

Anger both causes and accompanies distress. Anger can result in tight muscles, teeth grinding, piercing stares, headaches, heart attacks, loud voices, projectiles, and smashed furniture. When we are angry our blood boils, we are fit to be tied, we have reached the end of our rope, and what

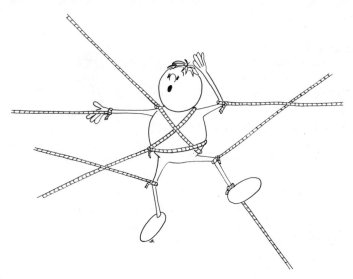

happened is the last straw. Anger is an emotion that occurs regularly in the life of every person, more often and with greater intensity at some times than at others. Failure to manage anger constructively can lead to alienation of loved ones, disrupted work performance, and even cardiovascular disorder. However, proper recognition, understanding, acceptance, and channeling of anger can make life more comfortable, productive, and exciting. In order for anger to be managed constructively, its components must be identified, and its major functions must be understood. The useful and constructive aspects of anger must be promoted while the destructive and useless aspects of anger are quelled. Rules for constructive anger management must be followed.

There are three main components involved in most human anger. First, anger is usually a defense against something. Second, anger occurs when we are not getting something we want or would like. We get angry when we are frustrated, thwarted, or attacked. Third, anger has in it a sense of righteousness and a belief that one's personal rights have been violated. When we are angry, we usually believe that we are rightfully angry because the other person has acted unjustly or irrationally. When we plan how to manage our anger constructively, we need to keep in mind that anger is a righteous but defensive reaction to frustration and aggression.

There are at least eight major functions of anger. Each is described briefly below.

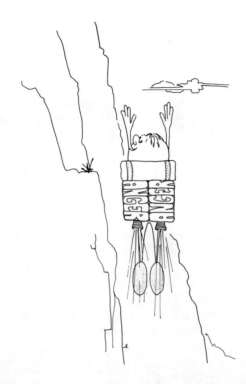

1. Anger provides energy and increases the vigor with which we act. Anger helps us to move toward action and to utilize the energy provided by the physiological stress reaction for productive activity. Anger mobilizes us for action and thereby provides considerable physical energy to apply toward achieving our goals.

2. Anger disrupts ongoing behavior by agitation, impulsivity, and interference with attention and information processing. Anger disrupts behavior, causing people to focus continually on the injustice that has been done to them or on the attack they are defending against rather than on tasks at hand or on receiving new information. It often causes us to act impulsively in ways aimed at correcting the perceived injustice or defending against the perceived aggressive actions of the other person.

3. Anger facilitates the expression of negative feelings and negative feedback, which might not be expressed if we were not angry. The constructive aspect of such communication is that it provides information we need for accurate identification of problems and high-qual-

ity decision making. Anger is a sign that something is going on that needs to be changed. It is only through facing such problems that they can be solved. Being angry and confronting another person in a way that leads to problem solving increases the trust within the relationship and increases confidence that the relationship is strong enough to handle future strains. Healthy relationships depend on the ability of both partners to give accurate but negative feedback to each other, and anger helps us do so. But the potential negative aspect of such forthrightness is that the strength of the negative feelings or feedback may be inappropriate to the provocation, may be overstated, or may be stated in such an offensive and threatening way that the conflict is escalated and the other person becomes fearful and angry.

4. Anger is a defense against vulnerability. It changes internal anxiety to external conflict. Anger can overcome anxiety and fear and encourage us to take actions we would never take otherwise. A small child may strike out in anger against a much bigger peer. A subordinate may confront a boss she is afraid of. A very shy person when angry may introduce herself to strangers. Such actions can be highly constructive or destructive, depending on the circumstances.

5. Anger initiates or strengthens antagonism as an internal, learned stimulus for aggression. Feeling angry can be a signal that aggressive actions are called for. Many times we become aggressive through habit when faced with a provocation and strike out verbally or physically at the other people in the situation.

6. Anger can be a signal that an event is a provocation or that something frustrating or unpleasant is taking place. Discovering that we are angry can help clarify or discriminate what is taking place within a situation.

7. Anger helps us maintain a sense of virtue and righteousness in the face of opposition. Anger helps us maintain a belief that we are right, justified, and superior.

8. Anger can intimidate other people and is therefore a source of interpersonal power and influence. When we want to overpower another person, get our way, or dominate a situation, being angry can often help us do so.

Being angry at another person can be an unpleasant experience. We can make the other person resentful and hostile when we express anger. We can become anxious after we have expressed anger as we anticipate rejection, counter-anger, and escalation of the conflict. Yet anger can have many positive effects on our problem solving if we learn to manage it constructively.

POINTS TO REMEMBER

1. When two people avoid discussing an issue, the issue will reappear in a different form. You cannot avoid conflicts. Open discussion of conflicts is the best way.

2. Being angry and upset, refusing to listen, and being defensive, while often justified, do not help resolve conflicts. They do not help the relationship continue and get stronger.

3. Feelings that are ignored or denied will come out later in one way or another. You must build healthy habits of managing your feelings.

COMPREHENSION TEST A

Test your understanding of stress and anger by answering true or false to the following statements. Answers are at the end of the chapter.

True	False	1. We are under stress only when we are angry.
True	False	2. Very high stress is damaging, but very low stress is beneficial.
True	False	3. The body reacts to stress by slowing down the heart and speeding up the digestion.
True	False	4. Most of our stress originates from interaction with other people.
True	False	5. Repressing anger can cause insomnia, headaches, and ulcers.
True	False	6. Although anger gives us energy, it disrupts our ongoing behavior.
True	False	7. Anger changes our internal anxiety into external conflict.
True	False	8. Feelings of anger are a signal that something frustrating or upleasant is taking place that you need to be aware of.

True	False	9. If you avoid discussing an issue, it will appear later in a different form.
True	False	10. "You are two days late for our date, and I'm feeling angry" is a more constructive expression of anger than "I'm going to cream you for being late."

RULES FOR MANAGING ANGER CONSTRUCTIVELY

In managing your anger constructively, there is a set of rules to follow. *The first rule in managing anger is to recognize and acknowledge the fact that you are angry.* Anger is a natural, healthy, nonevil human feeling. Everyone feels it. You need not fear or reject your anger. For one thing, repressed, denied anger does not vanish but often erupts suddenly in verbal and physical assaults on people and property as well as overreactions to minor provocations. In addition, repression and denial of your anger can create headaches, ulcers, muscle pains, and other physiological ailments. Remember that anger and aggression are not the same thing. You can express anger without being aggressive.

The second rule is to decide whether or not you wish to express your anger. Usually it is better to keep your life clear, dealing with issues and provocations when they arise and when you feel angry, not after days or weeks of being upset. It is a good idea *not* to take flight by avoiding the person or situation, thus waiting and letting resentment and hostility build up. But there are times when avoidance may be the most effective action to take. When the expression of anger will be ineffective or destructive, you need to be able to switch to a more productive and suitable pattern of behavior.

The third rule is to have ways of responding to provocations other than anger or depression. One alternative is relaxation. Learn to relax when you wish so that you can relax yourself when your anger has been triggered. As you learn to relax more easily, your ability to regulate your anger will improve. Another alternative is to change the way you view the provocation, thereby changing your feeling of anger. Through modifying your interpretations of what the other person's behavior means, you can control your feelings, responding with amusement or indifference rather than with anger. This skill is discussed at length later in this chapter. By learning alternative ways of reacting to provocations, you will be able to choose the most effective response. Such freedom gives you an advantage in situations in which other people are trying to provoke you, as the best way to take charge of such a situation is *not* to get angry when most people would expect or even want you to do so.

The fourth rule is to express your anger directly and effectively when it is appropriate to do so. There are several advantages to expressing anger directly. Anger conveys to other people what your commitments are and which commitments must be respected or changed. Expressing anger can clear the air so that positive feelings can once again be felt and expressed. Keeping feelings hidden usually causes problems in the relationship in the future as well as creating physical discomfort in the person repressing and hiding them. So it is less expensive in the long run for you and your friends if you express anger directly when it is appropriate to do so. If you repeatedly fail to express anger in words, you may give the impression that you don't care. Also, concealed anger is often displaced onto other people, so that members of your family may suffer because you displace anger at a friend onto them.

There are guidelines to keep in mind in expressing your anger directly. The *first* is to make the expression cathartic. *Catharsis* refers to the feeling of release of pent-up emotion that people experience either by talking about their troubles or by crying, laughing, shouting, or otherwise engaging in very active emotional release. Anger needs to be expressed in a way that terminates it and gets it over and done with. Anger is *not* a feeling to hold on to. If you have expressed it correctly, you should no longer feel angry afterwards.

A *second* guideline for the direct and constructive expression of anger is to ask for clarification before responding when someone has done something that you feel is aggressive or provocative in nature. Do not assume that aggression was intended without checking it out. It may be a misunderstanding, and you have nothing to be angry about.

A *third* guideline is to express your anger to the appropriate person and make it to the point. Do not generalize. Be specific about the provocation. "When you do such and such, it makes me feel angry."

A *fourth* guideline is to recognize that by expressing your anger you are taking responsibility for your feelings, and therefore (a) *you* got angry at what happened—the other person did not "make" you angry (this is discussed later in this chapter)—and (b) you are willing to become more involved with the other person and the situation as your anger becomes clarified.

A *fifth* guideline is to remember that heightened anger makes you agitated and impulsive, and that impulsive, antagonistic acts can escalate conflict and get you into trouble. Your information-processing capacity will also decrease as your anger increases, making your analysis of what actions are needed somewhat suspect.

The *sixth* guideline is to beware of the righteousness of your anger. In most situations it is not a matter of punishing people you think have acted in an unjust way, it is a matter of ensuring that a constructive outcome results from the situation. Do not attempt to prove you were right or that you are morally superior. Try to solve the problem and manage the situation constructively.

The *seventh* guideline is that you can control and contain your anger and usually be far more effective in managing the situation by staying *task oriented*. This means staying focused on what must be done in the situation to get the outcome you want. Taking insults personally distracts you from your task and involves you in unnecessary conflict. Do not let yourself get sidetracked or baited into a quarrel. Recognize what the other person is doing, but do not be provoked by it; rather, stay task oriented and focused on the issue. There is evidence that anger directed toward a person will be far more destructive than will anger directed toward an issue. Viewing an incident as a personal affront is likely to result in disruptive and defensive anger, while viewing an incident as a problem to be solved is likely to result in discriminative, expressive, and energizing anger.

The *eighth* guideline is to take into account the impact your anger will have on the other person. While you will usually feel better after expressing anger constructively and directly to another person, the other person may feel alienated and resentful. After expressing anger directly, it is important to make sure that the other person has a chance to respond and clarify his or her feelings before the interaction is ended.

The *ninth* guideline is to use the skills of accurate communication and constructive feedback discussed in chapters 2, 4, 5, and 6 of this book. Nonverbal messages are more powerful in expressing feelings than are words, but they are also more difficult to understand. To communicate your anger clearly, you need to be skilled in both verbal and nonverbal communication, and you need to be able to make your words and nonverbal messages congruent with each other. Make the statement of your anger descriptive, accurate, and to the point, and express it to the appropriate person. Keep in touch with yourself and say it all. State the anger directly without being sarcastic. Use honest, expressive language and avoid name calling, accusations, put-downs, and physical attacks.

The *tenth* guideline is to express positive feelings as well as your anger while discussing the situation. Besides being angry, you may have genuine respect and liking or some other positive emotion for the other person. While discussing your anger, it is often helpful to express your positive feelings as well.

The fifth rule for managing your anger constructively is to express it indirectly when direct expression is not appropriate and when the anger cannot be avoided. Feelings do need to be expressed. The stronger the feeling, the stronger the need for expression. In privacy you can swear at your boss, hit a punching bag, or swim hard while imagining what you would like to say to a certain acquaintance. There may be many times when you cannot express your anger directly to the people provoking you. Yet it is important to express your anger in a way that ends it. You do not want to stay angry forever. The sooner you get rid of the feelings, the happier your life will be. Expressing and terminating anger indirectly usually involves the following:

1. There is a general maxim that when one is angry and wants to feel better tomorrow, then one should exercise today. Vigorous exercise like jogging, swimming, tennis, or volleyball provides physical release of energy that is important in releasing anger.

2. Strongly express the feeling in private by shouting, swearing, crying, moaning, throwing pottery, pillow fights, and even hitting a pillow against a wall while yelling. This will provide a physical release of energy and anger.

3. Resolve the situation in your mind or resign yourself to it. Tell yourself things that can help. Give up thoughts of revenge and getting back at other people. You want to resolve the problems. You can put up with an unfair boss. An obnoxious coworker is not really that bad. Let the negative feelings go, do not hang on to them. They will only make your life unpleasant.

Don't disregard small irritations and little frustrations. Express them indirectly. Small feelings, if they are kept inside and allowed to build up, become big feelings. You may explode in an overreaction someday if you store up all your little frustrations and annoyances. Do not keep them.

The sixth rule is to analyze, understand, and reflect upon your anger. Get to know yourself so that you recognize (a) the events and behaviors that trigger your anger and (b) the internal signs of arousal that signal you are becoming angry. You can control your anger. You can find your own buttons so that you know when someone else is pushing them. It is important for you to understand the regularities of your anger patterns—when, in what circumstances, and with whom you become angry. You can then plan how to avoid frustrating, anger-provoking situations. And you can explicitly decide what you want and plan in detail how to manage situations to obtain it without getting angry. As you become more and more sharply tuned to the signs of tension and upset inside you, you will achieve greater ability to short-circuit the anger process. You can train yourself to use the initial flash of anger as a signal that anger is on the way and that you may therefore need to switch to a more productive and suitable behavior pattern. Signs of internal arousal can be alerting signals that you are becoming upset and that effective action is called for if a positive outcome is to result. Thus you can learn to stop anger before it develops.

In a second analysis, you might focus on anger's defensiveness, its reactiveness to frustration or deprivation, and its righteousness. Anger often results from your believing that things are not going the way you want them to go or that you are powerless in a situation in which you want to be able to influence other people. Remember, you gain power and influence when you keep calm and refuse to get angry. Since anger is sometimes due to doubting yourself or letting yourself feel threatened by someone else, it is important to remember that you are a worthwhile person and that you have many strengths and competencies. This can keep you from feeling angry. And you should always beware of the righteousness of your anger. It can be blind.

Another means of analysis that is useful in determining the function of your anger is to look at what your anger does for you. Review the functions of anger discussed in the previous section of this chapter and apply them to your anger.

The seventh rule is to congratulate yourself when you have succeeded in managing your anger constructively. Feel good about your success. Don't focus on your mistakes and failings or on the nastiness of other people. Focus on your ability to manage your anger constructively.

In addition to these seven rules, there are a number of specific skills needed when you express your anger at another person directly. These skills are detailed in the next section.

COMPREHENSION TEST B

Test your understanding of rules for managing anger constructively by answering true or false to the following statements. Answers are at the end of the chapter.

True	False	1. You can't express anger without being aggressive.
True	False	2. The first rule in managing anger is to recognize and acknowledge the fact that you are angry.
True	False	3. For the sake of honesty, you should always express your anger in a situation.
True	False	4. You can control anger by learning to relax or by changing your interpretation of what has happened.
True	False	5. When people want to get you angry, you should oblige them.
True	False	6. If you want people to know your commitments or if you want to clear the air, you should express anger directly.

True   False   7. Anger needs to be expressed in a way that ends the anger.

True   False   8. Don't get angry until you are certain there is a reason.

True   False   9. You can't help being angry when someone provokes you.

True   False   10. When you are angry, you don't think very clearly.

True   False   11. It is less destructive to direct your anger toward an issue than toward a person.

True   False   12. If you view an incident as a problem to be solved, it is less destructive than directing your anger toward the other person involved.

True   False   13. Make sure the person you've expressed anger to has a chance to respond and clarify his or her feelings.

True   False   14. Sarcasm, name calling, put-downs, and physical attacks are good ways to express anger.

True   False   15. Don't ever express positive feelings in a conflict, or you'll lose the effect of your angry expression.

True   False   16. Angry feelings can be eliminated by vigorous exercise, by strong private expression of feelings, or by resolving the situation in your mind.

True   False   17. Don't worry about expressing little irritations. They will disappear in time, if ignored.

True   False   18. If you can identify the beginning feelings of anger in yourself, you can learn to stop your anger from developing.

True   False   19. How you feel about yourself has very little to do with controlling your anger.

True   False   20. Praise yourself when you have managed your anger constructively.

EXPRESSING ANGER CONSTRUCTIVELY

To express your anger constructively, you describe the other person's behavior, you describe your feelings, and you make your nonverbal messages congruent with your words. The purpose of asserting your anger is to create a shared understanding of the relationship so it may be improved or so you may be more effective in achieving your goals. You want the other person to know how you perceive and feel about his or her actions, and you wish to end up knowing how the other person perceives and feels about your actions. You want to discuss the situation until you and the other person have a common perspective or frame of reference in viewing the relationship and your interactions with each other.

Behavior Descriptions

In describing the other person's provocative actions, you need to be skillful in observing what actually occurred and in letting the other person know what behavior you are responding to by describing it clearly and specifically. To do this, you must describe visible evidence, behavior that is open to anyone's observation. Restrict yourself to talking about the actions of the other person. Using personal statements is also a good idea so that it is clear that you are taking ownership for your observations. An example of a good behavior description is, "Jim, by my count, you have just interrupted me for the third time." (*Not,* "Jim, you are really being rude," which is negative labeling or, "Jim, you always want to be the center of attention," which imputes an unworthy motive.)

Descriptions of Your Own Feelings

You describe your feelings by using personal statements (referring to "I," "me," or "my") and specifying the feeling by name or by action-urge simile or some other figure of speech (see chapter 5). Your description will be more helpful and effective if it is *specific* rather than general ("You bumped my arm" rather than "You never watch where you are going"), *tentative* rather than absolute ("You seem unconcerned about completing our project" rather than "You don't care about the project and you never will"), and *informing* rather than demanding ("I haven't finished yet" rather than "Stop interrupting me"). This latter point needs reemphasizing because of its importance; the description of your anger should be *non-coercive* and should not be a demand that the other person change. Avoid judgments of the other person ("You are egocentric"), name calling or trait labeling ("You're a phony"), accusations and imputing undesirable motives to the other person ("You always have to be the center of attention"), commands, demands, and orders ("Stop talking and listen!"), and sarcasm ("You're really considerate, aren't you?" when the opposite is meant). By describing your feelings about the other person's actions, your feelings are seen as temporary and capable of change rather than as permanent. It is better to say, "At this point, I am very annoyed with you" than "I dislike you and I always will."

Making Nonverbal Messages Congruent

In describing your feelings you need to make your nonverbal messages similar to your verbal ones. When you express anger verbally, your facial expression should be serious, your tone of voice cold, your eye contact direct, and your posture rather stiff. Contradictory verbal and nonverbal messages will only indicate to the other person that you are untrustworthy and will make the other person anxious. The nonverbal expression of feelings is discussed in chapter 6.

Listening Skills

While discussing your anger with another person it is important to use good listening skills. Use *perception checks* to make sure that you are not making false assumptions about the other person's feelings and intentions ("My impression is that you are not interested in trying to understand my ideas. Am I wrong?" "Did my last statement bother you?"). And when negotiating the meaning of the other person's actions and in clarifying both your feelings and the feelings of the other person, use *paraphrasing* to make sure you accurately understand the other person and that the other person feels understood and listened to.

Summary

To express anger constructively, first describe the other person's provocative behavior and then describe your anger verbally while making your nonverbal messages congruent with your words. An example would be, "Jim, by my count you have just interrupted me for the third time in the past half hour, and I am both frustrated and angry as a result" (while maintaining a serious facial expression, a cold tone of voice, direct eye contact, and a rather stiff posture). You should then be ready to negotiate on the meaning of Jim's actions and on whether or not anger is the appropriate feeling to have.

In expressing anger your attitude should not be, "Who's right and who's wrong?" but rather, "What can each of us learn from this discussion that will make our relationship more productive and satisfying?" As a result of the discussion, each of you will act with fuller awareness of the effect of your actions on the other person as well as with more understanding of the other person's intentions. One, both, or neither of you may act differently in the future because of this increased awareness. Any change in future behavior needs to be self-chosen rather than compelled by a desire to please or a need to submit to the other person.

Finally, make sure the timing of the expression of your anger is appropriate. Generally, express your anger when there is time enough to discuss the situation and the provocation. The closer in time your reaction is expressed to the provocation, the more constructive the discussion will be.

ASSERTIVENESS, NONASSERTIVENESS, AND AGGRESSIVENESS

All people have a perfect right to express their thoughts, feelings, opinions, and preferences and to expect that other people will treat them with respect and dignity. In interpersonal situations involving stress and anger, you may behave nonassertively, aggressively, or assertively. When you behave *nonassertively*, you say nothing in response to a provocation, keeping your feelings to yourself, hiding feeling from others, and perhaps even hiding your feelings from yourself. Nonassertive behavior is often dishonest and involves letting other people violate your personal right to be treated with respect and dignity.

Aggressive behavior involves expressing your feelings indirectly through insults, sarcasm, labels, put-downs, and hostile statements and actions. Aggressive behavior involves expressing thoughts, feelings, and opinions in a way that violates others' rights to be treated with respect and dignity.

Assertive behavior involves describing your feelings, thoughts, opinions, and preferences directly to another person in an honest and appropriate way that respects both yourself and the other person. It enables you to act in your own best interests, to stand up for yourself without undue anxiety, to express honest feelings comfortably, and to exercise personal rights without denying the rights of others. Assertive behavior is direct, honest, self-enhancing self-expression that is not hurtful to others and is appropriate for the receiver and the situation.

In general, it is a good idea to raise your restraints and inhibitions against aggressive and nonassertive behavior and to lower any inhibitions, restraints, or anxieties you have about being assertive.

In summary, because we are human, we are constantly under stress, some of which is pleasant and desirable and some of which is unpleasant and undesirable. We react to both types of stress in a stereotyped, physiological reaction that provides energy and motivation for action. The primary source of stress, both good and bad, is other people, and interpersonal stress usually involves anger. Anger both causes and accompanies distress and is usually a righteous but defensive reaction to frustration and aggression. Through understanding the major functions of anger and the rules and skills for its constructive management and expression, the constructive aspects of anger can be promoted while the destructive aspects can be quelled. Below are three exercises aimed at helping you clarify your actions when you are angry. We will then turn to the issue of how to control your emotional reactions to events that could cause anger, depression, guilt, or sadness.

COMPREHENSION TEST C

Test your understanding of expressing anger constructively by answering true or false to the following statements. Answers are at the end of the chapter.

True   False   1. Expressing your anger constructively involves describing the other person's behavior, describing your feelings, and making your nonverbal messages match your words.

True   False   2. The reason for showing your anger is to let the other person see how you feel about her actions, but not to know how she feels about your actions.

True   False   3. "Edye, you are a pest!" is a good behavior description.

True   False   4. When describing your feelings, you should be personal, specific, tentative, informing, and noncoercive.

True   False   5. It doesn't matter if your nonverbal message fits your verbal message.

True   False   6. Good listening skills are important in expressing your anger.

True   False   7. Good listening skills include using perception checks and paraphrasing.

True   False   8. Nonassertive behavior involves hiding your feelings and letting people "run over" you.

True   False   9. Aggressive behavior is the best way to express anger.

True   False   10. Assertive behavior involves standing up for yourself without hurting others.

EXERCISE 12.1: UNDERSTANDING MY ANGER

Being aware of our feelings is an important and somewhat difficult task. Many of us were taught to hide our feelings. We learned to pretend we did not have them. This is especially true of feelings we consider negative, such as anger. We often keep our anger inside and act as if it were not there. We deny to ourselves that we are angry. In order to be aware of our anger and express it appropriately, we must understand what makes us angry.

The purpose of this exercise is to increase your awareness of what makes you angry. The procedure is:

1. Working by yourself, complete the statements given below on a separate sheet of paper. Be sure to write out your answers fully.
2. Form into groups of four. Take the first statement and discuss the answers of each member. Then go on to the second statement.
3. After you have finished discussing all sixteen statements, write down:
   a. The five major things that make your group members angry
   b. The five major ways in which your group members express their anger
   c. The five major conclusions your group has come to about what happens when anger is expressed
4. Share your conclusions with the other groups, while they share their conclusions with you.
5. In your group of four, discuss how your group's conclusions compared with the conclusions of the other groups. Do you all feel anger for the same reasons? Do you all express your anger in the same way? Do you all feel the same way when someone is angry at you? Do you all agree on what consequences will result from expressing anger?

My Anger

Complete the following statements. Be specific. Try to think of times when you were angry or someone was angry at you. You may wish to substitute "coworkers" or "fellow students" for "friends" and "parents," or "boss" for "teacher."

1. I feel angry when my friends . . .
2. When I'm angry at my friends, I usually . . .
3. After expressing my anger, I feel . . .
4. The way I express anger usually makes my friends . . .
5. When my friends express anger toward me, I feel . . .
6. When I feel that way, I usually . . .
7. After reacting to my friends' anger, I feel . . .
8. My reactions to my friends' anger usually results in their . . .
9. I feel angry when my teacher . . .
10. When I'm angry at my teacher I usually . . .
11. The way I act when I'm angry at my teacher makes me feel . . .
12. The way I act when I'm angry at my teacher usually results in my teacher's . . .
13. When my teacher expresses anger at me, I feel . . .
14. When I feel that way I usually . . .
15. After reacting to my teacher's anger, I feel . . .
16. My reactions to my teacher's anger usually result in my teacher's . . .

EXERCISE 12.2: DEFUSING THE BOMB EXERCISE

The purpose of this exercise is to discuss how you manage provocations. The procedure for the exercise is:

1. Divide into groups of three.
2. Read the following incident, and as a group answer these questions:
   a. How would you feel?
   b. What would you do?
   c. How would you maximize positive outcomes and minimize negative outcomes?
   d. What would you say to yourself to manage your feelings constructively?

Incident

You are a teacher at a suburban junior high school. You are sitting in your office when a parent, Ms. Jones, walks in without an appointment. Ms. Jones, in a very loud and angry voice, begins to demand that you reprimand one of your students, stating that the student is vicious and picks on Ms. Jone's son (who is a student in your class). Ms. Jones refuses to listen to your explanations, criticizes your ideas, and even brags about how well she understands teaching and child development. For the most part, she is uninterested in anything you have to say. Finally, as you present your view once again, Ms. Jones calls you a stupid jerk.

EXERCISE 12.3: MANAGING PROVOCATIONS

Novaco (1975) described a sequence of stages in managing a provocation constructively. Those stages are:

1. When possible, be prepared for a provocation.
2. Experience the provocation.
3. Cope with arousal and agitation.
4. Reflect on the experience and engage in self-reward for coping successfully.

For each stage, there are a number of statements people make to themselves to help them manage the provocation successfully. The assumption is that through controlling what you say to yourself before, during, and following a provocation you can change your conflict behavior and instruct yourself in more constructive behavioral patterns. The purpose of this exercise is to give you some practice in differentiating among the self-statements for each stage and applying them to a conflict situation you have recently been involved in. The procedure is:

1. Form into triads and classify the self-statements below according to the four stages of managing a provocation constructively.
2. Have each member of the triad then identify a conflict situation that usually creates anger and distress in him.
3. Working as a triad, take each conflict situation and work out a series of self-statements that can be used during each stage of managing the provocation constructively. Each member of the triad should leave the triad with a set of self-statements that will help her manage the conflict situation more constructively next time it appears.

Managing Provocations by Talking to Yourself

Given below are a number of statements that you could say to yourself to help yourself manage a conflict situation constructively. Working as a triad, classify each statement given below as belonging in one of Novaco's four stages of managing a provocation constructively.

Stage   Self-Statement

1. ____ I can work out a plan for handling this.
2. ____ As long as I keep cool, I'm in control here.
3. ____ Getting upset won't help.
4. ____ It worked!
5. ____ If I find myself getting upset, I will know what to do.
6. ____ You don't need to prove yourself.
7. ____ It's not worth it to get so angry.
8. ____ I could have gotten more upset than it was worth.
9. ____ I actually got through that without getting angry. Way to go!
10. ____ My anger is a signal that it's time to start talking to myself.

11. _____ If I start to get mad, I will just be banging my head against the wall. So I might as well just relax.

12. _____ This could be a bad situation, but I believe in myself.

13. _____ I'm doing better at handling myself in these situations all the time.

14. _____ My muscles are starting to feel tight. Time to relax and slow things down.

15. _____ Don't assume the worst or jump to conclusions. Look for positives.

16. _____ Before I go in, I need to take a few deep breaths, relax myself, make sure I feel comfortable and at ease.

17. _____ I didn't take anything personally. I sure feel better that way!

18. _____ I'm not going to let them get to me.

19. _____ He would probably like me to get really angry. Well, I'm going to disappoint him.

20. _____ I'll be able to manage this situation. I know how to regulate my anger.

21. _____ Calm down. I can't expect people to act the way I want them to.

22. _____ I've been getting upset for too long when it wasn't necessary. I have really improved in not getting angry!

23. _____ There won't be any need to get angry or upset.

24. _____ Don't get upset; just keep thinking about what I want to do to make sure I get what I want out of this situation.

25. _____ Keep focused on the task. Don't let them distract you into a quarrel.

26. _____ What is it I have to do to stay calm and be effective?

27. _____ There is no need to doubt myself. What he says doesn't matter.

28. _____ I am excellent at not reacting with anger when people provoke me.

MANAGING YOUR FEELINGS

There are times when your relationships may result in great happiness, satisfaction, growth, and joy. There are other times when your relationships may result in depression, sadness, anger, worry, frustration, or guilt. Everyone will be depressed occasionally about a relationship or angry at the way in which other people are treating him. If the feelings are dealt with constructively, they will not last very long. But if you have destructive patterns of interpreting what is happening in your life, you can be depressed and upset all the time. You can turn small events into tragedies. You could, for example, react as if a coworker's not liking you were as serious as finding out you have incurable cancer. There are people who are talented at taking an occasional small event and creating major feelings of depression or anger that stay with them for several days or weeks.

How you feel is important for your enjoyment of life and for your ability to relate effectively to other people. If you are depressed, angry, worried, and anxious about your relationships, then you need to take some

sort of action. You need to get rid of negative feelings and to promote positive feelings, such as happiness, contentment, pride, and satisfaction.

To change negative or destructive feelings, you have two choices. You can try to change things *outside* of yourself. You can change jobs, friends, location, and careers. Your second choice is to change things *within* yourself. You can change your interpretations of what is happening in your life. As was discussed in chapter 5, changing your interpretations will change your feelings. In choosing whether to try to change something outside of yourself or inside yourself, it is important to remember that *the easiest thing to change in your life is yourself.*

Let's take an example. Sam believes his boss is always picking on him. He thinks that his boss gives him the dirtiest jobs to do. Sam thinks that his coworkers aren't made to work as hard as he is. The boss always seems to be criticizing Sam but not his coworkers. All this makes Sam angry, depressed, worried, and frustrated. Sam also feels that the situation is hopeless. "What can I do?" asks Sam. "My boss has all the power. He can fire me, but I can't do anything to him."

Sam has two choices. He can try to change his boss. Or he can try to change his feelings. Psychologists would tell Sam it is easier to change his feelings than to change his boss. What do you think?

TIPS ON SURVIVAL: HOW TO LIVE A LONG LIFE

Want to live a long time? Research studies have been done on survival in concentration camps, in prisoner-of-war camps, on cancer and heart-disease victims, and on old age. Five factors seem to be the most important for survival:

1. *Having deeply held goals and commitments.* These goals and commitments need to involve relationships with other people. People who lived the longest in concentration and prisoner-of-war camps, for example, were people who turned their concern outward and worked to help other people survive.

2. *Sharing your distress with other people.* Quiet, polite, passive, accepting, and well-behaved persons die. A person who openly shares her suffering with other people and is aggressive in getting her needs met will tend to live longer.

3. *High morale is important.* Depression kills. In concentration camps, in POW camps, and among cancer patients, people who become depressed die.

4. *Physical activity is an important survival factor.* Keeping yourself physically active will help you survive.

5. *Friendships and love relationships are vital.* Lonely people die. Isolated people die. People with good friends and loving relationships survive. Many psychologists believe that loneliness is the biggest personal-adjustment problem in the United States.

Want to live a long and happy life? Then build goals and commitments that are important to you and that involve other people's welfare. Share your moments of distress and discomfort with other people. Learn how to talk with other people about how you feel. Avoid depression and keep your morale high. Keep physically active. And constantly build and renew friendships and love relationships. We will all die someday. Let us hope that we don't die from lack of commitments, passivity, depression, inactivity, or loneliness.

DISPOSABLE FEELINGS: LIKE IT OR DUMP IT

Do you remember the five aspects of expressing feelings discussed in chapter 5? They are:

1. Gather information through your five senses.

2. Interpret the information.

3. Experience the feelings appropriate to your interpretations.

4. Decide how you intend to express your feelings.

5. Express your feelings.

Do you remember that it is your interpretations that cause your feelings, not the events in your life? Feelings are not caused by events and people around you; they are caused by the ways in which you interpret your experiences. Your boss cannot upset you; only the interpretations you make about your boss's behavior can upset you. Your friends cannot upset you; only the interpretations you make about your friends' behavior can upset you. This means that you can control your feelings. You can decide which

feelings you would like to keep and expand. You can decide which feelings you would like to dump and get rid of. Your feelings are disposable!

Depending on your interpretations, you can feel satisfaction, pride, enjoyment, fun, contentment, and challenge about your relationships. Or you can feel depressed, anxious, worried, angry, sad, hopeless, and helpless about your relationships. When your interpretations result in feelings that contribute to a painful and troubled life, you are managing your feelings destructively. When you have feelings of depression and anxiety, your work suffers, the people around you suffer, and you are just no fun to be around. Maintaining relationships means that you are able to manage your interpretations so that you are not overly depressed, anxious, angry, or upset.

Your interpretations are heavily influenced by the assumptions you make about what is good or bad, what you do or do not need, and what causes what in the world. Sometimes people have assumptions that cause them to be depressed or upset most of the time. You can assume, for example, that your boss has to like you more than any other employee. Since there is always somebody your boss will like better than you, such an assumption will keep you unhappy. You will be depressed because your boss does not like you best! Assumptions such as this one are irrational. An *irrational assumption* is a belief that makes you depressed or upset most of the time. The belief (such as, the boss has to like me best or else my life is ruined) is accepted as true without any proof. If you believe your boss has to love you or else life is unbearable, you have an irrational assumption. If you believe that you have to be perfect or else you are absolutely worthless, you have an irrational assumption. If you believe that everyone in the world has to think you are absolutely marvelous or else you will be miserable, you have an irrational assumption. If you think you are unemployable because you can't immediately find a job, you have an irrational assumption. *Irrational assumptions can only make you feel miserable because they lead to depressing interpretations.* All you have to do to ruin your life is to make a few irrational assumptions and refuse to change them no matter how much pain they cause!

It takes energy to have destructive feelings. It takes energy to hold on to irrational assumptions. It takes energy to make interpretations that lead to miserable feelings. It takes energy to try to ignore, deny, and hide these miserable feelings. *The fewer irrational assumptions you have the more energy you will have for enjoying yourself and your relationships! The more quickly you get rid of your irrational assumptions and the destructive feelings they cause, the more energy you will have for enjoying yourself and your relationships!*

To maintain constructive relationships you need to:

1. Be aware of your assumptions.

2. Know how they affect your interpretation of the information gathered by your senses.

3. Be able to tell how rational or irrational your assumptions are.

4. Dump your irrational assumptions.

5. Replace your irrational assumptions with rational ones.

You can change your irrational assumptions. The easiest way is to: (1) become highly aware of when you are making an irrational assumption; (2) think of a rational assumption that is much more constructive; (3) and argue with yourself until you have replaced your irrational assumption with a rational one.

Irrational assumptions are learned. Usually they are learned in early childhood. They were taught to you by people in your past. Irrational assumptions are bad habits just like smoking or alcoholism. What was learned as a child can be unlearned as an adult. If you keep arguing against your irrational assumptions, you will soon develop rational ones! *Do not let yourself feel bad just because you have bad thinking habits!*

> *I have known a great many troubles, but most of them never happened.*
>
> Mark Twain

COMPREHENSION TEST D

Test your understanding of managing your feelings constructively by answering true or false to the following statements. Answers are at the end of the chapter.

True   False   1. The stages in managing provocations constructively are prepare, experience, cope, reflect, and reward.

True   False   2. You can change your conflict behavior by controlling what you say to yourself before, during, and after a provocation.

True   False   3. To change negative or destructive feelings, you can change things outside yourself or you can change yourself.

True   False   4. Changing your interpretations of events will not change your feelings about them.

True   False   5. The easiest thing to change in your life is something outside yourself.

True   False   6. Feelings are caused by the events and people around you, not by your interpretations of those events.

True   False   7. Irrational assumptions make you unhappy because they cannot come true.

True   False   8. The fewer irrational assumptions you have, the more energy you will have for enjoying yourself.

True   False   9. "Habits learned in childhood can't be changed" is an irrational assumption.

True   False   10. If you keep arguing against your irrational assumptions, you can get rid of them and develop rational ones.

EXERCISE 12.4: ASSUMPTIONS, ASSUMPTIONS, WHAT ARE MY ASSUMPTIONS?

What are common irrational assumptions? How do you know if your assumptions are rational or irrational? One way is to compare them with the following list of rational and irrational assumptions taken from the writings of Albert Ellis (1962). Do you make any of these assumptions? Do you have any of the irrational assumptions listed below? Do you make any of the rational assumptions listed below? Can you tell the difference between the rational and the irrational ones?

Read each of the statements listed below. Write *yes* for any assumption that describes how you think. Write *no* for any assumption that does not describe how you think. Then reread each statement. Write *R* for the rational assumptions. Write *I* for the irrational assumptions. Keep your answers. You will use them in a later lesson.

_____ 1. I must be loved, liked, and approved of by everyone all the time or I will be absolutely miserable and will feel totally worthless.

_____ 2. It would be nice if I were liked by everyone, but I can survive very well without the approval of most people. It is only the liking and approval of close friends and people with actual power over me (such as my boss) that I have to be concerned with.

_____ 3. I have to be absolutely 100 percent perfect and competent in all respects if I am to consider myself worthwhile.

_____ 4. My personal value does not rest on how perfect or competent I am. Although I'm trying to be as competent as I can, I am a valuable person regardless of how well I do things.

_____ 5. People who are bad, including myself, must be blamed and punished to prevent them from being wicked in the future.

_____ 6. What is important is not making the same mistakes in the future. I do not have to blame and punish myself or other people for what has happened in the past.

_____ 7. It is a total catastrophe and so terrible that I can't stand it if things are not the way I would like them to be.

_____ 8. There is no reason the world should be the way I want it to be. What is important is dealing with what is. I do not have to bemoan the fact that things are not fair or just the way I think they should be.

_____ 9. If something terrible could happen, I will keep thinking about it *as if* it is actually going to take place.

_____10. I will try my best to avoid future unpleasantness. Then I will not worry about it. I refuse to go around keeping myself afraid by saying, "What if this happened?" "What if that happened?"

_____11. It is easier to avoid difficulties and responsibilities than to face them.

_____12. Facing difficulties and meeting responsibilities is easier in the long run than avoiding them.

_____13. I need someone stronger than myself to rely on.

_____14. I am strong enough to rely on myself.

_____15. Since I was this way when I was a child, I will be this way all my life.

_____16. I can change myself at any time in my life, whenever I decide it is helpful for me to do so.

_____17. I must become upset and depressed about other people's problems.

_____18. Having empathy with other people's problems and trying to help them does not mean getting upset and depressed about their problems. Overconcern does not lead to problem solving. How can I be of help if I am as depressed as others are?

_____19. It is terrible and unbearable to have to do things I don't want and don't like to do.

_____20. What I can't change I won't let upset me.

The assumptions we make greatly influence our interpretations of the meaning of events in our life. These interpretations determine our feelings. The same event can be depressing or amusing, depending on the assumptions and interpretations we make. The purpose of this exercise is to focus a group discussion on the ways in which assumptions affect our interpretations and how we feel.

1. Form groups of four. Take the ten episodes below and discuss the following questions:
    a. What irrational assumptions is the person making?
    b. How do these assumptions cause the person to feel the way she does?
    c. What rational assumptions does the person need in order to change her feelings into more positive feelings?
2. In your group, discuss assumptions each of you have that influence your feelings of depression, anger, frustration, distress, and worry. When you are experiencing each of these feelings, what assumptions are causing you to feel that way? How can you change these assumptions to make your life happier?

Episodes

1. Sally likes to have her coworkers place their work neatly in a pile on her desk so that she can add her work to the pile, staple it all together, and give it to their supervisor. Her coworkers, however, throw their work into the supervisor's basket in a very disorderly and messy fashion. Sally then becomes very worried and upset. "I can't stand it," Sally says to herself. "It's terrible what they are doing. And it isn't fair to me or our supervisor!"

2. Jill has been given responsibility for planning next year's budget for her department. This amount of responsibility scares her. For several weeks she has done nothing on the budget. "I'll do it next week," she keeps thinking.

3. John went to the office one morning and passed a person he had never met in the hallway. He said, "Hello," and the person just looked at him and then walked on without saying a word. John became depressed. "I'm really not a very attractive person," he thought to himself. "No one seems to like me."

4. Dan is an intensive-care paramedic technician and is constantly depressed and worried about whether he can do his job competently. For every decision that has to be made, he asks his supervisor what he should do. One day he came into work and found that his supervisor had quit. "What will I do now?" he thought. "I can't handle this job without her."

5. Jane went to her desk and found a note from her supervisor that she had made an error in the report she worked on the day before. The note told her to correct the error and continue working on the report. Jane became depressed. "Why am I so dumb and stupid?" she thought to herself. "I can't seem to do anything right. That supervisor must think I'm terrible at my job."

6. Heidi has a knack for insulting people. She insults her coworkers, her boss, customers, and even passersby who ask for directions. Her boss

has repeatedly told Heidi that if she doesn't change she will be fired. This depresses Heidi and makes her very angry at her boss. "How can I change?" Heidi says. "I've been this way ever since I could talk. It's too late for me to change now."

7. Tim was checking the repairs another technician had made on a television set. He found a mistake and became very angry. "I have to punish him," he thought. "He made a mistake and he has to suffer the consequences for it."

8. Bonnie doesn't like to fill out forms. She gets furious every day because her job as legal secretary requires her to fill out form after form after form. "Every time I see a form my stomach ties itself into knots," she says. "I hate forms! I know they have to be done in order for the work to be filed with the courts, but I still hate them!"

9. Bob is very anxious about keeping his job. "What if the company goes out of business?" he thinks. "What if my boss gets angry at me?" "What if the secretary I yelled at is the boss's daughter?" All day he worries about whether he will have a job tomorrow.

10. Jack is a very friendly person who listens quite well. All his coworkers tell their problems to Jack. He listens sympathetically. Then he goes home deeply depressed. "Life is so terrible for the people I work with," he thinks. "They have such severe problems and such sad lives."

EXERCISE 12.6: CHANGING YOUR FEELINGS

Now that you have discussed how people can make their assumptions more constructive, you may want to apply your own advice to yourself. The purpose of this exercise is to give you a chance to discuss your own negative feelings and see what assumptions are causing them. The procedure is:

1. Form groups of four. Draw straws to see who goes first in your group. Then go around the group in a clockwise direction. Each member completes the following statements:
    a. What depresses me about school or work is . . .
    b. When I get depressed about school or work I . . .
    c. The assumptions I am making that cause me to be depressed are . . .
    d. Constructive assumptions I can adopt to change my depression to more positive feelings are . . .
    Listen carefully to what each group member says. If he is not sure of his assumptions, help him clarify them. Give support for making his assumptions more constructive.
2. Now go around the group again and discuss how each member completes these statements:
    a. The things I worry about are . . .
    b. What I do when I get worried is . . .
    c. The assumptions I am making that cause me to be worried are . . .
    d. Constructive assumptions I can adopt to change my worry to more positive feelings are . . .
3. Now try anger:
    a. The things I get angry about are . . .
    b. What I do when I get angry is . . .

    c. The assumptions I am making that cause me to be angry are . . .

    d. Constructive assumptions I can adopt to change my anger to more positive feelings are . . .

4. Let's see how you feel about your career!

    a. The negative feelings I have when I think about my career are . . .

    b. The things I do when I have those feelings are . . .

    c. The assumptions I am making that cause the feelings are . . .

    d. Constructive attitudes I can adopt to change these feelings to more positive ones are . . .

5. Discuss in your group what the members learned about themselves and the ways in which they manage their feelings.

EXERCISE 12.7: HOW DO I MANAGE MY FEELINGS?

There are five questions below. Each question has two parts. Check *a* if your way of managing feelings is best described by the *a* part of the question. Check a *b* if your way of managing feelings is best described by the *b* part of the question. Think about each question carefully. Be honest. No one will see your answers. The results are simply for your own self-awareness.

1.   ____ **a.** I am fully aware of what I am sensing in a given situation.

    ____ **b.** I ignore what I am sensing by thinking about the past or the future.

2.   ____ **a.** I understand the interpretations I usually make about other people's actions. I investigate my feeling by asking what interpretation is causing it. I work to be aware of interpretations I am making.

    ____ **b.** I deny that I make any interpretations about what I sense. I ignore my interpretations. I insist that I do not interpret someone's behavior as being mean. The person *is* mean.

3.   ____ **a.** I accept my feeling as being part of me. I turn my full awareness on it. I try to feel it fully. I take a good look at it so I can identify it and tell how strong it is. I keep asking myself, "What am I feeling now?"

    ____ **b.** I reject my feeling. I ignore it by telling myself I'm not angry, upset, sad, or even happy. I deny my feeling by telling myself and others, "But I'm not feeling anything at all." I avoid people and situations that might make me more aware of my feelings. I pretend I'm not really feeling the way I am.

4.   ____ **a.** I decide how I want to express my feeling. I think of what I want to result from the expression of my feeling. I think of what is an appropriate way to express the feeling in the current situation. In my mind, I review the sending skills.

    ____ **b.** Since I've never admitted to having a feeling, I don't need to decide how to express it! I don't think through what might happen after I express my feelings. I never think about what is appropriate in a situation. When my feelings burst I am too emotional to remember good sending skills.

5.   ____ **a.** I express my feelings appropriately and clearly. Usually, this means describing my feeling directly. It also means using nonverbal messages to back up my words. My words and my nonverbal messages communicate the same feeling.

___ **b.** I express my feelings inappropriately and in confusing ways. Usually, this means I express them indirectly through commands, accusations, put-downs, and evaluations. I may express feelings physically in destructive ways. My nonverbal messages express my feelings. I shout at people, push or hit them, avoid people, refuse to look at them, or don't speak to them. I may hug them, put my arm around them, give them gifts, or try to do favors for them. My words and my nonverbal messages often contradict each other. I sometimes smile and act friendly toward people I'm angry at. Or I may avoid people I care a great deal for.

MANAGING STRESS
THROUGH SOCIAL-SUPPORT SYSTEMS

One of the most effective ways of managing stress is through utilizing social-support systems involving other people who care about you and/or are sympathetic to your plight. Discussing stressful situations with friends and clarifying one's feelings through describing them to a sympathetic person are some of the most helpful strategies for managing stress. One of the first actions you should take when you find yourself experiencing stress, therefore, is to seek out friends and sympathetic acquaintances with whom to discuss the situation and your feelings.

There is a biological precedent for such a procedure. In the course of evolution, colonies of individual cells combined to form a single cooperative community in which competition was amply overcompensated for by mutual assistance (because each member of the group could depend on the others for help). Different cells specialized, each undertaking different functions, some to look after food intake and digestion, others to provide the means for respiration, locomotion, and defense, still others to coordinate the activities of the entire colony. The evolution of diverse species was largely dependent on the development of processes that permitted many cells to live in harmony, with a minimum of stress between them, serving their own best interests by ensuring the survival of the entire complex structure. Stress within the body is managed within this complex division of labor in which different specialized cells work collaboratively to deal with threats to the productiveness of the entire colony. The indispensability of disciplined, orderly, mutually cooperative support is illustrated by its opposite—the development of cancer, whose most characteristic feature is that it cares only for itself. Cancer feeds on the other parts of the biological system to which it belongs until it kills the entire system, thus committing biological suicide, since a cancer cell cannot live except within the body in which it started its egocentric development.

Loneliness, isolation, and lack of social support during periods of stress do create physiological damage and aggrevate the effects of stress. Isolating ourselves during stressful times is the equivalent of committing social suicide, as destroying or failing to maintain our relationships when we need them the most is self-destructive. When we are experiencing stress, we need other people to turn to for support. Yet many people have too few relationships they can count on as sources of support. In our complex, technological, bureaucratic world, a broad base of interpersonal support is important. In addition to whatever family we may have, we need friends and acquaintances who respect us, challenge us, provide resources for us, and to be our mentors, evaluators, experts, and energizers. When we are experiencing stress, it is important to feel that we are not alone and to realize that by discussing situations with other people, we can alleviate stress and provide ourselves with relief from pain.

CHAPTER REVIEW

Test your understanding of anger, stress, and managing your feelings by answering true or false to the following statements. Answers are at the end of the chapter.

True	False	1. A certain amount of stress is beneficial.
True	False	2. It is important to deal with anger in some way.
True	False	3. The first step to managing angry feelings is to identify the feelings as they begin.
True	False	4. You can change anger by looking at events differently or talking yourself out of it as you feel anger arise.
True	False	5. You can deal with anger constructively by repressing your feelings.
True	False	6. Hitting someone in the mouth is not a constructive way to deal with anger.
True	False	7. The best way to deal with anger is to talk over the situation with the person who made you angry.
True	False	8. If you can't talk over the problem, you can get rid of your angry feelings by vigorous exercise or private yelling or crying.
True	False	9. A good way to deal with stress is to discuss your feelings with a friend.
True	False	10. Isolating yourself during times of stress is self-destructive.

Indicate below which skills you have mastered and which skills you still need more work on.

1. I have mastered the following:
    ____ an understanding of stress and how to deal with it
    ____ an awareness of what makes me angry
    ____ an understanding of how I behave when angry
    ____ an understanding of my irrational beliefs and how to minimize them
    ____ an understanding of how to express anger constructively
    ____ an understanding of how to change my interpretations of situations

2. I need more work on:
    ____ an understanding of stress and how to deal with it
    ____ an awareness of what makes me angry
    ____ an understanding of how I behave when angry
    ____ an understanding of my irrational beliefs and how to minimize them
    ____ an understanding of how to express anger constructively
    ____ an understanding of how to change my interpretations of situations

You have read about how to deal with stress, anger, and managing your feelings. You should have a greater awareness of what makes you angry, how to minimize anger, and how to express anger constructively. As you practice the suggestions in this chapter, you will find that you have more constructive control over your feelings and relationships. As you continue to practice the skills you have learned in this book, you will learn how to "reach out" to others in a way that will result in more rewarding relationships for them and for you.

ANSWERS

Comprehension Test A: 1. false; 2. false; 3. false; 4. true; 5. true; 6. true; 7. true; 8. true; 9. true; 10. true.

Comprehension Test B: 1. false; 2. true; 3. false; 4. true; 5. false; 6. true; 7. true; 8. true; 9. false; 10. true; 11. true; 12. true; 13. true; 14. false; 15. false; 16. true; 17. false; 18. true; 19. false; 20. true.

Comprehension Test C: 1. true; 2. false; 3. false; 4. true; 5. false; 6. true; 7. true; 8. true; 9. false; 10. true.

Comprehension Test D: 1. true; 2. true; 3. true; 4. false; 5. false; 6. false; 7. true; 8. true; 9. true; 10. true.

Chapter Review: 1. true; 2. true; 3. true; 4. true; 5. false; 6. true; 7. true; 8. true; 9. true; 10. true.

Epilogue

Interpersonal skills are vital for interpersonal effectiveness and self-actualization. As was noted in the first chapter, there is no way to over-emphasize the importance of interpersonal skills in our daily lives. We are not born with these skills; they must be developed.

You have now completed a variety of experiences aimed at improving your interpersonal skills. You should now be more self-aware, self-accepting, and self-disclosing. You have had a variety of experiences in building trust, in giving and receiving constructive feedback, and in communicating ideas and feelings accurately and without ambiguity. You have had practice in expressing support and acceptance, confronting other people, and modeling appropriate behavior. You have been exposed to ways of reinforcing both your own and another person's behavior. You have had practice in handling conflicts constructively. You may find that you wish to repeat many of the exercises and reread much of the material in this book in order to learn how to utilize it fully in your relationships. There is, however, a concluding exercise that may be helpful in applying the material covered in this book to your relationships.

RELATIONSHIP SURVEY

The objectives of this exercise are to help you become more aware of the qualities of the relationships in your life and to commit you to applying the skills and insights you have gained from this book to increase the richness of them. You will need a large sheet of paper and a felt-tipped pen for the exercise. The procedure for the exercise is as follows:

1. Write your name at the top of the paper and divide it into two columns. On one side, list four of your relationships that you value highly, and on the other side, write what it is that you value about the relationship. These could be relationships you are presently involved in or ones you have had in the past.

2. Share this information with the group as a whole. This gives you an opportunity to practice self-disclosure and listening skills. After each person has shared his information, the group should suggest what they perceive as the essential qualities of a good relationship for that person. The person should then write down the suggestions of the group in the appropriate column on the sheet of paper.

3. Divide into groups of three. Within the triad have each person review the strengths, skills, and insights learned from this book. Each person then picks several of the relationships she is now involved in and sets a series of goals about how she will behave in order to improve them. Discuss the goals within the group.

4. Address an envelope to yourself. Plan how you will behave in the next six months to accomplish the goals you have just set. Write a letter to yourself specifying your goals and your behavior in the relationships selected during the next six months. Seal the letter. Open it six months from today.

SUMMARY OF INTERPERSONAL SKILLS

1. Self-Disclosure
    a. Be aware of and accept your thoughts, feelings, needs, and actions.
    b. Express your thoughts, feelings, reactions, and needs to other people when it is appropriate; let other people know you as you really are.
    c. Seek out feedback from other people.
    d. Give feedback to other people when they request it.
2. Trust
    a. Take risks in self-disclosure when it is appropriate.
    b. Respond with acceptance and support when other people self-disclose.
    c. Reciprocate other people's self-disclosures.
3. Communication
    a. Speak for yourself by using personal pronouns when expressing thoughts, feelings, reactions, and needs.
    b. Describe other people's actions without making value judgments.
    c. Use relationship statements when they are appropriate.
    d. Take the receiver's perspective into account when sending your message.

e. Ask for feedback about the receiver's understanding of your message.
f. Make your nonverbal messages congruent with your words.
g. Describe your feelings.
h. Describe what you think the other person is feeling and then ask if you are correct.
i. Paraphrase accurately without making value judgments about the sender's thoughts, feelings, and needs.
j. Negotiate the meaning of the sender's message.
k. Understand what the message means from the sender's perspective.
l. Make your nonverbal messages communicate clearly what you are feeling.

4. Responses
    a. When appropriate, engage in an evaluative response.
    b. When appropriate, engage in an interpretative response.
    c. When appropriate, engage in a supportive response.
    d. When appropriate, engage in a probing response.

      e. When appropriate, engage in an understanding response.

5. Acceptance and support
      a. Describe your strengths when it is appropriate to do so.
      b. Express acceptance of other people when it is appropriate to do so.

6. Influence
      a. Reinforce others' actions in order to increase, decrease, or maintain the frequency of their behavior, depending on what is in their best interests.
      b. Arrange for your behavior to be reinforced in order to increase, decrease, or maintain the frequency of desired behavior.
      c. Model interpersonal skills for others who wish to acquire them.

7. Conflicts
      a. Be aware of your habitual conflict style. Modify your conflict style according to the situation and the person you are dealing with. Whenever possible, manage conflicts like an Owl. View conflicts as a problem to be solved. Be aware of their potential value. And seek a solution that achieves both your own goals and the goals of the other person. Try to improve your relationship with the other person by resolving the conflict.
      b. Define conflicts in Stage 6:
          (1) Describe the other person's actions without labeling or insulting her.
          (2) Describe the conflict as a mutual problem to be solved, not as a win-lose struggle.
          (3) Describe the conflict as specifically as possible.
          (4) Describe *your* feelings and reactions to the other person's actions.
          (5) Describe *your* actions that help create and continue the conflict.
      c. Know when and how to confront—to begin open discussions of the conflict aimed at resolving it constructively.
      d. Define the conflict jointly with the other person.
      e. Be sure the conflict is defined according to issues, not personalities. Make it clear that you disagree with the other person's ideas or actions, not with him as a person. Do not take criticism of your ideas and actions as criticism of you as a person.
      f. Find out how you and the other person differ before seeking to resolve the conflict.
      g. See the conflict from the other person's viewpoint.
      h. Increase both your motivation and the other person's motivation to resolve the conflict.
      i. Manage your feelings so that they do not make the conflict worse.

j. Reach an agreement about how the conflict is to end and not recur.

k. Avoid common misperceptions that intensify the conflict.

8. Stress and anger

    a. Follow the rules for the constructive management of anger.

        (1) Recognize and acknowledge that you are angry.

        (2) Decide whether or not you wish to express your anger.

        (3) Have ways of responding to provocations other than anger and depression.

        (4) Express your anger directly and effectively when it is appropriate to do so.

            (a) Make the expression cathartic.

            (b) Ask for clarification before responding to a provocation.

            (c) Make it to the point and express it to the appropriate person.

            (d) Take responsibility for the anger, owning it as yours, and becoming more involved with the other person in expressing it.

            (e) Remember that heightened anger makes you agitated and impulsive.

            (f) Beware of the righteousness of your anger.

            (g) Stay task oriented rather than letting yourself get sidetracked by taking others' actions personally.

            (h) Take into account the impact your anger will have on the other person.

            (i) Use the skills of accurate communication and constructive feedback.

            (j) Express positive feelings as well as your anger while discussing the situation.

        (5) Express your anger indirectly when direct expression is not appropriate.

        (6) Analyze, understand, and reflect on your anger.

        (7) Congratulate yourself when you have succeeded in managing your anger constructively.

    b. Assert your anger through behavior descriptions, descriptions of your own feelings, congruent nonverbal messages, and good listening skills.

    c. Manage your feelings constructively:

        (1) Recognize your irrational assumptions that lead to negative feelings.

        (2) Build more rational assumptions.

        (3) Argue with yourself, replacing your irrational assumptions with your rational ones.

Appendix

Square Arrangement I: One-Way Communication

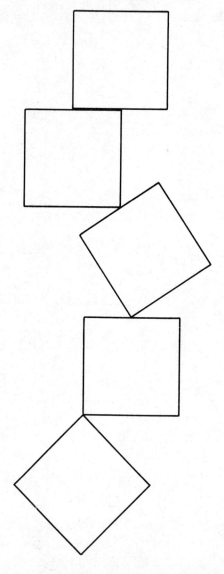

Instructions: The sender is to study the figures above. With his back to the group, he is to instruct the members of the group on how to draw them. He should begin with the top square and describe each in succession, taking particular note of the placement relationship of each to the preceding one. No questions are allowed.

Square Arrangement II: Two-Way Communication

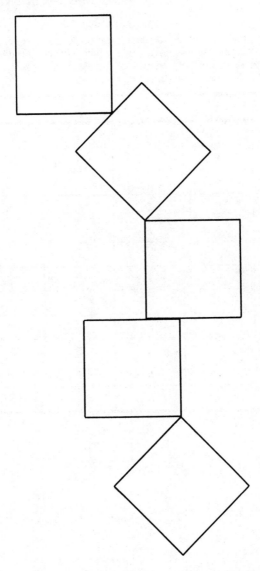

Instructions: The sender is to study the figures above. Facing the group, she is to instruct the members on how to draw them. She should begin with the top square and describe each in succession, taking particular note of the placement relationship of each to the preceding one. She should answer all questions from participants and repeat her descriptions if necessary.

After you have completed Answer Sheet 7.1B, use this scoring key to score the types of responses you gave for each item on Answer Sheet A. Then divide into groups of three and score the accuracy with which you identified the different responses for each item on Answer Sheet B. In groups of three, discuss each answer until everyone understands it.

Item	1 A	2 B	3 C	4 ○	5 E
1.	I	S	E	U	P
2.	E	U	I	P	S
3.	U	I	P	S	E
4.	P	U	E	S	I
5.	S	P	U	I	E
6.	P	U	I	E	S
7.	E	I	P	S	U
8.	S	E	U	P	I
9.	U	P	E	S	I
10.	P	U	E	S	I
11.	I	E	S	U	P
12.	U	P	S	E	I

After you have completed Answer Sheet 7.3B, use this scoring key to score the type of phrasing you personally gave for each item on Answer Sheet A. Then divide into groups of three, score the accuracy with which you identified the different types of phrasing for each item on Answer Sheet B, and discuss each answer in your group until everyone understands it.

Item	1	2	3	4
1.	I	A	P	S
2.	S	I	P	A
3.	A	S	I	P
4.	P	A	S	I
5.	I	P	A	S
6.	P	S	A	I
7.	A	P	I	S
8.	P	I	S	A
9.	I	S	A	P

FEELINGS OF REJECTION EXERCISE: INSTRUCTION SHEET

Person No. 1

You are to try to get the person sitting opposite you in your circle (Person 3) rejected from your group. Use any reason you can think of—he has big feet; she's the only person with glasses; he's got chapped hands—anything you think of. Stick to this, and try to convince the other members of your group that this is the person who should be rejected. You can listen to the arguments of the other members in the group, but don't give in. Be sure to talk about the person and not about rules for rejecting.

Person No. 2

You are to try to get the person sitting opposite you in your circle (Person 4) rejected from your group. Use any reason you can think of—he has big hands, she's the only person in a dress, he's got chapped lips—anything you can think of. Stick to this, and try to convince the other members in your group that this is the person who should be rejected. Be sure to talk about the person and not about the rules for rejecting. You can listen to the arguments of other group members, but don't give in.

Person No. 3

You are to try to get the person sitting at your left (Person 2) rejected from your group. Use any reason you can think of—he has large ears, she has freckles, he has dandruff—anything you can think of. Stick to this, and try to convince the other members that this is the person who should be rejected. You can listen to the arguments of other members, but don't give in.

Person No. 4

You are to try to get the person sitting on your right (Person 1) rejected from the group. Use any reason you can think of—he misses too many meetings, she's the only one in the group wearing a sweater, she's the shortest person—anything you can think of. Stick to this, and try to convince the other group members that this is the person who should be rejected. You can listen to the arguments of other people in the group, but don't give in. Be sure you talk about the person and not about rules for rejecting.

FEELINGS OF DISTRUST EXERCISE: INSTRUCTION SHEET

Instructions A

Do not share these instructions with the other person in your pair. Your task for the next five minutes is to talk as positively and warmly as you can to the other person. Say only positive and friendly things, showing especially that you want to cooperate and work effectively with him or her in the future. Your conversation is to concentrate on him or her about your impression of that person; and the need for cooperation between the two of you. Don't talk about yourself. No matter what happens, you say only positive things. Keep the conversation moving along quickly. You are to speak first.

Instructions B

Do not share these instructions with the other person in your pair. The other person will speak first. Your task for the next five minutes is to talk with the other person in a way that shows distrust of him or her. Whatever the other person says, say something in return that communicates suspicion, distrust, disinterest, defiance, disbelief, or contradiction. Talk only about the things the other person talks about, and avoid starting conversation or bringing up new topics. Try not to help the other person out in any way. As an example, should your partner comment, "Say, I like the shirt you're wearing," you might respond, "What do you say that for? It's ugly. I don't like it at all. What are you trying to accomplish by complimenting my shirt?"

References

DEUTSCH, M. Cooperation and trust: Some theoretical notes. In M. Jones, ed., *Nebraska symposium on motivation*. Lincoln: University of Nebraska Press, 1962, pp. 275–319.

ELLIS, A. *Reason and emotion in psychotherapy*. Secaucus, N.J.: Lyle Stuart, 1962.

GURMAN, A., AND RAZIN, A., eds. *Effective psychotherapy*. Elmsford, N.Y.: Pergamon Press, 1977.

HAMACHEK, D. *Encounters with the Self*. New York: Holt, Rinehart & Winston, 1971.

JACKSON, D. Family interaction, family homoeostasis, and some implications for conjoint family therapy. In J. Masserman, ed., *Individual and familial dynamics*. New York: Grune & Stratton, 1959, pp. 122–141.

JOHNSON, D. W. Role-reversal: A summary and review of the research. *International Journal of Group Tensions* 1 (1971): 318–34.

JOHNSON, D. W. *Contemporary social psychology*. Philadelphia: Lippincott, 1973.

JOHNSON, D. W. *Educational psychology*. Englewood Cliffs, N.J.: Prentice-Hall, 1979.

JOHNSON, D. W. Attitude modification methods. In F. Kanfer and A. Goldstein, eds., *Helping people change*. 2nd ed. Elmsford, N.Y.: Pergamon Press, 1980.

JOHNSON, D. W., AND JOHNSON, F. *Joining together: Group theory and group skills*. Englewood Cliffs, N.J.: Prentice-Hall, 1975.

JOHNSON, D. W., AND JOHNSON, R. *Learning together and alone: Cooperation, competition, and individualization*. Englewood Cliffs, N.J.: Prentice-Hall, 1975.

JOHNSON, D. W., AND MATROSS, R. Interpersonal influence in psychotherapy: A social psychological view. In A. Gurman and A. Razin, eds., *Effective psychotherapy*. Elmsford, N.Y.: Pergamon Press, 1977, pp. 395–432.

JOHNSON, D. W., AND NOONAN, M. The effects of acceptance and reciprocation of self-disclosures on the development of trust. *Journal of Counseling Psychology* 19 (1972): 411–16.

LEAVITT, H. *Managerial psychology*. Chicago: University of Chicago Press, 1958.

LUCE, R., AND RAIFFA, H. *Games and decisions*. New York: John Wiley, 1957.

LUFT, J. *Of human interaction*. Palo Alto, Calif.: National Press, 1969.

McCROSKEY, J., LARSON, C., AND KNAPP, M. *Introduction to interpersonal communication*. Englewood Cliffs, N.J.: Prentice-Hall, 1971.

MILLER, S.; NUNNALLY, E.; AND WACHMAN, D. *Alive and aware: Improving communication in relationships*. Minneapolis: Interpersonal Communication Programs, 1975.

NOVACO, R. *Anger control*. Lexington, Mass.: D. C. Heath & Co., 1975.

POWELL, J. *Why am I afraid to tell you who I am?* Niles, Ill.: Argus, 1969.

ROGERS, C. *Client-centered therapy*. Boston: Houghton-Mifflin, 1951.

ROGERS, C. Dealing with psychological tensions. *Journal of Applied Behavioral Science* 1 (1965): 6–25.

ROGERS, C., AND ROETHLISBERGER, F. Barriers and gateways to communication. *Harvard Business Review*, July–August 1952, pp. 28–35.

WATSON, G., AND JOHNSON, D. W. *Social psychology: Issues and insights*. Philadelphia: Lippincott, 1972.

WEISS, R., ed., *Loneliness*. Cambridge, Mass.: MIT Press, 1973.

Index